D1270498

Orff Schulwerk
Reflections and Directions

Proceedings of the Symposium
Global Connections in Orff Schulwerk: Reflections from Kentucky

Orff Schulwerk
Reflections and Directions

Proceedings of the Symposium
Global Connections in Orff Schulwerk:
Reflections from Kentucky

Cecilia Chu Wang
Editor

D. Gregory Springer
Assistant Editor

Contributors
Carlos R. Abril
Judith W. Bond
Jay Broeker
Jane Frazee
Ana Lucía Frega
Lori F. Gooding
Cindy Hall
Kuo-Huang Han
Jo Ella Hug
Terri Brown Lenzo
K. Michelle Lewis
Nicola F. Mason
Kimberly McCord
Mary Shamrock
David Sogin
Robyn Staveley
Arvida Steen
Margaret Thong

GIA Publications, Inc.
Chicago

Orff Schulwerk
Reflections and Directions
by Cecilia Wang

G-8611
ISBN: 978-1-57999-998-8

GIA Publications, Inc.
7404 S. Mason Ave.
Chicago, IL 60638
www.giamusic.com

Cover and Layout Design by Martha Chlipala

TABLE OF CONTENTS

SECTION ONE
Orff Schulwerk: A Global Perspective

SECTION TWO
Reflections

SECTION THREE
Directions for the Twenty-First Century

LESSON PLANS
for the Twenty-First-Century Classroom

PREFACE

Cecilia Wang

In the summer of 2011, a group of music educators and pedagogues gathered together to reflect on how best to promote music learning in the new century. Among the presenters were the movers and shakers from both the past and present who have passionately dedicated their professional lives to better music education through the promotion of Orff Schulwerk. These people are master teachers of teachers, serious thinkers, authors, scholars, and most of all, expert practitioners who inspired countless students toward quality music teaching and learning. Having served as presidents of the American Orff-Schulwerk Association collectively spanning several decades, these passionate music educators were invited to share their thoughts in a special symposium titled "Global Connections in Orff Schulwerk: Reflections from Kentucky." This symposium coincided with the celebration of twenty-five years of Orff-Schulwerk Teacher Education at the University of Kentucky. However, the real purpose of this symposium was to look at Orff Schulwerk from a global perspective, to learn from the past, to take a critical look at the present, and to design an agendum for the future of Orff Schulwerk in the schools and for teacher training. The event provided a forum for scholarly debate as well as an open and honest critical discussion about the status of Orff Schulwerk.

Orff Schulwerk, as Orff referred to it as "his wild flower" in a speech given at the opening of the Orff Institute in Salzburg on October 25, 1963, has spread and blossomed in many parts of the world as Carl Orff had envisioned it would several decades ago. Many teachers have embraced the Orff approach as the most stimulating way to teach children and for the children to learn music. Yet, the search to adapt its application to learners in the twenty-first century of the information age is sorely needed in order to maximize the effect of music education. The attendants of this symposium, from several continents, participated in identifying some of the changes occurring in our schools and suggested an agendum for action for music education in general, and specifically for Orff-Schulwerk educators.

This book contains not only critical thoughts for using the Orff-Schulwerk approach, but also provides examples of field-tested lessons that exemplify some fresh directions to follow in the immediate future. The content of this book is for music teachers of all levels, teacher trainers, teachers of children with special needs, and university professors/researchers. If you are curious about Orff Schulwerk, or want to have a deeper understanding of best practice in teaching music, or are eager to try out some alternative innovative ways to teach your students music, you may find this book most helpful.

Nota Bene: *The term 'Orff Schulwerk' is used throughout this book in various ways. Although the term is commonly used as a noun, it can also be used as an adjective. In these cases, the term is presented with a hyphen for grammatical accuracy.*

ACKNOWLEDGEMENTS

I am indebted to my assistant editor D. Gregory Springer, who has read every word of the manuscript with utmost care and suggested changes in both the style and in the content of writing. He has shown great professionalism and joy in this task. I want to thank all the contributing authors whose work has inspired me for many years, and consultants who reviewed different parts of this project. My sincere thanks goes to Carroll Gonzo whose expertise in music education is most valued as a copy editor here. Thank you Martha Chlipala, for the beautiful design of this book. I am grateful for the University of Kentucky for their support with a *Research Conference and Workshop Award*, and for Alec Harris of GIA Publications Inc. for his recognition of our passion in and for music education.

Much love goes to Nancy (Dancy) Miller, our guru of movement pedagogy in Orff Schulwerk.

—*Cecilia Wang*

Chapter 1

WHY ORFF SCHULWERK?
Cecilia Wang

"Why Orff Schulwerk?"
"Why not?"
"We must!"

For many music educators, Orff Schulwerk is just one of many approaches in teaching music. However, for those who take time to understand its philosophy, practice, process, and techniques, Orff Schulwerk is considered by many to be the most stimulating way for teaching and learning music. As a director of an Orff-Schulwerk teacher-education course for twenty-five years, I am accustomed to having teachers telling me that Orff-Schulwerk training has changed their way of teaching forever. These are happy teachers, guiding their motivated students to learn music and think creatively.

Why does Orff-Schulwerk pedagogy work so well? It is because this approach embodies what latest research has identified as brain-based learning. We learn best when the lessons allow the brain to process the information most effectively, make new neural connections, and store the neural patterns securely. According to Caine and Caine (1991, 1997), the core principles directing brain-based education are as follows:

- the brain is a complex adaptive system—it can do multiple tasks simultaneously;
- the brain is a social brain—students learn better when engaged in interactive activities;

- the search for meaning is innate—meaningful materials are learned better;
- the search for meaning occurs through "patterning";
- emotions are critical to patterning—human expression aids learning;
- every brain simultaneously perceives and creates parts and wholes;
- learning involves both focused attention and peripheral perception;
- learning always involves conscious and unconscious processes— both active processing and memory retrieval are at work, using multiple neural pathways;
- we have at least two ways of organizing memory: spatial and by rote;
- learning is developmental;
- complex learning is enhanced by challenge and inhibited by threat; and
- every brain is singularly organized.

Furthermore, three principles emerge for best practices in teaching.

- Orchestrated immersion—teacher creates a social environment for active learning.
- Relaxed alertness—teacher provides challenges while minimizing stress.
- Active processing—teacher delivers activities that encourage students to engage in processing and internalizing information, making connections to previous learning; teacher also makes quick assessment of students' performances.

A typical Orff-Schulwerk lesson fits nicely into this framework. In an archetypal Orff-Schulwerk classroom, students are immediately engaged in music-making activities that require attention, focus, alertness, and multisensory responses. Singing, chanting, moving, playing, and listening constitute most of the activities that are fast-paced, often occurring simultaneously, and changing on demand, according to the cues given by the instructor. The teacher chooses materials and resources that relate to the student's life and community and thus are meaningful for the students.

The teacher would reinforce previous materials and skills introduced earlier, and challenge the students to create new versions of songs, chants, movement patterns, or accompaniments. Music making is organic and always in a social environment, whether students work in small groups or with the whole class. The teacher provides a safe environment for students to explore, improvise, and express their ideas. For example, students would practice improvising a given part together until they are comfortable to share their own creation separately. The music ensemble setting is conducive to accommodating different abilities when each person or small group can play parts they can perform well. Each student has a specific role and at the same time contributes to the musical outcome of the whole class. Under this highly interactive environment, students not only grow musically, but also they build confidence, critical thinking, and interpersonal skills.

The first brain-based learning principle mentioned earlier is to stimulate the brain by providing instruction that requires it to adapt to complex activities. Orff-Schulwerk activities such as chanting a poem, e.g., "One Two Touch My Shoe," while playing body percussion of "stamp, clap, pat knee, and snap" in common time requires students to multi-task often. Such combined tasks would excite neural actions in motor execution, language production, and sequencing of events. Making music in the ensemble settings provides the social setting as well as the interactivity that promotes focused attention and peripheral perception at the same time, embodying two other brain-learning principles. Singing and moving to music, or singing and playing instruments require different but simultaneous processing in the brain, involving both conscious thoughts and retrieval of subconscious skills learned earlier. Orff ensembles are comprised of multiple *ostinati* in speech, playing, and moving. These patterns are first transmitted by rote through listening. These typical activities of Orff Schulwerk help the brain to form patterns in language, motor skills, sound discrimination, and spatial orientation. The materials used in the Schulwerk classroom often include song lyrics, and poems with rhymes that easily arouse rich visual or aural imagery and emotion. Furthermore, stories and dramatization are often included. One may come to realize that the infinite ways a teacher can combine these different multisensory activities using different materials creatively can epitomize brain-based learning in music education. The Orff-Schulwerk approach provides the ingredients for the music teacher to create optimal learning experiences.

The Carl Orff approach does not dictate what the teachers or students must do, nor the sequential order of materials to be presented, but relies mostly on the insight and wisdom of the teachers to guide their students, based upon the Schulwerk philosophy and sample materials. Carl Orff was strongly influenced by the work of Jaques-Dalcroze, who believed that the mind, body, and spirit work in an integrated manner to produce expressive music. Orff believed that a joyous atmosphere is indispensable for children to learn music and that such an atmosphere would be attained if we allow children to be spontaneous and natural. Children learn to speak naturally, and thus chanting and speech provides a comfortable medium for children to feel the rhythm of the language, especially if the words are those familiar to the learner. Orff also noticed that music and dance are often performed together in many cultures. He believed that music, movement, and speech are all intertwined and provide the foundation for children to learn music, and must be integrated in music education.

Music teachers who use the Schulwerk approach can guide students toward optimal learning only if they are creative, well-prepared yet flexible in delivering their teaching. This practice is a student-centered approach in which the learners are encouraged to express their musical ideas whenever it is appropriate to do so. This notion means that the teacher must make astute assessments of students' performances and responses on demand, and grasp all expected and unexpected teachable moments that present themselves. Fortunately, Carl Orff and his principal organizer and teacher Gunild Keetman (Regner & Lange-Ronnefeld, 2004) provided us with many good techniques to use in the Schulwerk process. Rhythm patterns derived from words, phrases, and poems are used as ostinato patterns that can be played or sung as different parts of the Orff ensemble. The melody part may be improvised or from an existing composition or song. Body percussion of four basic body movements—snapping fingers, clapping hands, patting thighs, and stamping feet—are used to practice rhythm patterns, making use of the kinesthetic sense to feel the rhythm and place it into motor memory.

The words can be chanted to form a speech piece. Compositional techniques such as canonic imitation and those used in fugues are employed to embellish the piece. The melody can be an original one created from poems, or from existing songs or compositions.

By using various combinations of pitched and non-pitched percussion instruments, singing, speech, and original movement and dance, often in ABA or Rondo forms, make it possible for an Orff ensemble to be arranged and performed in infinite ways. Carl Orff had metallophones and xylophones designed and made especially for children learning. He wanted the instruments to sound mellow and that bars be removable so that only correct notes are available for the piece being played. This technique is a device that minimizes risk-taking, reduces the stress of playing wrong notes, and enables children to perform and create freely with good results. The recorder is often used as the instrument assigned to play the melody and/or for descant, though other instruments that fit into the ensemble sound can also be used.

The Orff process is one that engages the students constantly in all modalities—listening, playing, moving, singing, and creative activities. Experiencing the music comes before learning the related terminology, description, and notation. First, students learn a musical idea or pattern usually by rote, relying on and sharpening their aural perception and memory, they then explore ways to expand this idea in alternative forms through singing, playing, or moving. Notational understanding, music reading, and improvisation complete the sequence of learning a new music concept. It is the teacher's responsibility to teach incrementally in small steps and in a logical order so students are successful in mastering each step throughout the teaching and learning process. The moment students can transfer the musical concept by freely improvising, they not only demonstrate a mastery of the concept, but also expresses the joy of creating original thoughts. One can easily understand why students in Orff classrooms are motivated to learn more. Regretfully, outside of the context of the Orff approach, it seems that improvisation is not taught regularly except in jazz music.

The five volumes of *Music for Children*, along with a variety of related books, authored by Carl Orff and Keetman (1957) comprise the main representation of repertoire of music used in the Orff Schulwerk. This collection serves as references and good musical examples for Schulwerk teaching and should be analyzed and studied. However, acquiring skills to adapt this and other music materials is of paramount importance for all teachers of the Orff approach. Indeed, it is crucial when using the Orff approach to employ music, language, traditional folk songs, dance, and games of the children's home culture as the primary materials in their music education. Folk songs and stories of other countries should also be used to provide well-rounded musical learning. Orff Schulwerk is one area that teachers can be innovative more often, and many teachers do integrate other subjects such as visual arts, drama, and literature into their lessons. Keetman's (1970) introductory text, *Elementaria: First Acquaintance with Orff Schulwerk*, has been translated into thirty-four languages; some include original songs and poem materials in the specific language. At least several English versions of *Music for Children* exist, in Britain, Canada, and the United States.

Orff Schulwerk was first introduced in Germany, where Carl Orff (1895-1982) lived. In 1924, Orff and Dorothee Günther founded a school for gymnastics, music, and dance for movement and music education in Munich. He received help from his friends Karl Maendler to make metallophones and xylophones; and from Curt Sachs to develop an instrument ensemble such that students could improvise easily to accompany movement in a spontaneous, personal way, and with musical expression. In 1930, aided by Gunild Keetman, the first edition of *Schulwerk Rhythmic-Melodic Exercises* was published, followed by several exercise books for various instruments of the ensemble. In 1932, *Orff Schulwerk: Music for Children* was in the plan to be published when the political climate changed and the Güntherschule was destroyed by fire. In 1948, Orff was invited by the Bavarian Radio to broadcast a series of music programs for children 8-12 years old, rekindling the work toward Orff Schulwerk. In 1951, Keetman was invited to teach at the Mozarteum in Salzberg, where the Orff Institute began in 1963. The five volumes for *Orff Schulwerk: Music for Children* were finally completed in 1954. From that point on, interest in the Schulwerk approach spread to different countries including Canada, USA, Japan, and other countries in

Europe and in Latin America. Moreover, music educators would study the Orff approach firsthand at the Mozarteum (Orff, 1963). In chapter three, written by Jane Frazee, she captures the dramatic historic situation in which Carl Orff went through, the struggle in the conception of Orff Schulwerk, and how this European beginning blossomed in the United States and has been sustained for fifty-five years.

Arnold Walter, a former Canadian, is credited for bringing Orff Schulwerk to North America. At the first conference of the Orff-Schulwerk Association held at Ball State University in Muncie, Indiana, April 1969, he cautioned that despite much enthusiasm, some people claiming to be Orff teachers still did not have a clear conception of how Orff Schulwerk should be applied. To Walter, the production of an elaborate and impeccable musical performance or teaching music mechanically is not what Orff Schulwerk is about. Orff Schulwerk is not a "method." The Schulwerk depends on the teachers who can guide their students with fantasy and creative intuitions. An Orff teacher must know how to improvise, and it is the *process* of improvising that counts! The process requires the teachers and students to sing, dance, listen, dramatize, play percussion instruments, compose, arrange, conduct, and most of all, "think music" (Walter, 1969)!

From 1969 to the present, the American Orff-Schulwerk Association (AOSA) has held at least one national conference each year, with strong leadership from the grassroots, state and local chapters, providing inspiration to an increasing number of educators toward this approach. Overall, 120 local Orff chapters have been formed in the U.S., though a few have since become inactive.

Yet, although what Arnold Walter had cautioned still lurks underneath the surface, many excellent musicians and dedicated educators have worked tirelessly to promote Orff Schulwerk for quality music education with optimal effectiveness. Jane Frazee's (1987) book *Discovering Orff* is a landmark publication that provides clear examples of the "what and how" to implement Orff activities for American teachers. Arvida Steen's (1992) book, *Exploring Orff*, provides extensive lesson materials in carefully planned sequences to promote musical growth. More books of quality were published in the last fifteen years, along with many other music materials and scores for Orff activities and ensembles.

One of the most significant developments, however, is the offering of Orff-Schulwerk teacher-education courses at institutes of higher education throughout the country. Although the Orff Institute in Salzberg is still offering their regular and summer institute programs, the AOSA-approved teacher training courses in the United States (numbering fifty this year) are mainly responsible for providing Schulwerk training for the majority of Orff teachers today in the United States. Arvida Steen, past president of AOSA, spearheaded the establishment of the AOSA guidelines for course contents in three levels of teacher training, criteria for teacher competencies, and requirements for apprenticeship and teacher trainers. Due to the popularity of these teacher-training courses, a new Director of Education was created to oversee the integrity of Orff-Schulwerk teacher training in America. Steven Calantropio, a longtime Orff-Schulwerk teacher of children and adults, is the first person selected to serve in that capacity.

Along with the development of Orff Schulwerk as a strong pedagogic approach, comes a body of related research. It is not surprising that this literature reflects the weaknesses and strengths as the Schulwerk grew from infancy to an established pedagogical approach. One notable finding from many of these current studies is that participants of all kinds who immerse themselves in the Schulwerk approach all express a positive attitude toward it. Most of the weaknesses of the earlier studies are a result of the research methodology used and the wide variability of research questions and treatments. However, in the last two decades, more relevant research studies have appeared. In chapter nine, this body of research is described in much greater detail.

In this chapter, this author has given an overview of Orff Schulwerk. Orff Schulwerk is not just another music-teaching approach, but has been established as a pedagogy that truly works in optimizing students' musical learning. It is an approach that employs brain-based learning, and it can seamlessly incorporate all the requirements of the National Standards for Music Education. Most important, this approach generates continuous excitement in teaching and learning and stretches the creative minds of both teachers and students. This approach provides the tools for teachers and students to experience joyfully *cooperation, collaboration, and creativity—* the goals of education for the twenty-first century. That is why we must be proactive in the practice of and research about Orff Schulwerk!

References

American Orff-Schulwerk Association (AOSA), Chagrin Falls, OH. (http://www.aosa.org).

Caine, R.N. & Caine, G. (1997). *Education on the edge of possibility.* Alexandria, VA: Association for Supervision and Curriculum Development.

Caine, R.N. & Caine, G. (1991). *Making connections: Teaching and the human brain.* Alexandria, VA: Association for Supervision and Curriculum Development.

Frazee, J. & Kreuter, K. (1987). *Discovering Orff: A curriculum for music teachers.* London: Schott.

Keetman, G. (1970). *Elementaria.* Stuttgart: Ernst Klett Verlag.

Orff, C. (1963). Orff-Schulwerk: Past & future. In Carly, I. M. Ed, (1977). *Orff Re-Echoes.* AOSA.

Orff, C. & Keetman, G. (1957). *Music for children.* Mainz : B. Schott's Söhne.

Regner, H. & Lange-Ronnefeld, M. (2004). *Gunild Keetman: A life given to music and movement.* New York: Schott.

Steen, A. (1992). *Exploring Orff.* New York: Schott Music Corp.

Walter, A. (1969). The Orff Schulwerk in American education. In Carly, I. M. (Ed.), (1977). *Orff Re-Echoes.* AOSA.

Chapter 2

CRITICAL ISSUES IN ORFF SCHULWERK

Carlos R. Abril

At a point in my work as an elementary general music teacher, after having studied at the Orff Institute, completed my Orff levels, attended a smattering of American Orff-Schulwerk Association (AOSA) conferences, and become interested in philosophy, research, and music teacher education, I decided to apply for PhD programs in music education. It was during an interview for one of those programs that I abruptly became aware of the tenuous relationship between Orff Schulwerk and the greater music education community. That tension was new to me then, but obvious now, and is relevant to this chapter.

The interview started as most do: I was asked questions relating to my professional experience, my research interests, and my long-term professional goals. About twenty minutes into the interview, it took a turn, steered by one professor who wanted to probe my Orff background and gain an understanding of its essence. She asked something similar to the following: "I can see you have a lot of training in Orff, and your teaching video is obviously influenced by that work. Since you must know a lot about Orff, I would like you to tell us how you are able to reconcile the premise upon which the Orff philosophy is laid in its historical context with teaching children in the United States today."

Her interrogation took me aback in that it made clear she assumed there was a problem that warranted reconciliation. My answers did not satisfy her because it was probably obvious to her that I did not perceive a problem. It was at that moment that the words of a few trusted mentoring professors, who had advised me to play down my Orff background in my applications, sounded in my head. I did not understand why this professor failed to understand that a creative, playful, child-centered, and active music-making program was valuable and meaningful to children. What I said in response to her is not important; what is important is that this interchange served as the moment when I realized there was a tension and became curious about the history and theoretical foundation upon which Orff practices were built. Over the years, in conversations with my colleagues and friends in the Orff community, I have come to realize that many are unaware of the voices of dissent that are heard in music education. Is this nothing more than a tension, a critical perspective, or an idea that transcends Orff Schulwerk?

Clearly, the professor in my interview was not the first to be critical of a given music education method or approach. On many occasions, both formal and informal, over dinner and at conference presentations, I have heard negative, critical, and even antagonistic remarks about and attitudes toward Orff—interestingly, only in my work outside of the world of Orff. I must confess, when I first used to hear these remarks or experienced these attitudes, I would react passionately and defensively. Later I began to think it more prudent to consider what others were saying, discerning if they were critiques of Orff organizations, practices, rituals, history, philosophy, or something else.

The purpose of this chapter is to provide an analysis of critical issues in Orff Schulwerk and search for commonly recurring themes that emerge from an examination of the literature. Moreover, I will reflect on the themes from my perspective as a general music teacher, music teacher/educator, a member of AOSA, workshop presenter, and former member of the *Orff Echo* editorial board. For those who find philosophical alignment with Orff Schulwerk, you are invited to temporarily suspend your current beliefs regarding Orff, open yourself to these ideas, and reflect upon our individual and collective practices in both teacher education and in the schools. This reflection can help leaders in the Orff movement to consider ways of moving practice, teacher education, and various Orff-related organizations forward. This chapter is not meant to provide answers but instead designed to provoke thought and encourage dialogue among music educators. It can also be viewed as a framework with which to read (or reread) the forthcoming chapters in this book.

In preparing for this chapter, I searched numerous indices and databases e.g., Google Scholar, International Index of Music Periodicals, and books and journal articles that critically examined Orff pedagogy. Each piece was read to find passages or sections in which its author advanced a critical stance, implicit or explicit, regarding Orff pedagogy. Twenty-four articles, book chapters, and dissertations that met the criteria were read and sections related to Orff Schulwerk were extracted. Works that only briefly or superficially mentioned Orff were excluded. Three major themes emerged from this process and serve as the conceptual framework for the chapter: (a) the theory, (b) the pedagogy, and (c) the ideology.

The Theory of Recapitulation

The first major theme that emerged from the literature was a recapitulation theory, which proposes that the development of the human parallels those of human evolution. In a cultural sense, it refers to the linear path of human development from savagery to barbarianism to civilization, repeating the evolutionary development of the species (Fallace, 2012). Psychologist and educator, G. Stanley Hall, was influential in translating the biogenetic theory to child development and believed that children must be given the opportunity to express their primitive impulses so that they would not be carried into adulthood (Chambliss, 1996). One example of the ways these ideas shaped pedagogy is in the principle that content should be presented to students in a linear direction, from the most simple to the more complex and sophisticated. These ideas were translated into popular teaching materials and pedagogies of the early twentieth century in Europe and the U.S. (Fallace, 2012).

It should come as no surprise that these popular ideas promulgated during the years Orff and Keetman were developing the Schulwerk, which would influence their rhetoric and pedagogy. In a 1962 speech at the University of Toronto, Carl Orff (1963) stated that "the Schulwerk concerns itself with the primary forces and forms of music," referred to as elemental. That is a "pre-intellectual" form of music that includes "simple sequential structures, *ostinatos,* and miniature rondos. It is earthy, natural ... [and] fitting for children" (p. 72). Many years later, Warner (1991) advanced the idea that Orff pedagogy is designed to tap into the ways children make music, which she claims "resembles in many ways the music-making of primal cultures," and "speaks to the child in a language he understands and is able to respond to instinctively" (p. 8).

Others demonstrate how recapitulation theory positions the learner and the materials of the Schulwerk. Arnold Walter (1977), instrumental in bringing Orff Schulwerk to North America, clearly recognized the approach's epistemological roots, stating, "[W]e encounter the fundamental law of biogenesis that the individual recapitulates the developments of the species, both before and after birth. This is the cornerstone on which Orff's Schulwerk is being based" (p. 22). He makes the connection more explicit, explaining that:

> [W]e do know that it [music] was closely associated with speech and intimately related to movement; that rhythm was its most powerful element to be slowly and gradually tamed by melody; that harmony came late into the picture. It is highly significant that the instinctive behavior of small children follows the historical pattern: they will move to music, combine it with emotionally charged speech; they will endlessly improvise and turn every utensil they can lay hands on into a percussion instrument. Melody shapes will appear later while harmony has to wait until it is taught. (p. 22)

Although Walter recognizes the need to modify the approach based upon where and to whom it is being taught, he believed that these underlying principles should be closely safeguarded to maintain the essence of the approach.

The materials of Orff pedagogy are grounded in the idea that music education, as with children's development, must traverse the history of Western art music, from its more primitive or elemental forms, to more evolved musics of higher levels of sophistication and complexity (Calantropio, 2010). The xylophone and metallophone too were modeled after so-called primitive musical cultures, such as those used in parts of Africa and Indonesia, respectively, and were viewed as a natural starting point for children as they progressed through their phylogenetic development in music (Orff, 1963).

The theory of recapitulation, however, has been strongly and unanimously discredited in the scientific literature. It has been called unsound, simplistic, racist, and lacking in support from the research (Fallace, 2012). It is also the most frequent critique of Orff Schulwerk in the literature. Following are a few examples. Music scholar, Robert Walker (2007), states:

> Empirically and logically, there can be no justification for applying the recapitulation theory of development to music education using the music of [so-called] primitive societies, especially as the theory posited that children pass through a stage of musical development equivalent to that of adults in primitive societies on their way to more sophisticated state of Western musical culture and its associated music. Such a view invalidates much music of the world in that it treats the 'adult' music as being something 'child-like' rather than fully developed, sophisticated, and evolved. (p. 277)

In her extensive study of the ways children make and transmit music on playgrounds around the world, Kathryn Marsh (2008) questions various pedagogies, including Orff Schulwerk. She states:

> [T]he underlying philosophical and methodological tenants of Orff Schulwerk and Kodály method have not been questioned by their practitioners, despite major changes in educational philosophy and ethnomusicological thought. The child as a 'primitive' paradigm was subject to criticisms even as the methodologies were developing....The whole notion of musical primitivism as applied to non-Western music has been discredited because it is rooted in the erroneous assumption that Western music has supposedly evolved from 'primitive' prototypes. (p. 11-12)

It seems clear from these and other critiques that the recapitulation paradigm underlying some contemporary approaches to music education cannot continue to be justified when the attributes of children's contemporary music making, listening, and engagement are recognized. It is a theory that privileges the white, European cultural view of the world and music. What does this mean for the use of the Orff volumes and the long-term sequence suggested for teaching music to children? Undoubtedly, many of the ideas from the Schulwerk are valuable, meaningful, and important, but how might it change if we were to find a new theory upon which to guide our teaching? Can we continue to justify or build our work on a theory that lacks credibility and validity?

The Pedagogy

The second theme relates directly to the first but is more focused on the specifics of Orff pedagogy, including music, materials, teaching, and learning. This focus is the most commonly discussed, written about, and modeled aspect of Orff. The pedagogical ideas that surround the practice were developed as a way to help children realize their musical and artistic potential by providing them with musical experiences that bear a strong resemblance to the music vocabulary, behaviors, and play of children. The Schulwerk was conceived of as a child-centered, play-based way of encouraging learning and making music (Frazee, 2006). However, the adult conceptions and assumptions of what children know, like, and can do has been challenged, questioned, and critiqued in the literature. Kathryn Marsh (2008) spoke of Orff as following a model in which

> 'Playlikeness' is equated with simple repetitive structures, materials with a restricted rhythmic and tonal palette, and use of movement to develop musical understanding, which make many false assumptions about the relative simplicity of children's musical play. The problem is that simple musical materials tend to be overemphasized in classroom practice. (p.12)

In the earliest years of Orff Schulwerk in North America, some were critical that the Schulwerk was overly simplistic and somewhat removed from the realities of children's lives and society in the twentieth century (Flagg, 1966). Dolloff (1993) notes that Orff pedagogy is thought to linger too long on specific, narrow, and limiting forms and styles e.g., pentatonic, rondo form, but reminds us that this was not Orff's intention. In fact, Orff stated, "it is impossible and undesirable to shut a child off from all other musical influences" (Orff, 1962, as cited in Dolloff, 1993, p. 15). Teachers must be cautious not to take suggestions for sequencing musical experiences (e.g., harmonic structures) to any limiting extreme, and not to equate child-like with "child-ish music," or elemental with simplistic music learning experiences.

Songs

Folk songs, for example, are often used in Orff Schulwerk because they are simple, have limited rhythms, and have simple tonalities. Although the simplicity of some songs may align with the philosophical precepts of Orff, it can disregard the musical palate of students and their musical lives outside the classroom (Harwood & Marsh, 2012). Arnold Walter (1977) believed that Orff Schulwerk could be adapted based upon where and who was being taught, suggesting the use of songs of the child's mother tongue, which is to say songs of the cultural backgrounds of children. This notion has proven to be a complex, if not a virtually impossible proposition in today's multicultural schools and classrooms (Kelly-McHale, 2011).

In the book, *Songs in their Heads*, a study of musical meaning and value in the lives of children, Patricia Campbell (2010) interviews Lateesha, an elementary aged girl who describes the things that go on in her music class. What is interesting is the disconnect between her musical world at home and that at school: there is a dichotomous role that rap music plays in her school, while she engages in much rhythmic chanting in the Orff-infused music classroom, she does not see it as "really" being rap. Even young children such as Lateesha are able to recognize the subtle difference, "describing the music class rendition as just 'kinda rap' without a rhythmically complex underlay of sound and with a text that is innocuous, safe, and remote" (p. 176). Children's musical lives are more sophisticated than we may give them credit for, as evidenced in the ways children are able to recognize, speak about, and perform music of their culture.

Pedagogical songs, or songs composed by an adult to teach a particular musical concept or to limit pitches or tonality are used in some general music workshops, courses, and even in publications. They have a pedagogical purpose, but they lack an authentic cultural root and are often of questionable relevance and musicality. In her article titled, "So Why So Mi?" Peggy

Bennett (2005) challenged music educators to consider what comes first, the pedagogy or the music. She explains:

> To stay true to a sequence [or pedagogical approach/method], song teachers use a 'forced delay' approach. They withhold musical information and experiences and require children to master one step before moving onto the next, treating certain melodies, intervals or songs as potential interference to their sequence. In some extreme cases, children are not allowed to sing or identify tones that they have not yet studied. (p. 47)

Such examples demonstrate how pedagogy can drive musical selections and music experiences, rather than the other way around. This form of pedagogy can lead to experiences that are of disconnected meaning and little relevance in the lives of students.

Learning and Teaching

As in the ethnocentric belief that music history followed a linear progression of evolution, some believe that learning— and teaching— should follow a similarly neat and tidy developmental trajectory. Current research suggests otherwise. Learning occurs in varied ways that are unevenly paced, messy, and unexpected (Campbell, 2010; Harwood & Marsh, 2012). Learning is thought to be most effective when someone is met with real challenges and problems that require creative and critical thinking to solve (Robinson, 2006). In his much discussed and viewed TEDtalk, Sir Ken Robinson (2010) calls out for the dismantling of overly linear and sequential approaches to teaching.

The Orff teaching process, which has been described as the essence of its pedagogy (Shamrock, 1997), has been subjected to scrutiny as well. Benedict (2009) asserted that its systematic nature can be problematic insofar as that structure or order (process) and sequence is delivered in an automatic fashion and takes "the place of critical thought and agency, and ... in the process of self-estrangement from the kinds of problem posing found in musicking situations that are less clearly delineated by sequential ordering, both students and teachers become alienated from themselves" (p 218).

Maud Hickey (2009), who has spent her career researching and teaching composition and improvisation, questioned the need for music teachers to start with small, rhythmic building blocks and patterns as "prerequisites for imitation," (p. 288) which then lead to improvisation experiences. Assumptions about children's capabilities, development, and artistry have lead to pedagogical practices that can be limiting, disconnected from the multicultural and complex culture of contemporary childhood, and overly rigid in their delivery.

The Ideology

Another theme that emerged from the literature is the danger of having a given approach (e.g., Orff) become ideology. Recall the words of Carl Orff (1963) when describing the Schulwerk in its earliest years in North America:

> Those who look for a method or a ready-made system are rather uncomfortable with the Schulwerk; people with artistic temperaments and a flair for improvisation are fascinated by it ... unfortunately, it has been misinterpreted, exploited, and falsified to the point of caricature ... a teacher is stimulated by the possibilities inherent in a work which is never quite finished, in flux, constantly developing. (p. 69)

Over time, the ideas that were once fresh and open to interpretation and adaptation have been codified and converted into a restrictive method of teaching by some. Collective evidence from the *Orff Echo* journal and the American Orff-Schulwerk Association National Conference, where these fundamental ideas are reinforced and preserved, support this perception from the profession. Is Orff Schulwerk always an approach as practiced today? At what point does it become a method or an ideology?

Conceptually, Orff Schulwerk is not supposed to be a method, as Orff practitioners and presenters will often remark. However, it can be viewed as methodological in both the practices and products of the Schulwerk. For example, they offer specific structures to lessons (e.g., from word to instruments); developmental (e.g., from simple to complex), conceptual (e.g., from rhythm to harmony), and theoretical (e.g., pentatonic to major modes) sequences to follow; and a common set of core materials (e.g., Five Volume, *Music for Children*). Benedict (2010) goes further suggesting that the normative thought processes, common-sense practices, and rituals renders Orff Schulwerk an ideology. In her critique of Orff and Kodály, she writes:

> It is not the concept of these methods that needs to be done away with; both Orff and Kodály envisioned musical processes that sprang from the innate desire to experience and create as a social, musical engagement. Rather, it is a need to interrogate the indiscriminate embracing of these methods as a possible form of control and coercion, as well as the possible appropriation of musicking as a way to increase the social capital of music teachers. (p. 222)

She views her own Orff teaching and training through the lens of Karl Marx: "[I]nstruments had become less [music-making] materials and more like tools in a production line that struck me as similar to the division of labor Marx was writing about … and finally it was the way in which for me the method had so often taken on an aura of fetish as the students simply became tools in the process." (p. 214)

She is not the first or the only person to warn music educators and general education teachers of the dangers of blind engagements with a given methodology. Thomas Regelski (2002) informed the music education community to be aware of "blind faith in and devotion to a technicist method" or what he coined "methodolatry" (p. 111). He states: "From the perspective of methodolatry, then, "good teaching is simply a matter of the standard use of a 'good method.' And, since the method itself is deemed good before the fact of use, and the training in the delivery of the method is standardized, any failure of students to learn … is attributed by default to 'uncontrolled variables.'" (p. 111)

We must be willing to challenge that which we take for granted and interrogate our beliefs. We must be cautious not to fall into what Robinson (2010) refers to as the tyranny of common sense, where people are afraid, unwilling, or unable to challenge their beliefs and ideologies. In his classic book, *Punished by Rewards*, Alfie Kohn (1993) warns:

There is a time to admire the grace and persuasive power of an influential idea, and there is a time to fear its hold over us. The time to worry is when the idea is so widely shared that we no longer even notice it, when it is so deeply rooted that it feels to us like plain common sense. At the point when objections are not answered anymore because they are no longer even raised, we are not in control; we do not have the idea; it has us. (p. 3)

Most would agree that uncritical actions, in any facet of one's life, are potentially dangerous. The moment we are no longer willing to critique ourselves or speak out without fear, we have become victim to blind faith. Faith may have a place in our lives, but we must question whether it is appropriate in education. The scholars, whose works are discussed in this chapter, are not saying the ideas of Orff and Keetman should be discarded. Instead, they are urging us to continually challenge ourselves and question our actions in the classroom. In recent years, public statements from AOSA claim that the Orff approach is *the* answer. Stating that any one approach is truth or the best is dangerous; we move from having a methodology to serve learning to being an idea we revere and idolize. The educational philosopher, John Dewey (1938), warned us that "For any theory and set of practices is dogmatic which is not based upon critical examination of its own underlying principles" (p. 10).

Lessons from the Field

The question the professor I described in the opening posed to me in my interview lingered with me long after I graduated from the program. What was most valuable to me from that experience was not the question itself or my response. What mattered was the inquisitive and critical disposition she was attempting to sense and later instill in me. How might a question like hers or critiques such as the ones presented in this chapter change our ways of thinking and acting as music educators in general and as practitioners of Orff Schulwerk in particular? I contend that approaches and methods to teaching music, both new and old, must be critically understood, examined, and reimagined for their potential in education. In so doing, we might begin to reimagine ourselves and our practices to best serve the needs and interests of children, not the interests of an organization or any one methodology. We must also engage in substantive dialogues about the need to rethink our curriculum and instruction in the twenty-first century, a time and context that is drastically different from when Orff Schulwerk was developed in Europe. Our future as general music educators might require our coming together in some new, innovative, and revolutionary way. We must not fear interrogating our common-sense practices, past actions, and revered teachers. People interested in Orff and music teaching should be in the business of finding ways to engage children in meaningful and relevant music learning and making, helping children become more curious about the world around them, and developing their artistry and humanity.

References

Benedict, C. (2010). Methods and approaches. In H. F. Abeles and L. A. Custodero (Eds.), *Critical issues in music education: Contemporary theory and practice* (pp. 194-214). New York: Oxford University Press.

Benedict, C. (2009). Processes of alienation: Marx, Orff and Kodály. *British Journal of Music Education, 26*(2), 213-224.

Bennett, P. D. (2005). So, Why Sol-Mi? *Music Educators Journal, 91*(3), 43.

Calantropio, S. (2010). Merging and emerging: The path of Orff Schulwerk. *Orff Echo, 43*(1), 14-18.

Campbell, P. S. (2010). *Songs in their heads, (2ⁿᵈ Ed).* New York: Oxford University Press.

Chambliss, J. J. (1996). *Philosophy of education: An encyclopedia.* New York: Garland Pub.

Dewey, J. (1938). *Experience and education.* New York: Macmillan.

Dolloff, L-A. (1993). Das Schulwerk: A foundation for the cognitive, musical, and artistic development of children. In (L. R. Bartel, Ed.). *Research Perspectives in Music Education* (pp. 1-51). Toronto, Canada: Canadian Music Education Research Centre.

Dullea, R. (2009). Populism and folklorism in Central European music pedagogy of the nineteenth and early twentieth centuries. *Journal of the Society for Musicology in Ireland, 4,* 35-53.

Fallace, T. (2012). Recapitulation theory and the new education: Race, culture, imperialism, and pedagogy, 1894-1916. *Curriculum Inquiry, 42,* 4, 510-533.

Flagg, M. (1966). The Orff system in today's world. *Music Educators Journal, 53*(4), 30.

Frazee, J. (2006). *Orff Schulwerk today: Nurturing musical expression and understanding.* Mainz, Germany: Schott.

Harwood, E. and Marsh, K. (2012). Children's ways of learning inside and outside the classroom. In G. E. McPherson & Welch, G. F. (Eds.), *The Oxford Handbook of Music Education* (pp. 322-340). New York: Oxford University Press.

Hickey, M. (2009). Can improvisation be taught?: A call for free improvisation in our schools. *International Journal of Music Education, 27*(4), 285-299.

Kelly-McHale, J. (2011). *The relationship between children's musical identities and music teacher beliefs and practices in an elementary general music classroom* (Unpublished doctoral dissertation). Northwestern University, Evanston, IL.

Kohn, A. (1993). *Punished by rewards: The trouble with gold stars, incentive plans, A's, praise, and other bribes.* Boston: Houghton Mifflin Co.

Marsh, K. (2008). *The musical playground: Global tradition and change in children's songs and games.* Oxford: Oxford University Press.

Locke, T. (2009). Orff and the 'ivory tower': Fostering critique as a mode of legitimization. *International Journal of Music Education, 27*(4), 314-325.

Orff, C. (1963). The Schulwerk: Its origin and aims. *Music Educators Journal, 49*(5), 69-74

Regelski, T. (2002). On 'methodolatry' and music teaching as critical and reflective praxis. *Philosophy of Music Education Review, 10* (2), 102–123.

Robinson, K. (2006, June). *Ken Robinson says schools kill creativity.* [Video file]. Retrieved from http://www.ted.com/talks/ken_robinson_says_schools_kill_creativity.html

Robinson, K. (2010, May). *Sir Ken Robinson: Bring on the learning revolution!* [Video file]. Retrieved from http://www.ted.com/talks/sir_ken_robinson_bring_on_the_revolution.html

Shamrock, M. (1997). Orff-Schulwerk: An integrated foundation. *Music Educators Journal, 83*(6), 41-44.

Walker, R. (2007). *Music education: Cultural values, social change and innovation.* Springfield, Ill: Charles C. Thomas.

Walter, A. (1977). *The Orff Schulwerk in American education.* In E. McNeill Carley (Ed.), Orff re-echoes: Book I (pp. 14-24). Cleveland, OH: American Orff-Schulwerk Association.

Warner, B. (1991). *Orff-Schulwerk: Applications for the classroom.* Englewood Cliffs, N.J: Prentice Hall.

Table 1

Critiques in the Literature: Themes and subthemes

Publication	Critiques			
Benedict (2009)	**Ideology**			
Benedict (2010)			**Method** Process *simplicity over creativity*	
Bennett (2009)				**Repertoire** *pedagogical song*
Campbell (2010)				**Repertoire** *relevance*
Dolloff (1993)			**Method** Limited *forms and styles*	
Dullea (2008)		**Recapitulation**		
Flagg (1966)				**Repertoire** *simplistic*
Hickey (2009)			**Method** Improvisation *immediacy and pleasantness*	
Jorgensen (2008)		**Recapitulation**		
Jorgensen (2011)		**Recapitulation**	**Method** Instruments *immediacy*	
Kelly-McHale (2011)				**Repertoire** *mother tongue*
Marsh (2009)		**Recapitulation**	**Method** Improvisation, Instruments *Immediacy*	
Walker (2007)		**Recapitulation**		

SECTION ONE

ORFF SCHULWERK:
A GLOBAL PERSPECTIVE

Chapter 3

FROM THE OLD WORLD TO THE NEW:
CULTIVATING ORFF'S WILDFLOWER FROM EUROPE TO THE USA
Jane Frazee

Today we celebrate fifty-five years of Orff Schulwerk in North America and twenty-five years of Orff Schulwerk at the University of Kentucky. Thank you for the opportunity to celebrate this important occasion with you. Congratulations! My contribution to global connections takes us to Europe as we attempt to discover the roots of Orff Schulwerk in Weimar Germany and on to the Mozarteum in Austria in 1954. We'll examine the North American work that began in 1956.

Orff Schulwerk in the Old World

Carl Orff described himself as a passionate gardener, so it is not surprising that he called his educational work a wildflower. He believed that the Schulwerk would flourish wherever it found suitable growing conditions. And, because he insisted that he was not the inventor of the Schulwerk but rather the synthesizer of the ideas that were already in the air, he was its first nurturer.

The seeds of the Schulwerk are to be found in the Bavarian cultural *milieu* in which Orff was born and lived for his entire professional life. To provide a context for the remarkable story of the birth of the Schulwerk in 1920s Munich, we will examine the convergence of several factors: (1) Weimar Culture; (2) the Concept of the Volk and Hausmusik; (3) the Hitler Youth; (4) the Body Culture Movement; and finally, (5) the Güntherschule.

My focus will be on the ways in which each of these affected Orff in a personal way, in order to deepen our understanding of the origins of the practice that we preach.

Historical Considerations:
Weimar Culture in Munich

If, as Orff often claimed, the seeds of the Schulwerk were in the air, we must first consider Weimar Germany in general, and Munich in particular, to discover the political and cultural atmosphere in which these seeds were sown. What were the conditions that encouraged an unknown music teacher and composer in his early thirties to believe that he could develop a music education approach that would be welcomed in this incomparable musical country of Bach, Haydn, Mozart, Beethoven, and Brahms—a country claimed by Richard Wagner to be so preeminent in music that he once remarked that only a German has the exclusive right to be called "musician"?

In fact, the seeds of the Schulwerk were planted in a troubled time and troubled place. Weimar, Germany arose from a country defeated in World War I, a war in which the twenty-two-year-old Orff served on the eastern front, but was sent home after suffering shock when a dugout collapsed and nearly buried him alive. The Treaty of Versailles ended the war in 1919, but the outrage against its terms created conditions that caused great social unrest. Bankruptcies, unemployment, and food riots led to a Bavarian revolution in 1918-1919, fought by the communists and the many right-wing parties who opposed them.

Orff was absent during the first year of the Munich uprising, working as a choirmaster in Mannheim and Darmstadt in 1918. He returned home to Munich to become a freelance composer and teacher the following year. Munich, with its dire economic, social, and political problems, was not a propitious place for an unknown music teacher and composer to establish himself. Labeled by some as the "dumbest city in Germany," Munich had a secure reputation (especially in Berlin) as a provincial town without an intellectual core.

And yet, such a characterization missed a vital dimension of the Munich environment. The city, it turns out, had its very own version of Greenwich Village: Schwabing. The lively bohemian culture in the district attracted such writers and artists as Thomas Mann and Franz Mark and promoted mysticism, Dionysian and ancient Germanic rites, pagan rituals, and nudity. Some of these ideas served Orff well twenty years later in *Carmina Burana*, which became a hit in Germany in the early 1940s. In addition, the roots of one of the most important currents in twentieth-century art—German Expressionism—are firmly rooted in Munich.

This highly charged climate of free thinking and loose living was in direct conflict with the conservative elements of the Weimar culture that censored art works considered indecent. Music was not exempt from suppression. In 1929, the Nazis founded the Combat League for German Culture to discourage such efforts as the avant-garde music organization (to which Orff belonged) that promoted festivals of new music and arrangements of old masters. Orff also aroused suspicion on the right because he set poems by the Jewish poet Bertold Brecht, and in fact he found it necessary to defend himself against accusations that he was a Communist. And so, although Orff claimed no interest in politics throughout his life, his creative work in Munich meant that he could not escape the political tensions of the city. Neither could Orff escape the creative ferment of the dance scene in Munich. From the revolution movement taking place around him, he was drawn to the idea that corporeal rhythm comes from body movement; from physical gestures of work or play. As music director at the Güntherschule, he was able to apply this principle in his musical accompaniments for the dance students. In this musical laboratory, he also became aware of the musical potential of percussion instruments to express rhythm. Drums, sticks, and gongs were soon augmented by pitched instruments: xylophones, recorders, and strings. This combination of uncomplicated instruments and amateur players was the breakthrough that Orff needed to realize that a democratic music education was theoretically available for everyone. And so, the Schulwerk was born.

Despite the political and social unrest, the Güntherschule actually flourished throughout the 1930s, given Dorothee Günther's cooperation with the regime and her Nazi party membership. The astonishing highlight of this period was the commission of a performance for the opening of the 1936 Olympic games in Berlin. This event offered international exposure to the new music and dance developed at the school: 6,000 Berlin school children performed a procession and round dance choreographed by Dorothee Günther and Maja Lex with music composed and conducted by Gunild Keetman. The success of this performance and the accompanying recognition of the musical and pedagogical achievements of Orff and his colleagues, together with Günther's support of the National Socialists, meant that they were safe from Nazi interference until a year before the war's end. The Schulwerk's first home in Munich lasted twenty years, but the wildflower would be transplanted to Salzburg only five years later, and from there take root around the world.

The Concept of the Volk and Hausmusik

In addition to the vibrant—but troubled—Munich context into which the Schulwerk came into being, it was also shaped by two significant German sensibilities: the concept of the Volk and the Hausmusik tradition. Both played important roles in the development of Schulwerk ideas and Orff's attempts to stimulate interest in them.

The Volk movement evolved at the end of the nineteenth century as Germany was moving its independent states toward nationhood. The Volk are the people, but only the people of the German nation. The term embraced history and spirituality as well as the idea of an overarching "national soul" that—of course—was Aryan. Incorporating legends, traditional folk songs, sayings, and fairy tales such as those collected by the Brothers Grimm, it was also tied to the land. The combination of Aryan blood and German soil produced the superior German, one who supported the submission of the individual to the state.

Orff, of course, inherited this Volk tradition and understandably made use of its resources in his Schulwerk. Traditional folk songs, proverbs, and rhymes became source material for rhythmic and melodic exercises as Orff shaped the language of his new educational ideas around old folklore. The result of these initial educational efforts were two Schulwerk publications of 1930-1931: *Rhythmic and Melodic Exercises*. In a Schott promotional publication produced ten years later, called *An Introduction to Carl Orff*, Schott referred to Orff's Schulwerk as striving for a "genuine basis, rooted in race and Volk" (Kater, 2000, p. 121).

In addition to his German Volk inheritance, Orff grew up with Hausmusik—amateur chamber music performed at home. However, in-house performances of classical music were on the wane at the turn of the century because young people did not want to cope with the technical demands of traditional instruments.

Weimar Youth music leaders, however, transformed the Hausmusik tradition of participatory music by organizing festivals featuring choral and group singing accompanied by recorders and guitars. During the 1930s, these events evolved into Nazi propaganda productions known as *Thingspiele*, based upon the blood and soil ideology. The term "Thing" harks back to old Germanic outdoor pagan gatherings of the people. *Thingspiele* featured speech, movement, singing choirs, and elaborate effects such as banners, marches, and lights, involving thousands of amateur performers.

The elements of speech, movement, song, and instruments that were characteristic of the *Thingspiele* became fundamental activities of Orff's Schulwerk. Further, the grand spectacle of the *Thingspiele* events was very much in evidence in the music and dance presentation created by Güntherschule faculty for the Munich Olympic games.

The Nazis embraced a return to Hausmusik throughout the 1930s for the purpose of molding young National Socialists, but it was slow to make an impact on the quality of music instruction in the public schools. It is this vacuum that Orff's Schulwerk was promoted to fill. The effort came too late; Orff's Jewish colleague Leo Kestenberg—the brilliant and influential director of the Ministry of Education and Arts and leader of the German music education reform movement—was relieved of his position in 1932. The leaders of the Hitler Youth would now direct music education.

The Hitler Youth

Similar to each of the topics we are considering, the subject of the role played by the Hitler Youth in the development of the Schulwerk is significant, yet somewhat impenetrable. To offer a way into the subject, the discussion will be presented in three parts: (1) The Hitler Youth Movement; (2) Music in the Hitler Youth; and (3) Orff's relationship to the Hitler Youth.

The Hitler Youth Movement

The roots of the Hitler Youth movement were alive and well long before Hitler came to power in Germany. It evolved from the *Wandervogel* [wandering birds] movement.

The young adult members of this group wanted to lead lives that were simple, honest, and free—away from the constraints of homes, parents, and teachers. Prizing emotion over reason, they sought independence on long, mountain hikes, camping out, and singing songs.

When Hitler became chancellor in 1933, he transformed the *Wandervogel* movement into the Hitler Youth to Nazify future generations of Germans. Although the organization claimed no gender bias, the inequality of the sexes is revealed by differences in opportunities. The girls received no political training and the elite Adolph Hitler schools were not open to them. Girls, however, revered Hitler, treating him with hysterical adulation in public—as a rock star. And, they often acted on their newly achieved sexual freedom. Following the 1936 Reich Party rally in Nuremberg—attended by at least half a million people—nine hundred girls came home pregnant. In only half the cases, were the fathers known.

Fuhrer worship was at the heart of all Hitler Youth school activities; he was a god-like figure to German young people. They were exploited to become obedient followers as well as to fight for their Fuhrer. Many lost their lives doing just that.

Music of the Hitler Youth

Even in the early years of the National Socialist regime, Hitler Youth schools were an attractive alternative to public school education. In addition to such traditional subjects as mathematics and languages, training in these schools included physical education and the arts. And of all the arts, music was preferred. Music, especially singing, was thought to be both character and community building. Singing was described by the Hitler Youth leaders as being particularly useful "at those moments when we want to waken the consciousness of being part of a community, in order to deepen the power of such an experience" ("Music and the Holocaust," n.d.).

In order to achieve the desired group cohesion and individual enthusiasm for the Nazi cause, composers were engaged to produce hundreds of songbooks for the Hitler Youth based upon political and ideological texts that promoted National Socialist principles. Carl Orff declined to contribute to this effort. But, the music touched a nerve. As one former Hitler Youth member said, "in the songs that we sang, in the poems that we recited, everything was bright, shiny and clear, the sun and the earth were ours, and tomorrow so too would be the whole world" ("Music and the Holocaust," n.d.)

The Reich Youth Leadership founded music schools and conservatories specifically for the Hitler Youth boys. By 1940, the Salzburg Mozarteum had joined the group of Hitler Youth high schools of music education, training students in conventional music subjects, but also in newly developed ideological ones such as "German Musicology," designed by the authorities to contrast so-called inferior Jewish music with the great German musical heritage.

A leader of the Weimar Institute for Music Instructors of the Hitler Youth, William Twittenhoff, developed a program to be used by educators to introduce their students to rhythmic education. Twittenhoff is representative of a group of composers and educators who were highly influential in the music section of the Hitler Youth. He also was a former student and colleague of Carl Orff.

Orff's Relationship to the Hitler Youth

We have previously noted that Orff's efforts to sell his Schulwerk books to the public schools in the early 1930s were unsuccessful. Another market, however, was available to him with the astonishing growth of the Hitler Youth music schools. He and his publisher, Schott, were eager to interest the authorities in the Schulwerk for financial reasons, as well as to fulfill his ambition to be acknowledged as the founder of a new approach to music education in Germany. Schott, in 1934, publicity indicated that they wanted "every Hitler girl and every Hitler boy to end up contented" with Orff-Schulwerk materials (Kater, 2001, p. 121). In his effort to compare his Schulwerk to the type of Hausmusik that was supported by the Nazis, Orff wrote to Schott that he believed his objectives to be "concurrent, to the highest degree, with what is being required today" (Kater, 2001, p. 121).

Twittenhoff tried out Schulwerk ideas in his role as teacher in several Nazi youth music-training centers. In spite of its emphasis on rhythm, which he so esteemed, he was unable to arouse support for the Schulwerk among Hitler Youth music instructors because of its musical demands. Further, it would be impossible to play a xylophone while marching, and singing political songs was not a featured ingredient of the Schulwerk program. So, in spite of Orff's ambitions for his wildflower—and friends who promoted it—the Schulwerk had not yet found a congenial place to flourish.

Body Culture

As discussed earlier, the early years of the twentieth-century young men were eager to join *Wandervogel* groups to satisfy their yearning for freedom and adventure. Young women, too, were eager to loosen the old constraints on their freedom. The Body Culture movement, developed in the 1920s, grew out of this aspiration. As it evolved in Germany, Body Culture was largely a female enterprise. Because women believed that their freedom and power depended on the expressive capabilities of the body, emancipation included nudity in order to fully project their individual and collective identities. The women's

Body Culture movement was seen as a release from a history of repression that denied passion, eroticism, and ecstasy, and that resulted in the alienation of the human mind from its emotions. It found its release in gymnastics and games, outdoor activities, and festivals but—most especially—in dance.

We've identified Body Culture as largely a women's movement, yet two of the three most influential visionaries of the movement were men. Emile Jaques-Dalcroze's work featured musicianship development through movement. He emphasized musicianship development—not expressive dance. Rudolph Laban, on the other hand, believed that dance made all parts of the body essential to aesthetic expression. A third major contributor to the Body Culture movement, Bess Mensendieck, was an American physician who established a network of schools throughout Europe during the 1920s and 1930s. Her gymnastics students (all of whom were women) were taught to develop conscious awareness and slow practice of isolated movements to develop strong bodies through everyday activities. Music had no role in a Mensendieck school.

Trained in all three methods as well as art, Dorothee Günther was well prepared to found a school that integrated these approaches to gymnastics and dance. One among many schools that flourished in Munich at the time, it admitted only young women ages eighteen through twenty-two and depended upon tuition income, state and city subsidies, and from proceeds of performances of the traveling *Tanzgruppe Günther*. As the sole owner of the school, competing with numerous others for students, one can understand Günther's documented unconditional cooperation with the Nazis, beginning in 1933—she had a school to run!

A modern dance frenzy existed in Germany in the 1920s and 1930s. Berlin, alone, had 157 dance schools in 1929. Most of these schools were run by women, for women. Expressing emotions could lead to loose instructional practice, but Günther believed that rapture and ecstasy were best expressed through a rigorous approach to analysis and demonstration of movement elements. Her emphasis on elements was especially well suited to her musical partner at the school who was busy developing his own theories of music based upon the elements of rhythm and melody: Carl Orff.

This fortuitous collaboration, begun in 1924, has had momentous repercussions for almost a century. For had there been no Body Culture movement in the early twentieth century in Germany, there would have been no Güntherschule, and had there been no Güntherschule, there would have been no Orff Schulwerk.

The Güntherschule

Our brief consideration of the influential forces in Weimar, Germany, that have provided a context for our exploration of the birth of the Schulwerk leads us to our last topic: the Güntherschule. Just twenty-nine years old when he was hired to teach music at the school, Orff had obviously not been living in a musical vacuum. In fact, he was well acquainted with early music and also that of his admired contemporaries, Richard Strauss and Igor Stravinsky.

Although Orff publicly attributed his musical debt to Monteverdi and arranged three of his large works, including *Orfeo*, for performance, I suggest that his true musical inspiration lay elsewhere. When Orff was only eighteen years old, Stravinsky introduced an entirely new approach to orchestral color in *The Rite of Spring*, using the full orchestra as a percussion instrument. *The Rite* also introduced such musical devices as additive motivic melodic development, ostinati, changing meters, and driving rhythms. This piece changed the course of music: Peter Schiekele said in a 1990s radio broadcast that the work had such a profound effect on composition that virtually all subsequent twentieth-century music could be said to be the "Rewrite of Spring" (http://www.classiccat.net/stravinsky_i/_tros.info.php). That remark surely includes Orff, for by 1930 he had developed a new music education system based upon musical motives, ostinati, changing meters, as well as additive rhythmic and melodic elements played on non-technical percussion and melodic instruments by non musicians. From this perspective, it seems to me defensible to argue that Stravinsky plus Günther equals Orff Schulwerk. From Günther we note the isolation of movement elements that lead to the artistic form; from Stravinsky comes the revelation of the color and rhythmic possibilities of percussion instruments and the application of these resources to create music from short rhythmic and melodic elements. These were the ideas that were "in the air," as Orff liked to say; his role was to codify them into a revolutionary approach to music education for children.

Orff's association with Güntherschule lasted for about ten years before he turned over the music teaching duties to Hans Bergese in 1932 and William Twittenhoff in 1934.

The school curriculum was based upon Günther's synthesis of the leading movement approaches: gymnastics (from Mendensiek), rhythmic dance (from Dalcroze), and expressive dance (from Laban). It also included courses in anatomy, physiology, movement notation, and the history of art—all of which were taught by Günther. Maja Lex, a brilliant dancer, was added to the movement staff after fifteen months of study at the school. Gunild Keetman was officially appointed to the music teaching staff in 1928, but she had been working out musical ideas with Orff since her arrival at the school two years earlier.

In only six short years, the Güntherschule had become a success story. By 1930, the *Tanzgruppe Günther* was receiving critical acclaim for its exceptional repertoire of primitive dances, including the *Barbaric Suite*, *Ecstatic Dance*, and the *Night of the Hovering Thoughts*.

In addition to its performances, the Güntherschule was also the birthplace of a flood of Orff-Schulwerk publications that were issued by Schott from 1930 – 1935. In these five short years, no fewer than twenty-two books addressed technique for playing percussion instruments, xylophones, recorders, piano, and even violin.

William Twittenhoff, who—as we have seen—was soon to become a leader in the music division of the Hitler Youth, contributed the last book from that period in 1935. Examples from this book illustrate notable similarities to *Music for Children*, published 15 years later.

Though Orff Schulwerk was born in Munich, it did not die there. In 1949—after the first successful Music for Children radio broadcasts of 1948—Keetman began teaching bi-weekly classes for children aged eight through ten at the Mozarteum in Salzburg. But, something striking happened to the wildflower in the trip from Germany to Austria. Instead of the Güntherschule's emphasis on dance, the new Mozarteum curriculum featured music. Instead of an educational program that addressed young adult women, the new participants were children who would now be involved primarily in music activities that were enhanced by dance.

Other significant developments that reinforced the new emphasis on music included the publication of *Music for Children* volumes in 1950 – 1954 and the release of the first Schulwerk recordings issued in 1956 – 1957. A further illustration of the shift in focus from dance to music is the first Orff-Schulwerk course curriculum that the Mozarteum organized for teachers in 1953. And, it was not accidental. Orff was now free to realize his dream of a musical education for teachers, and as he states in his autobiography: "This meant another approach to the work for Keetman, for these students would be mostly music teachers in the making" (Orff, 1978, p. 239). Clearly, Orff Schulwerk had been reborn. Music was now the driving force, supported by dance.

As interest in Orff Schulwerk increased, a new four-semester curriculum sequence for adults was developed at the Mozarteum in 1961 under the direction of Carl Orff, Gunild Keetman, and Wilhelm Keller. Two years later, on October 25, 1963, a new home especially designed for Orff-Schulwerk pedagogy was dedicated. The Orff Institute offered the necessary facilities to support the development and implementation of curricular plans for pre-service and in-service teachers. The following chart offers us the opportunity to look at the way those special course plans evolved over twenty-year intervals from 1962-2002.

Table 2

Forty Years of Orff-Schulwerk Training Courses

1962 – 2002

	MOZARTEUM 1962 Four Semesters	ORFF INSTITUTE Special Course 1981-1982 1 Semester	ORFF INSTITUTE Special Course 2002-2003 1 Year
PEDAGOGY	(10%) Pedagogy / Didactics	(4%) Pedagogy	(23%) O-S Sources; Didactics; Pedagogy/Practice Teach
MUSIC *	(70%) Theory; Folk songs; Choral Conducting; Literature Analysis; Rhythmic, Melodic Exercises; Improvisation Recorder, Gamba, Instrumental Ensemble Training on Percussion, Wind, String, and Keyboard Instruments	(44%) Percussion; Ensemble and Improvisation; Active Music Listening Recorder; Music & Mvt. Composition	(18%) Ensemble & Improvisation Composing with and for Children
MOVEMENT	(20%) Movement Training Gymnastics	(44%) Movement Technique, Gymnastics; Movement Forms; Music and Mvt.; Mvt. Accompaniment; Mvt. Improv; Trad. Dances	(41%) M & M Projects; Mvt./Dance Technique; Basic Choreography & Improvisation; Mvt. Accompaniment
SPECIAL TOPICS	(0%)	(8%) Colloquium	(18%) Lectures with Special Themes; Weekly Round-Table Discussion

* A course for building instruments was also offered. In 1962, it was taught by Klaus Becker-Emck, the founder of Studio 49.

So we can see that the wildflower was budding and ready to bloom in favorable conditions beyond its new Austrian home. We will follow it to North America in the next section.

Orff Schulwerk in the New World

Cultivating the Wildflower in the New World

As you know, wildflowers arrive spontaneously—often in surprising places. The Schulwerk was no exception! Quite by accident, it was discovered at an International Society for Music Education (ISME) meeting in Europe by a German musical administrator working in Canada. Dr. Arnold Walter, Director of the Faculty of Music at the University of Toronto, offered the first United States presentation of Orff Schulwerk in April 1956 at a Music Educators National Conference meeting presented by ISME. In addition to his paper, the session included a children's demonstration. This introduction was followed by workshops, demonstrations, and courses throughout the United States under the leadership of Doreen Hall, a Walter protégé. And so, the transformation from wildflower to North American cultivar was underway.

We will examine several factors that have coalesced to produce American Orff Schulwerk, as we seek to discover how the wildflower was cultivated in this country. These factors include the music education climate in the mid-twentieth century, the role of the American Orff-Schulwerk Association, local chapters, conferences, training courses, scholarships, and books.

The American Climate

Music education in mid-twentieth-century America was suffering from a pedagogical drought. Traditional practice was based upon passive music appreciation and teacher-directed performance activities. The profession itself acknowledged the need for reform in the 1960s with the Yale Seminar (1963) and Tanglewood Symposium (1967). Indeed, if music educators had been providing hands-on, playful approaches to music learning, it is unlikely that Orff's wildflower would have taken root here. But, Orff Schulwerk was just what imaginative American music teachers were seeking: a developmentally sound, discovery-based, musically valid, joyful approach to music teaching and learning, and they set to work to adapt it to the musical landscape of this country.

It is not at all surprising that the music education establishment in the United States was not particularly welcoming to this immigrant pedagogical approach. College and university professors who typically espoused theory over application resisted the participatory model of the Schulwerk. In addition, the early efforts of some young Orff teachers with more enthusiasm than experience who demonstrated the delight, if not the essence, of the Schulwerk caused doubts about the effectiveness of Orff Schulwerk.

My own experiences as a young practitioner illustrate the prevailing attitudes among music education leaders. I was invited to present summer Orff courses at several prestigious universities because of student demand, but faculty support was non existent. I was once introduced as "the foreign expert," and was invited to present a session for a Music Educators National Conference meeting in the late 1970s, with the stipulation that I never mention the word Orff. However, the climate began to warm somewhat during the 1980s and by the 1990s Orff was no longer a four-letter word. In fact, we are currently witnessing a transformation in U.S. university programs, with young professors, including Orff among the so-called "eclectic approaches," worthy of consideration by undergraduates. In addition, several American universities now offer a master's degree with an Orff emphasis.

It is unlikely that such progress would have occurred without the backing of a strong, supportive organization. The American Orff-Schulwerk Association has met that need for almost a half century.

Organizational Support: The American Orff-Schulwerk Association

Growing interest in Orff Schulwerk around the country inspired Arnold Burkart, then teaching at Ball State University in Muncie, Indiana, to convene a group of midwestern Orff proponents in May of 1968 to establish a professional organization. The American Orff-Schulwerk Association

(AOSA) was founded to support and encourage interest among teachers, as they discovered and explored this fresh approach to teaching music. In order to publicize these efforts, the organization established a newsletter, *The Orff Echo*, and promoted annual national conferences. The first conference was held at Ball State University in April of 1969, with Arnold Walter and Doreen Hall headlining the event. The meeting attracted 165 participants, an unexpectedly healthy number for a fledgling organization not yet a year old.

The initial sprinkle became a full-fledged storm of interest as membership increased 360 percent (from 330 to 1185) during the first five years of the organization's existence. Membership continued to grow throughout the next decade, peaking at 5,000 in 1998. Membership numbers declined to about 3,000 during the first decade of the twenty-first century, attributable—at least in part—to a new emphasis on reading and math that resulted in cutbacks in school music.

Local Chapter Activity

The wise founders of AOSA realized that promoting Orff's educational ideas could best be realized at the local level. At the outset, seven chapters were chartered in 1970; the number has grown to ninety-five as of fall 2010. The total number of members in local chapters is currently 5,400. Chapter Annual Reports indicate that forty-one percent of local chapter members also hold national membership in AOSA.

With the founding of local Orff chapters, the largest network of regularly scheduled in-service opportunities for music teachers in the nation was established. The notion of teachers teaching teachers in workshops organized and financed by local chapters was remarkably successful, illustrating that grass-roots efforts could provide opportunities for collaborative learning and mutual support. Minnesota chapter and AOSA member Shana Wagner put it this way: "For many of us, Minnesota Orff has offered the extra momentum, the new energy to put into work we loved, a community of great friends and learners, and a renewing of our musical and creative spirits." Many local chapters partner with colleges and universities to offer workshops at discounted rates for music education students. Others have gone further, providing experienced chapter members as resource teachers for Orff pedagogy classes in college and university music education courses, volunteering time as mentors to young teachers, and welcoming student teachers into their classrooms. For a decade, the Rocky Mountain chapter in Denver has sponsored the College Liaison Program, bringing Orff workshops and information to pre-service teachers at colleges in the area.

Publicity: Publications and Media

As we have previously noted, *The Orff Echo* was founded in 1968 to promote a national community of Orff practitioners. The original three-issues-a-year publication has become a quarterly, with a professional editor and volunteer editorial board that determines content and provides oversight. Each issue offers a collection of articles that illuminate a selected theme of importance to Orff teachers.

The Orff Echo has been joined by a number of complementary publications such as the quarterly newsletter, *Reverberations*, conference videos and DVDs, and related print monographs. Remarkably, all this publicity activity, with the exceptions of the *The Orff Echo* editor and Webmaster, has been achieved by volunteer efforts.

An archive collection of materials from a half-century of Orff Schulwerk in America is housed in the Isabel McNeill Carley Library at the Eastman School of Music. However, Orff teachers who are primarily interested in the practical application of Orff Schulwerk to their classrooms (and the excitement of its possibilities) make their way to the annual AOSA conference, hosted by local chapters throughout the country.

The AOSA Professional Development Conference

Since 1969, the AOSA conference has attracted music educators from throughout the U.S. as well as Canada and—increasingly—international participants. Attendance at these annual meetings has increased over ten times the 165 that were present at the first conference. In fact, in some years more than 2,000 teachers and visitors have been attracted to this gathering: a community of educators connecting with like-minded friends to improve their practice, make music, and dance. All Orff teachers have special conference memories of people and ideas that have changed their professional—and perhaps—personal lives. The participatory sessions at these conferences have offered opportunities to encounter materials, curriculum ideas, and pedagogical applications in an atmosphere that fosters community and discovery.

Forty-four Professional Development Conferences have been held in the U.S. since 1969 (two conferences were held in the years 1974 and 1975). As with local chapter meetings, these conferences demonstrate the most likely explanation of the dynamic growth and acceptance of Orff's ideas in this country: teachers actively teaching one another. Many music educators who attend these meetings are inspired to seek more intensive Orff training that is available at college and university summer courses throughout the country.

Summer Courses

American teachers who sought training in Orff Schulwerk initially had to make their way to Toronto, where special summer courses under the leadership of Doreen Hall and Arnold Walter were first established in 1957. The 1962 course included a weekend of presentations by Carl Orff and Gunild Keetman. A few weekend Orff workshops for teachers had been conducted in the U.S. during the 1960s; however, American three-level, three summer teacher-training courses were first established in 1963 at Ball State University in Indiana. The charismatic Belgian teacher, Jos Wuytack, then a member of the Toronto faculty, established two-week, three-level courses in the United States based upon the Canadian model: first at Memphis State (TN) in 1970 and the University of Minnesota in 1971. These programs have offered levels courses in consecutive summers for forty years—training teachers who now staff courses throughout the country.

Because Orff was not interested in overseeing the international spread of the Schulwerk, two species of his wildflower emerged in the United States. Wuytack's work represented a shift in emphasis from rhythmic and melodic counterpoint illustrated in the five volumes of Orff's *Music for Children* to classical melody and harmony, based upon his own teaching material.

American courses featured Salzburg or Wuytack, depending on the course director and faculty.

A specific area of contrast in approach is the use of instruments. Wuytack students learn to accompany folk songs with Orff instruments, but typically do not play instrumental pieces, particularly from the Orff/Keetman volumes. Salzburg courses use the instrumental pieces in the volumes as inspiration for improvisation and take a different approach to song accompaniment.

Both Salzburg and Wuytack represent a selective American application of the original Schulwerk model of music and movement education. Courses were developed that recognized the limitations of time and space in the schools and thus resulted in an emphasis on music over movement training.

Another important consequence of transplanting the wildflower to American practice has, in my opinion, been the emphasis on outcomes that has transcended the kind of experimentation encouraged by Orff. He intended his pieces in the *Music for Children* volumes to be used as models for children and teachers as they developed their own original expressions, but the performance ideal has retained its authority in most music programs. The outcome has been that improvisation has not been central to the adaptation of Orff Schulwerk in America.

A further problem encountered by the transfer of Schulwerk to America is the summer course structure. The two-week Level I program must include basic Orff skills and vocabulary as well as movement and recorder, leaving little time for pedagogical application of these skills. Because teacher modeling does not a curriculum provide, teachers may find themselves unprepared to bring their joyous Orff learning experiences to the daily realities of their own classroom situations. As a result, they may conclude that the best use of Orff instruments is in performance situations.

American teachers will have to come to grips with these issues as they also attempt to address the many cultures that are present in their classrooms. A new emphasis on speech activities will be one avenue to highlight this diversity, along with songs and dances of the various ethnic populations. Although it has been adapted in many cultures, the original *Music for Children* music is Western in orientation and so will need to be supplemented with examples from other cultural frameworks.

The dichotomy of the approaches to content described above has proven to be a difficult hurdle to overcome for those designing guidelines for Orff-Schulwerk Training Courses that outlined ensemble, movement, and recorder proficiencies with time allocation suggestions for a two-week, sixty-hour, three-level program. Three documents published in 1976, 1980, and 1997 reflect the two divergent approaches to harmonic progression, resulting in alternative program specifications for Levels II and III. A new guidelines committee introduced a single approach to content in 2012 that will serve all U.S. courses in the future. With this standardization of Schulwerk elements, the wildflower is well on the way to becoming a cultivar.

Now let's return to our Training Courses chart. We've already seen that the course developed by Orff at the Mozarteum stipulated that seventy percent of the coursework would be devoted to music. In twenty years you can see it has been reduced to forty-four percent, and finally to eighteen percent of the curriculum. However, at George Mason and Southern Methodist Universities (whose programs are almost identical and fairly typical of programs around the country), music constitutes fifty-eight percent of the total program. The unavoidable conclusion from this chart: a student who attends a three-level program in the United States receives virtually the same amount of music training in six weeks as an Orff Institute student receives in a full year of study. There are many attractive reasons to visit Salzburg, but it would seem that the study of elemental music theory and application is not an important one.

Table 3

Fifty Years of Orff-Schulwerk Training Courses

1961 – 2011

	MOZARTEUM 1961 4 Semesters	ORFF INSTITUTE Special Course 1981-1982 1 Semester	ORFF INSTITUTE Special Course 2002-2003 1 Year	GEORGE MASON; SMU Levels Programs 2011 2 Weeks
PEDAGOGY	(10) Pedagogy / Didactics	(4%) Pedagogy	(23%) O-S Sources; Didactics; Pedagogy/Practice Tch	(15%) Pedagogy
MUSIC *	(70%) Theory; Folk songs; Choral Conducting; Literature Analysis; Rhythmic, Melodic Exercises; Improvisation Recorder, Gamba, Instrumental Ensemble Training on Percussion, Wind, String, and Keyboard Instruments	(44%) Percussion; Ensemble and Improvisation; Active Music Listening Recorder; Music & Mvt. Composition	(18%) Ensemble & Improvisation Composing with and for Children	(58%) Ensemble/Improvisation Recorder
MOVEMENT	(20%) Movement Training Gymnastics	(44%) Movement Technique, Gymnastics; Movement Forms; Music and Mvt. Movement Accompaniment; Mvt. Improv; Trad. Dances	(41%) M & M Projects; Mvt. Dance Technique, Basic Choreography & Improvisation; Mvt. Accompaniment	(19%) Movement Technique; Mvt. Improvisation; Mvt. Pedagogy; Rhythmic Movement; Traditional Dances
SPECIAL TOPICS	(0%)	(8%) Colloquium	(18%) Lectures with Special Themes; Weekly Round-Table Discussion	(8%) Community Music & Movement Activities; Lectures

* A course for building instruments was also offered. In 1962, it was taught by Klaus Becker-Emck, the founder of Studio 49. SMU/George Mason: 27.5 hours of music per level x 3 = 82.5 hours of music over 3 levels Orff Institute: three hours of music per week x 28 weeks = 84 hours of music over one year.

AOSA-approved teacher education courses have enjoyed healthy growth over the forty years they have been offered in the United States. Following the appointment of Steve Calantropio as Education Director in 2007, summer course content and faculty are carefully reviewed before AOSA course approval is granted.

During the last five years, the number of courses held at universities across the country has ranged from forty-two to fifty-three, serving an average of 1,515 students each summer. Considering the relatively unfavorable economic environment and school climates (all arts left behind in the age of No Child Left Behind) during this period, these numbers seem to me to be reasonably healthy. The survival of Orff programs around the country is actually somewhat surprising when we take into account the inevitable university tuition increases and the fact that most Orff teacher training efforts are self-supported. That is what makes tuition scholarships a crucial AOSA endeavor.

Financial Support

AOSA recognized early in its history the importance of offering scholarship help to students wishing to begin or continue Orff study. The idea of a grass-roots organization based upon the concept of mutual support and primarily funded by teacher/members is no better illustrated than in the scholarship efforts that have been established by AOSA. Since 1976, a staggering total of $344,907 has been given to enhance the work of 362 Orff teachers, supported—for the most part—by the generosity of music teachers. Put another way, almost $10,000 a year since 1976 has been given to Orff teachers and schools to further the implementation of Orff-Schulwerk music programs.

Table 4

Scholarships and Financial Aid

Name of Fund	Established	Current Assets	Total Award Amounts	Recipients
Gunild Keetman	1976	$230,500	$216,147	249
Research	1986	$78,000	$26,482	27
Shields/ Gillespie	1987	$57,000	$43,753	32
TAP	1996	$104,000	$44,616	43
International Outreach	2002	$17,000	$4,709	8
Barbara Potter	2007	$54,000	$9,200	3
TOTALS		$540,500	$344,907	362

Books

The enthusiastic reception of Orff Schulwerk in the U.S. encouraged Schott to begin an American publication program. The initial effort toward realizing this possibility was led by the director of the Orff Institute, Hermann Regner. His strong commitment to an indigenous American materials collection led to the three-volume set of *Music for Childen American Edition* (1977 – 1982). This collection has inspired thirty-seven supplemental books for classroom use, and the list continues to grow.

Many other books for American teachers have joined these supplements. Songs with Orff instrumental accompaniment have proliferated, given the rich heritage of pentatonic folk songs in America. In addition, the growth of immigrant populations in this country has encouraged production of materials and recordings that reflect a variety of ethnic music and dance contributions.

Beginning in the 1980s, American teachers began the process of sifting, clarifying, and ordering the elements of Orff Schulwerk for practical classroom application. Major contributors to this effort include Brigitte Warner's *Orff Schulwerk: Applications for the Classroom* (1991), Konnie

Saliba's *Accent on Orff* (1990), Arvida Steen's *Exploring Orff* (1992) and my own *Discovering Orff (1987), Orff Schulwerk Today (2006), and Artful, Playful, Mindful (2012)*. Doug Goodkin's *Play, Sing, and Dance* joined the list in 2004.

Summary

It is clear that much effort has been expended in the U.S. to convert Orff's wild plant into a cultivar with gratifying pedagogical outcomes. A half-century of careful—and caring—work has been devoted to the application of original Schulwerk material and international folk resources to the American school curriculum.

But, we didn't create this musical garden on our own. Our half-century of success is due—in large part—to two courageous women who planted the seeds: Doreen Hall and Margaret Murray. Hall's work included the first North American edition of *Music for Children* and the organization and administration of Schulwerk courses in Toronto that provided the momentum for the first generation of American Orff teachers. Murray taught us how the music could be realized through the *Music for Children* recordings, how elemental style unfolded through the *Music for Children* volumes, and how it might be taught in her translation of Keetman's *Elementaria*.

And so, we have come full circle from the trio of gifted women who established and nurtured elemental music and dance at the Güntherschule in Germany (Dorothee Günther, Gunild Keetman, and Maja Lex). It is the English duet—Doreen Hall and Margaret Murray—who organized and produced the books and courses necessary for its North American dissemination. The male visionaries (Jaques-Dalcroze, Laban, and Orff) offered the original inspiration, but the trio—followed by the duet—of courageous women brought the ideas to fruition. For the gifts of musical resources and inspiration, we acknowledge the visionaries, while expressing our profound gratitude to the five women whose work made our own possible.

Table 5

From the Old World to the New
Cast of Characters in the Orff Drama
The Old World

Hans Bergese	1910-2000	Orff student and collaborator and co-editor (with Orff and Keetman) of Orff-Schulwerk editions 1932-1935. Composer, developer of Orff instruments for Sonor 1953. Güntherschule teacher from 1932.
Cesar Bresgen	1913-1988	Professor of composition at Mozarteum in 1939 and again in 1947. Hitler Youth composer, Orff friend and colleague, ardent National Socialist.
Dorothee Günther	1896-1975	Founder of the Güntherschule, a dance school. Gymnastics teacher, author, and costume designer for Tanzgruppe Günther, the school, performing group. She insisted on artistic dance expression based upon technique.
Emile Jaques-Dalcroze	1865-1950	Visionary teacher who developed rhythmic gymnastics, body awareness linked to music. First school in Hellerau 1922-1924, and then founded Institute in Geneva in 1925. School continues today.
Gunild Keetman	1904-1990	Orff Schulwerk co-creator and teacher. Compositions developed from elements of dance for teachers and children. Author of *Music for Children*, *Elementaria*, and more than twenty other didactic books.
Leo Kestenberg	1882-1962	Reformer who established a unified system of instruction for school music and private lessons. Removed from office by the Nazis before he could establish Orff Schulwerk as the foundation of German music study.
Rudolph Laban	1879-1958	Dancer, author, choreographer, founder of fourteen schools of dance in Europe. Ballet master in Berlin. He contributed to the modern ideal of emotional expression in dance. Developed dance notation system: Labanotation.
Maja Lex	1906-1986	Brilliant dancer, choreographer, and teacher who developed Güntherschule dance curriculum based on structural technique leading to improvisation.
Bess Mensendieck	1864-1957	American physician who developed the System of Functional Movements reflecting women's daily activities. Author of eight books; established schools throughout Europe based on her physical exercise regimen without music.
Carl Orff	1885-1982	German composer and music educator who developed pedagogy based upon elemental music and movement. Students are active participants in improvisation involving speech, movement, song, and instrument playing.
Eberhard Prussner	1889-1964	Staff of Mozarteum for Hitler Youth music in 1939; Director in1948. Began an Orff-Schulwerk program in 1949; supported new Orff Institute 1963.

Hermann Regner	1928-2008	Director of Orff Institute; composer, teacher, radio broadcaster, founder of Orff Schulwerk Forum and executive board member of the Orff-Schulwerk Foundation. Edited the American Edition of *Music for Children*.
Igor Stravinsky	1882-1971	One of the most influential composers of the twentieth century, this Russian changed musical expression with emphasis on rhythmic energy, melodies created from two- to three-note cells, and emancipated percussion instruments.
William Twittenhoff	1904-1969	Orff student and Güntherschule colleague; led music department from 1934. Authored *Music for Children* in 1935; instructor in the Weimar Hitler Youth who believed in the power of rhythmic indoctrination.

Table 6

From the Old World to the New
Cast of Characters in the Orff Drama
The New World

Arnold Burkart	Founding member and first president of AOSA. Executive Secretary of AOSA 1970-1974. Teacher, music administrator, clinician in U.S. and Orff Institute. Author of *Keeping Up With Orff Schulwerk in the Classroom* 1971-1981.
Steve Calantropio	First AOSA Education Director. Teacher of children (thirty-one years), author of *Pieces and Processes* and articles on Orff Schulwerk. National and international clinician; developed and teaches master classes in elemental music.
Isabel Carley	First editor and author of many articles for *The Orff Echo* (1968-1983). Graduated from Orff Institute in 1964. Recorder performer and composer, studio teacher of children, and national presenter of Orff workshops for teachers.
Jane Frazee	Founder and director of first M.A. program with Orff concentration, teacher of children and teachers, Fulbright Professor at Orff Institute 1981-1982, author of five books of Orff pedagogy, AOSA Past President and Distinguished Service Award; recipient of Pro Merito Award.
Doug Goodkin	Author of seven books on music education and many articles on Orff pedagogy, teacher of children (thirty-four years), international presenter of Orff workshops and courses, director of San Francisco Orff summer course; Pro Merito Award winner.
Doreen Hall	Introduced Orff Schulwerk to North America. Founded Canadian Orff Society and summer course in Toronto (1957); co-authored first adaptation of *Music for Children* in English, Salzburg study (1954-1955), Pro Merito and Order of Canada awards.
Grace C. Nash.	Early proponent of Orff Schulwerk in the U.S. Author of four volumes of *Music With Children* and other publications including Creative Approaches to Child Development. First recipient of AOSA's Distinguished Service Award.
Margaret Murray	Founder of UK Orff Society. Produced first recordings of *Music for Children* (1956) and authored the second translation of the five volumes in English and Keetman's *Elementaria*. Teacher and author of articles on Orff Schulwerk.
Mary Shamrock	Past President of AOSA, second *The Orff Echo* editor, author of monographs on Orff Schulwerk (*Background and Commentary; Issues in Global Dispersal*). Distinguished Service Award from AOSA; editor of *Guidelines for Orff Training Courses* 1980.
Arvida Steen	AOSA Past President and Distinguished Service Award winner, author of *Exploring Orff* and co-author of two books of Orff pieces for children, *Chair of Guidelines for Orff Training Courses* revision, 1997. Teacher mentor, clinician in US, Canada, Salzburg, and Australia.
Brigitte Warner	Author of *Orff Schulwerk: Applications for the Classroom*, studied Orff at the Mozarteum with Orff and Keetman; taught children and teachers from 1966 until her death in 1998.
Jos Wuytack	Developed the two-week, three-level plan of Orff-Schulwerk courses now standard practice in the US. International presenter, author of Orff-Schulwerk articles and various collections of pieces for instruments and voices in many languages.

From the Old World to the New:

Chronology

1854-1957	Bess Mensendieck
1879-1958	Rudolf Laban
1889-1964	Eberhard Preussner
1895-1950	Emile Jaques-Dalcroze
1895-1982	Carl Orff
1896-1975	Dorothee Günther
1904-1990	Gunild Keetman
1906-1986	Maja Lex
1917	Orff's brief military service
1921	Margaret Murray born
	Doreen Hall born
1924	Güntherschule founded
1931-1934	First Schulwerk publications: Orff, Keetman, Bergese
1937	*Carmina Burana* premiere
1948	Schulwerk radio broadcasts begin.
	Preussner appointed Mozarteum President
1949	Orff Schulwerk children's classes begin at Mozarteum under Keetman
1950-1954	*Music for Children* by Orff and Keetman published (Volumes I – V)
1954-1955	Doreen Hall in Salzburg to study with Orff and Keetman
1956-1961	Hall English edition of *Music for Children* published
1956	First Orff Schulwerk recordings issued
1957	First summer course in Toronto
1958-1966	Murray English edition of *Music for Children* published
1961	Opening of Orff Schulwerk Information Center at the Mozarteum
1962	First Conference: *Orff Schulwerk in the School* at the Mozarteum
	Orff and Keetman weekend presentations at University of Toronto course
1963	Orff Institute opens
	First American summer course – Ball State University
1968	Birth of the American Orff-Schulwerk Association
1969	First AOSA Professional Development Conference
1970	First Wuytack U.S. course – Memphis State University
1976	AOSA Guidelines for Orff Training Courses published – Level I

1977	*Paralipomena* published
1977-1982	American Edition of *Music for Children* published
1980	AOSA Guidelines for Orff Training Courses published: Levels I – III
1997	Revised AOSA Training Course Guidelines published: Levels I – III
2007	AOSA Education Director appointed

BIBLIOGRAPHY

Books

Blom, P. (2008). *The vertigo years.* New York: Basic Books.

Kater, M. H. (1997). *The twisted muse.* New York: Oxford University Press.

Kater, M. H. (2000). *Composers of the Nazi era.* New York: Oxford University Press.

Kater, M. H. (2004). *Hitler youth.* Cambridge: Harvard University Press.

Large, D. C. (1997). *Where ghosts walked.* New York: W.W. Norton.

Mellers, W. (2008). *Caliban reborn.* New York: Harper and Row.

Orff, C. (1967). *The Schulwerk.* New York: Schott Music Corp.

Regner, H., & Ronnefeld, M. (Eds.). (2004). *Gunild Keetman.* Mainz: Schott.

Ross, A. (2007). *The rest is noise.* New York: Farrar, Strauss, and Groux.

Shirer, W. L. (1960). *The rise and fall of the Third Reich.* New York: Simon & Schuster.

Thomas, W. (1977). *Musica poetica.* Tutzing: Verleagt Bei Haus Schneider.

Toepfer, K. (1997). *Empire of Ecstasy.* Berkeley: University of California Press.

Twittenhoff, W. (1935). *Orff Schulwerk.* Mainz: B. Schott's Sohne.

Warner, B. (1991). *Orff-Schulwerk: Applications for the classroom,* Englewood Cliffs NJ: Prentice Hall.

Articles

Keetman, G. (1985). Reminiscences of the Güntherschule. In AOSA, *Orff Re-Echoes Book II* (pp. 3-7).

Maier, H. (1995). Carl Orff in His Time. Mainz: Schott.

Orff, C. (1972). The Schulwerk – Its Origins and Aims. In MENC, *The Eclectic Curriculum in American Music Education* (pp. 152-161).

References

Kater, M. H. (2000). *Composers of the Nazi Era*. New York: Oxford University Press.

Music and the holocaust: Music amongst the Hitler Youth. (n.d.). Retrieved from http://holocaustmusic.ort.org/politics-and-propaganda/third-reich/music-hitler-youth/

Orff, C. (1978). *Documentation, Vol. III*. New York: Schott Music Corp.

Chapter 4

Orff Schulwerk in Latin America:
Diverse Experiences
Ana Lucía Frega[1]

To describe the way Orff Schulwerk was introduced in Latin America, I found myself remembering my PhD studies about "methods," and some of these methods had a great impact in Latin America. Outlining this introduction of Orff Schulwerk turned out to be a great challenge because Latin America is a complex subject. Why is it such a large subject? Latin America is a huge subject in itself— as an expansive continent, as an area of varied people and cultures, as the diversity of pre-colonial realities, and finally because of the mixture and sometimes overlapping of colonial influences, all of which influence contemporary states/countries.

Though I am not a certified Orff educator, I was involved with it at the beginning of my professional life—first at my home in Buenos Aires, and then at the Orff Institute in Salzburg nine years after completing my degree at the National Conservatory in Buenos Aires, Argentina. Following that, I immediately became a teacher of music at the kindergarten, primary, and secondary levels. I became involved in all the graduate courses available at the time in my town, which, of course, included Orff. I then met Guillermo Graetzer, a key person in the history I intend to share with you.

So, I am not a "specialist" because there were no classes in the Orff approach in my undergraduate study at that time, but when I traveled to Europe to visit the main center of the methods I was interested in and acquainted with e.g., Willems and Martenot in France, Jaques-Dalcroze in Switzerland, and Orff in Austria, I studied in Salzburg in the early 1960s. When attending my lessons at the Orff Institute in Salzburg, I met Herman Regner, with whom I had some interesting discussions and attended several classes with various teachers. Among them was Barbara Haselbach, who was in charge of the important area of movement. I was a friend of José Posada, who was from Uruguay and became a known Orff teacher, teaching several courses in Buenos Aires and in different Spanish countries in Latin America as well.

Orff Schulwerk in Argentina

As early as 1884, the Argentinean National Law of Education required music to be a single, required subject in the schools for two primary purposes: (1) to reinforce the compulsory study of Spanish all over the country, which was then facing a permanent increase of immigrants; and (2) through singing, to develop the national anthem and patriotic songs that represent national identity of primary students. For these reasons, music was compulsory in primary school in Argentina (Frega, de Couve, & Dal Pino, 2010), starting at the kindergarten level and proceeding through the end of the secondary level. From 1950 on, Argentinean music educators have been very interested in contemporary approaches to music teaching, which means that commonly known "methods" around the world have been studied and applied.

In Argentina, the Spanish version of the Orff Schulwerk was first published as *Orff Schulwerk: Adaptación castellana para Latino-América realizada por Guillermo Graetzer*. The formal Orff Institute Yearbook acknowledged this version of the Schulwerk, and consequently, a practical introductory booklet was published by Guillermo Graetzer with Antonio Yepes. This booklet was the "introduction" to the actual series of books containing songs, rhymes, and arrangements. To prepare this volume, Graetzer had the valuable help of Antonio Yepes, a well-known percussionist. Graetzer, however, was the individual who led the movement on the Orff approach and who oversaw the publication of the five small volumes with songs and rhymes titled, *Musica para niños* [*Music for Children*]. The international leaders of Orff Schulwerk immediately acknowledged this version because it was included in the official list of available versions of the Orff approach printed in the 1962 Orff Institute Yearbook.

After publication, several problems emerged. First, many ethnomusicologists did not agree with Graetzer's musical selections. Even though the Orff supporters tried to make it a compulsory method to be used all over the country, this intention did not work for the following reasons:

- money for instruments was not always available;
- it did not fit the Argentinean musical tradition of the entire curriculum;
- Argentinean music employs three-, four-, and five-note scales, but they were not the identical European scales used by Orff; and
- the instrumental timbres were non-traditional. Drums such as the *bombo*, *caja*, and *kultrun* were a part of the Argentinean tradition and folklore, but none of them were initially included as classroom material.

The set of instruments did not meet the musical Argentinean traditions, and the kind of folk music that was taught in the general educational system differed from traditional European folk music of the time. Musical timbre is not innocent, and as a result, the musical arrangements *did not sound Argentinean*.

Art composers were immersed in a combination of a "nationalistic movement" (circa 1920-1930), an emphasis on the folklore traditions (circa 1940-1950), and a move toward the Western academic rules of composition, including all the common avant-garde tendencies of the time. For this reason, people such as the world-renowned Argentinean composer Alberto Ginastera were seriously opposed to the Orff approach, especially when some people tried to make it a kind of "official," compulsory method to be used exclusively. Other methods were becoming known at that time as well, including Jaques-Dalcroze (since the 1930s), Edgar Willems and Maurice Martenot (since the 1960s), and Zoltan Kodály. Additionally, all Latin American countries normally handle music on the basis of a fixed-*do* system, which uses no letters (or movable *do*, as such). The use of fixed *do* was another reason to argue against the Orff approach at that time. Nevertheless, the impact that the Orff approach and Graetzer had in the teaching of music at the kindergarten and primary levels greatly influenced the contents of the programs at that time, which were dictated by national authorities in the tradition of a country with strong centralized governments.[2]

From a cultural point of view, Latin America should not be reduced to cultural stereotypes i.e., a warm region, mariachi as the Mexican music, etc. A much too synthetic approach toward the subject of Latin America results in an oversimplification. So, the fact that Graetzer made a Spanish version did not ensure that the musical material was truly valid for the entire vast and diverse region.

Orff Schulwerk in Mexico

In Mexico, Cesar Tort, a Mexican composer who was also interested in music education, reacted against the international Orff approach—not really in principle, but instead concerning the kinds of instruments used. He said the Orff Schulwerk had nothing to do with Mexico because it did not have the Mexican identity that he wanted to retain. This point of view was the same the one held in Argentina.

An instrument's construction can retain national identity. The physical construction of the instrument can symbolize other greater things, such as culture and a country's heritage. For this reason, Tort used traditional instruments of the local Mexican cultures to integrate a new "Orff-style ensemble." He also wrote a *Music for Children* book for Mexican children, incorporating both Orff-Schulwerk principles and local traditional instruments. For Tort, Orff principles were locally based on both geographic location and local instrumental traditions.

Orff Schulwerk in Colombia

In Colombia, it was simply another case of the dissemination of Orff in Latin America. In Colombia, music educators benefited from the donated instrument settings in many schools, but they rejected some of the Orff materials because they did not directly refer to the Colombian tradition. As previously stated, musical timbre is not innocent; it has a cultural meaning!

We would not have the ninth symphony of Beethoven's if the world restricted him in terms of musical timbre.

Conclusion

Although Carl Orff's contribution was tremendous, its use should be culturally questioned. What makes his contributions so profound? Is it the actual sounds, or is it the impact of being able to offer musical opportunities to all children, even those with developing skills? Composers in the United States have dealt with native musical traditions, as have composers in Latin America. The concept-forming component of Orff is profound. Allowing children to discover their own knowledge is also wildly profound. So, my idea is that the Orff approach, as it has been used in the region, reflects some of the influence of valid principles and is still alive. I dare to recommend a comparative survey in the Americas about the use of the Orff approach based upon the areas listed below.

- Principles
- Instruments
- Repertoire
- Planning
- Evaluation

Such a descriptive and comparative study may help to build a more regional, multicultural approach to Orff Schulwerk, which would offer numerous benefits for the improvement of music education.

Summative Ideas

- The Graetzer's concept of "Latin American" was neither special nor complete.
- Orff Schulwerk was an important growth as a "tool," but cultural decisions had to be made about its use and improvement in the region.
- Some of the activities included in the curricula of different countries in the region were very much Orff oriented (echo, imitation, etc.), while others were not (fixed *do* versus moveable *do*, different timbres, etc.).

I understand that music education practice and research has grown in many ways since the 1960s. Practitioners and researchers have expanded the field with a vast amount of information such that we now may take further steps to develop and even enlarge the scope conceived by great people such as Carl Orff and followers such as Guillermo Graetzer and César Tort. As stated by Charles Elliott (1996),

> Music education has been referred to by some critics as 'a profession without a discipline,' implying that there is no separate and distinct body of knowledge making up that area of study called music education.... Not too long ago, much of the research in music education was done by doctoral students completing their dissertations. Continuing and long-term research related to music teaching and learning is now beginning to become rather commonplace and is being conducted by researchers in music education.... That discipline we call music education is beginning to take place. (p. 2)

As practitioners and researchers, we should invest both time and energy to improve the field of our profession. I am ready to help in this regard.

References

Elliott, C. A. (1996). Forward. *Update: Applications of Research in Music Education, 14*(2), 2.

Frega, A. L. (1997). *Metodología comparada de la educación musical.* Buenos Aires: Collegium Musicum.

Frega, A. L., de Couve, A., & Dal Pino, C. (2010). Argentina: From 'música vocal' to 'educación artística: Musica.' In G. Cox & R. Stevens (Eds.), *The origins and foundations of music education* (pp. 139-151). London: Continuum International Publishing Group.

End Notes

1   First of all, I want to especially thank Cecilia Wang for her kind invitation for me to speak at the Global Connections in Orff Schulwerk: Reflections from Kentucky symposium. I also want to thank Dina Graetzer of the Collegium Musicum of Buenos Aires, Argentina, where a part of the history of Orff in Latin America occurred back in the early 1960s. I also want to particularly thank Michelle Lewis and Gregory Springer for allowing me to use their notes of my presentation to write this final report.

2   An example of the variety of musics in the region may be found in the book, *Songs of Latin America: From the Field to the Classroom* by Patricia Shehan Campbell with Ana Lucía Frega, Warner Brothers publications, 2001.

Chapter 5

ORFF SCHULWERK IN AUSTRALIA

Robyn Staveley

How Are We Similar?

We feel in Australia that we have a great affinity with the United States Orff family through the many publications we all have and visits by many eminent United States presenters. We share this common heritage of Orff Schulwerk that binds us in a joyous, exhilarating, spiritual union with learning and music. In this chapter, you are introduced to Orff Schulwerk in Australia.

In a later chapter are some points that were discussed in our "Skyped" talk at the *Global Connections in Orff Schulwerk: Reflections from Kentucky*. I have elaborated on a number of points, especially on the use of technology as an issue that is of interest to all educators worldwide. I hasten to add that the discussion about technology represents my own views, based upon my own studies toward a PhD in cognitive neuroscience, although in discussions with my colleagues, the challenge of meaningful, musical use of technology is one that engenders much debate. The current research regarding embodied cognition has much to offer to this debate (see chapter 18, "Neuroscience, Technology, and Music Education").

Orff Schulwerk in Australia

Orff Schulwerk came to life in Australia as a result of the work of three people: Diana Humphries, Lorna Parker, and Keith Smith. Diana had heard about Orff Schulwerk at Teachers College in the 1960s through a teacher there, though the impact on her music teaching and learning was more evident to her as she began her teaching career. Soon after, she met Lorna Parker and the two began researching and offering workshops about creative music and movement education. Diana attended a special course in Salzburg and when she returned to Australia, the movement grew until there was, by the 1980s, an Orff-Schulwerk association in every state.

Lorna and Diana introduced the Orff approach in special education for children with mild to severe disabilities. Many families have felt the impact of the joy and life that these two ladies engendered in their children's learning through their involvement with music and movement and the philosophy of Orff Schulwerk. At her school for students with severe disabilities, Diana yearly organized the opportunities for all the students to perform in the local town hall. All the students had costumes and make-up and were taught songs and movements. Professional musicians offered their services for the performance. The students played to large audiences, and from the minute the music began and the lights were on, people were amazed at how the students musically and physically came to life and responded.

For many years, Lorna and Diana provided professional development activities for teachers. They offered camps, workshops, weekend retreats, courses, and together with others, established a national organization to oversee state Orff-Schulwerk organizations and the running of a biannual national conference. Today, though both retired, Lorna and Diana continue their tireless work for children with disabilities along with adults and their families through the establishment of centers in which adults with disabilities can continue to thrive and learn as they grow older in respite care centers for families and care givers.

Teacher Training in Australia

In many countries, the fight to keep the arts alive in teacher training is always a battle. Many teacher-training programs have as little as two hours in their entire training devoted to music. For a number of years in the 1990s, there was an Orff-Schulwerk accredited university diploma and degree course offered at the Australian Catholic University in Melbourne. Unfortunately, that offering has now finished and there are no other accredited Orff-Schulwerk courses in our universities.

However, the Australian Orff-Schulwerk organization has developed teacher-training courses similar to the levels courses in the U.S. Dr. Carol Richards, known to many in the U.S. as a former music teacher from Indiana, oversaw the development of these teacher-training courses. Australia has four levels of teacher training, and most states offer courses during school holidays. In some states, the courses have been accredited by The Institute of Teachers. This institution registers and determines that courses, teachers, and training organizations comply with national teacher-training guidelines and that the course content and presenters are of high academic and musical standards. This circumstance means that teachers who complete our courses are accredited through a recognized, official registered organization. Consequently, these accredited courses are highly sought after.

At present, the Australian government is going through a long process to develop national curricula for all Australian schools. Moreover, each state has their own set of curricular offerings, with obvious ramifications for students who change states during their school education. The curriculum for "The Arts" contains music, dance, drama, visual arts, and media arts. The "curriculum draft" has had many revisions, but the chief fear for Orff educators is the omission of movement and dance from the music curriculum. Music teachers are lobbying hard for a revision to include movement as part of the Orff curriculum.

Nota Bene: *Robyn Staveley joined us via a "Skyped" video conference call during the Symposium. She described Orff Schulwerk in Australia and responded to questions from the audience. This chapter is a summary of her conversation.*

Chapter 6

SOUTH AFRICA:
DEVELOPING IDENTITY IN A PLURALISTIC COMMUNITY
Nicola F. Mason

Having been in the USA for almost four years now, I have had the privilege of being able to compare, contrast, and reflect on many aspects of music education from the USA and my home country of South Africa. This is also true of specific teaching approaches such as the Orff Schulwerk. In South Africa, the approach has adapted and evolved in order to meet the needs of children in a changing political and educational climate.

South Africa is a country rich in musical heritage. It is often referred to as the "Rainbow Nation" because of the immense diversity of cultures, religions, and inclusion of indigenous, European, and eastern traditions. Music education in South Africa, as with so many countries across the continent, shares a multicultural heritage because of the vast array of influences from other countries. As an ex-colony of Britain, English was adopted as the primary language in schools beginning in the early 1600s. In music education, a strong culture of choral traditions included the European Tonic Sol-fa system and a repertoire of hymns, European songs, and folk traditions with the complete exclusion of indigenous music (Herbst, De Wet, & Rijdjkiv, 2005). Malay and Indian Cultures influenced song and dance throughout the country from the early 1800s, and the early 1900s saw the influence of North American Jazz blended with African rhythms.

Until recently, African music education was only seen in informal music training—mostly through enculturation. This enculturation was greatly due to apartheid, a system of racial segregation that influenced all aspects of society, including education. But, in 1994 the world watched as the country held its first democratic elections after forty-six years of legalized segregation. Prior to the elections, white children received all forms of music education that often included multiple music specialists within schools. Under the Bantu Education Act of 1953, black children received no arts education, which included no extramural activities in the arts. At the height of the discrimination, matriculation examinations were only offered in English, resulting in very few black children receiving their high school diplomas.

Today, under the Revised National Curriculum (RNC), all eleven official languages are acknowledged and implemented throughout the curriculum (Msila, 2007). The foundation of the 2002 Revised National Curriculum states that,

> The curriculum aims to develop the full potential of each learner as a citizen of a democratic South Africa. It seeks to create a lifelong learner who is confident and independent, literate, numerate and multi-skilled, compassionate, with a respect for the environment and the ability to participate in society as a critical and active citizen. (Revised National Curriculum Statement, n.d., p. 8)

To address the many indigenous needs of the people of South Africa, each of the nine provinces governs the implementation of the RNC. A system of outcomes-based education provides the framework for assessment and curriculum development. There is a strong focus on the integration of the arts within the RNC. The combined Arts and Culture curriculum forms part of eight learning areas for grades R through nine. The broad learning outcomes within each area of the Arts and Culture curriculum require students to demonstrate knowledge and skill in dance, drama, music, and visual arts (Department of Education, 2002).

- Learning Outcome 1: Creating, Interpreting and Presenting
- Learning Outcome 2: Reflecting
- Learning Outcome 3: Participating and Collaboration
- Learning Outcome 4: Expressing and Communicating

The inherent flexibility, adaptability, and constantly developing nature of the Orff-Schulwerk approach parallels so many elements of change in South Africa and plays a pivotal role in helping children understand their own identities in a newly developed pluralistic community. Orff Schulwerk lends itself so naturally to the inclusion of folk songs and traditional melodies that it seems only natural to emphasize the significance of the approach in the current curriculum, especially because there is still constant debate regarding the amount of focus given to indigenous music in South Africa.

Orff Schulwerk was introduced in South African schools during the early 1970s. Today, the approach is mostly centralized in the northern provinces in Johannesburg and Pretoria. However, it is used to varying degrees within primary schools across all nine provinces. Miriam Schiff, president of the Orff-Schulwerk Society of South Africa (OSSSA) states,

> Private Schools in South Africa offer Orff Schulwerk, usually from the early childhood classes through primary school, though this is not the case in all schools. Very few high schools offer much Schulwerk. Public school teachers will incorporate some Schulwerk if they have the requisite knowledge and experience. The vast majority of public school teachers have no knowledge of the approach at all. (M. Schiff, personal communication, March 2011)

Founded in 1972 by Hazel Cunnington (Walker) and Janet Hudson, the OSSSA serves as a resource for teachers. In 2012, the society celebrated its fortieth year. It is an active organization with members from around the country. Their annual publication, *The Orff Beat,* is subscribed to by universities and readers around the world and provides articles and lesson plans for teachers of all grades. Their Web site, www.orff.org.za, provides information about levels course training, links to international Orff-Schulwerk organizations, and information about workshops. Approximately three workshops a year are provided for teachers, and although most workshops are only offered in Johannesburg, some have been hosted in Cape Town and Durban because of the limited availability of instruments. The organization also awards an annual bursary of $1,250 to one candidate for attendance at an Orff-related course. In 2012, the bursary recipient, Gail Levitt from Cape Town, attended the International Orff-Schulwerk Symposium in Salzburg.

OSSSA also supports annual Orff-Schulwerk levels training, however, teacher training was suspended a few years ago to provide the organization time to develop and redesign its curriculum. The new levels teacher training will focus more on meeting the needs of African children and will correspond more closely with the national curriculum. There will also be a conscious shift away from the previously emphasized Eurocentric approach to music education. Schiff says:

> We ran all three Levels for many years but then felt that they were perhaps too 'Eurocentric' for our local teachers. A decision was made to revise the Levels Courses, making sure that, while Orff's principles were covered, the repertoire, songs and movement content would be more African and geared to our curriculum. Our Levels will be more or less as before, but instead of always using material from the Orff Volumes, we will try to use more from the local languages and songs. (M. Schiff, personal communication, March 2011)

In preparation for the 2012 teacher training, the organization consulted with local members who have received international teacher training in San Francisco with Doug Goodkin. They also followed the guidelines provided by the American Orff-Schulwerk Association forum. The movement curriculum was designed based upon consultation with the education department. The level one teacher training courses resumed in Johannesburg on June 2012 with Sofía López-Ibor.

Amoaku, author of *African Songs and Rhythms for Children* (1990), reiterated the current standing of OSSSA twenty years ago when he demanded that an African version of the Orff Schulwerk was necessary (Amoaku, 1982). He makes a close comparison between African musical traditions and the Orff Schulwerk with regard to speech, rhythm, movement, tuned percussion, and the process of imparting musical knowledge through imitation, improvisation, and exploration. In their attempts to shift away from the past Eurocentric approach, an Africanized approach to the Orff Schulwerk can be found in many primary school classrooms throughout South Africa. Examples include the use of log xylophones and African marimbas, the use of traditional recorder repertoire such as the *Africorder* (Malan, 2003), and the inclusion of indigenous languages in traditional songs.

Figure 1.

Chakalaka (Peas Porridge Hot) arr. Penny Jackson & Liz Mills
(*Orff Beat,* 2010)

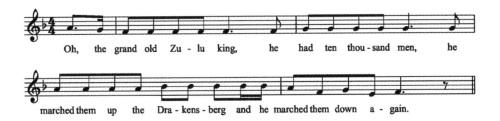

Figure 2.

Grand Old Zulu King (Grand Old Duke of York) arr. Penny Jackson &
Liz Mills (*Orff Beat,* 2010)

Figure 3.

Jabulanie Went to Town (Yankee Doodle) arr. Penny Jackson & Liz Mills
(*Orff Beat,* 2010)

African marimba ensembles are commonly found in schools. They are often heard in tourist "hot spots" and have become the iconic sounds of African music. Similar to the Orff instrumentarium, they are available in bass, tenor, alto, and soprano ranges and in standard or chromatic sets.

The standard set can be played in C or G and includes F-sharp. The log xylophone is an unresonated keyboard instrument that is commonly played by more than one person at a time. Unlike the African marimba or traditional Orff xylophones, it is struck on the ends of the keys. The sounds of the African marimba and log xylophone rely heavily on improvisation and collaborative music making, hence their adaptability for the traditional Orff ensemble setting. Schiff states that, "Marimbas have become very popular with children and teachers, and these complement and enhance the sound of the more traditional Orff instruments" (M. Schiff, personal communication, March 2011). Traditional Orff instruments suppliers are also available in South Africa.

Despite the financial, political, and cultural challenges of the past forty years, the OSSSA has been able to maintain a consistent presence in South African music education. It has also continued to provide their members with world-class teachers and clinicians, including Doug Goodkin (USA), Ulli Jungmair (Austria), Gerard Van Der Geer (Australia), Jos Wuytack (Belgium), Lois Birkenshaw-Fleming (Canada), Janet Greene (USA), Christoph Maubach (New Zealand), and Komla Amoaku (Ghana). Their commitment to education is unquestionable and their influence undeniable. The society's dedication to maintaining the authenticity of the approach while preserving the indigenous integrity of South African music and movement supports the fundamental principles upon which the Orff Schulwerk was created.

References

Amoaku, W. K. (1982). Parallelisms in traditional African system of music education and Orff Schulwerk. *International Library of African Music*, 6(2), 116-119.

Amoaku, W. K. (1990). *African songs and rhythms for children*. Schott Music & Co.

Department of Education. (2002). *Revised national curriculum statement. Introducing the arts and culture learning area*. Pretoria: Government Printer.

Herbst, A, De Wet, J, & Rijsdjik, S. (2005). A survey of music education in the primary schools of South Africa's Cape Peninsula. *Journal of Research in Music Education*, 53(3), 260-283.

Jackson, P. (2010). Chakalaka: A medley of South African nursery rhythms for junior choir. *Orff Beat, 39,* 9-18.

Malan, W. (2003). *Africorder.* South Africa: Ritenotes Music Publishers.

Msila, V. (2007). From Apartheid education to the Revised National Curriculum Statement: Pedagogy for identity formation and nation building in South Africa. *Nordic Journal of African Studies, 16*(2), 146-160.

Revised National Curriculum Statement. (n.d.). Retrieved from http://www. education.gov.za.

Chapter 7

At Home with Global Connections:
Understanding Diversity in Our Schools
Arvida Steen

In 1999, I began my official journey into retirement. After that, I was an employee or long-term volunteer in three positions that were quite different from my career at the Blake School and in summer courses, including the University of Kentucky and the University of St. Thomas, St. Paul. These three teaching situations fulfilled a longtime wish to return to public school education in some capacity: (1) In 2000 I became director of an after-school program in West St. Paul called "Encore," a partnership between Augustana Lutheran Church and Garlough Environmental Magnet School. We met with approximately twenty-four third graders on one day and with fourth graders on another. Although sponsored by a church, Encore was a nonsectarian program; (2) I volunteered both in music and in third through fifth grade classrooms at Indian Mounds Elementary School in Bloomington; and (3) I volunteered at the bilingual preschool at Hamline Methodist Church in St. Paul.

These situations brought me face-to-face with some twenty-first century classroom realities. I sensed that I knew less about these children and the influences that mold them. The student diversity challenged my understanding of their economic situations, their cultural behavioral norms, and my ability to communicate and to be flexible and effective. I realized that in order to connect with these students, I needed to be open to trying different, more effective teaching strategies. To establish some perspective, I went back to a diagram from my curriculum book, *Exploring Orff* (Steen, 1992, p. 11), which is shown in Figure 1 below.

Given the teaching task in each classroom situation, I needed to ask myself some basic questions: (1) What do I know about these students and their cultural, academic and social environments? (2) What do I bring to the equation—my skills and experience, but also unconscious biases from my earlier career that may hinder my ability to make connections with the students? I thought about my philosophy and about resources that could help me renew my sense of direction as I faced new challenges. I was leaving a more focused environment for several different environments outside my comfort zone.

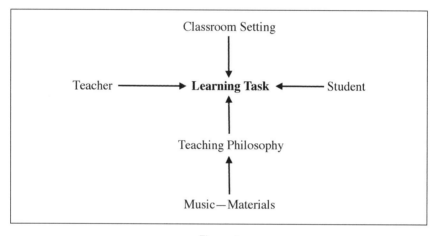

Figure 1.

A Minnesota Diversity Profile*

Blake School

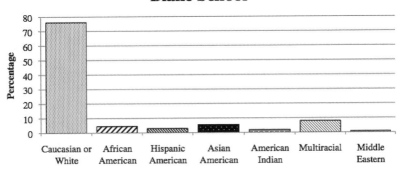

Figure 2.
*Source: www.blakeschool.org

The Blake School chart represents the school setting I knew best, the private school where I taught for twenty-eight years. The attendance area overlaps that of other private and parochial schools, though the majority of students come from Minneapolis. The popular notion is often that private and parochial schools are nearly 100 percent American-born Caucasians. Today, this statistic is frequently not so. These schools search for qualified students in order to reflect the pluralism of the cultures around them. Blake School definitely serves a broader cultural base today than it did ten years ago. When considering preschool through twelfth grade, the percentage of students of color is twenty-five percent; in elementary grades it is closer to thirty percent. The various languages of the student body represent forty-two countries. Blake School also supports diversity through travel programs that take faculty and students to a variety of other countries. In a recent conversation with a teacher there, I learned that at St. Paul Summit Academy, a "friendly rival" of Blake, in the Lower School, twenty-five percent of the students are of color. This student body represents five continents and the various languages spoken by this diverse group comprises thirty languages. Other private schools would supply similar statistics. Below are graphs that show the cultural diversity in the public school districts of the children I presently teach, including Minneapolis, St. Paul, and two first-ring suburban schools.

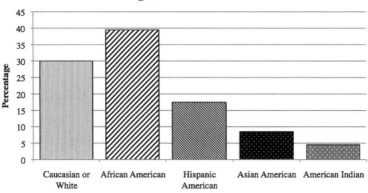

Figure 3.

Source: Report of the Annual Racial/Ethnic Count of Students K-12, October 2011, Minneapolis Schools Web site.

Most striking in the entries of the above graph is that the Euro-American student population is in the minority—about thirty percent compared to forty percent African-American and twenty-nine percent combined other groups. There are forty-five elementary schools, seven middle schools, seven high schools, eight special education schools, eight alternative schools, nineteen contract alternative schools, and five charter schools in the district. The various languages spoken by the student body comprise ninety different languages. Home and most school communications are printed in English, Hmong, Spanish, and Somali. Another fact: in the past ten years, the Minneapolis schools have lost 12,000 students due to a decrease in the city's population in general due to flight to the suburbs, often because of "school choice" issues. This district is home to the largest concentration of African-American students in the state.

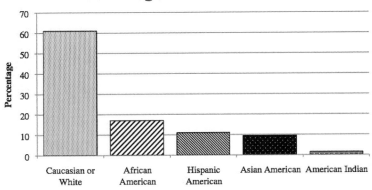

Figure 4.

Source: Bloomington Public Schools Web site, Annual Report

This suburban school district is directly south of Minneapolis and is divided into east and west by Highway 35 West. To the east, Kennedy High School, Oak Grove Middle School, and Indian Mounds Elementary School, fifty percent of the students are of color. In contrast, west of Highway 35 the school population is mostly white. Indian Mounds Elementary has a large Hispanic population; English is often a second language, and fifty-one percent of the students receive free lunch. The change in the east district has been rapid over the last ten years, shifting from the working middle class to large pockets of poverty in fifty percent of the population. I admit a fondness for the Indian Mounds faculty. They are young, talented, and committed to helping their students succeed.

St. Paul Public Schools

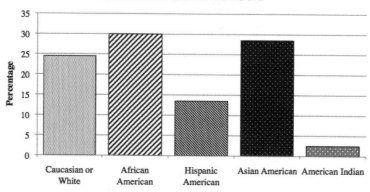

Figure 5.

Source: St. Paul Public Schools Web site

I volunteered to teach music in the bilingual preschool program in St. Paul, where my grandchildren attended at that time. The lead teachers were culturally Spanish, and all staff members spoke Spanish except for the volunteer music teacher! All students in the program were residents of St. Paul and likely would go on to public schools in the city. St. Paul is the home of the second largest Hmong population in America; this fact is especially visible in several elementary and middle schools. As shown in the above graph, the Asian (mostly Hmong) cultural component here is comparable in numbers to the African-American group. To complicate matters, the Hmong people had no written language until the 1960s. The language has five prominent dialects, with stories and customs that are orally passed on. As shown in the graph, the Asian and the African-American students each outnumber the Caucasian students.

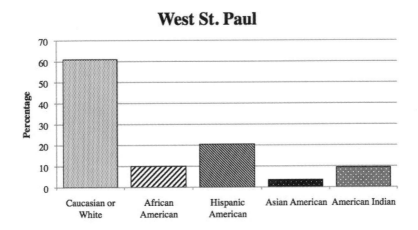

Figure 6.

Source: West St. Paul Schools Web site

The area known as West St. Paul is noteworthy for the size of its Hispanic population. In recent years, it has become more a migrant rather than a residential population. It is common for up to twenty percent of the students in the Encore after-school program to just disappear suddenly because of changing family jobs, housing losses, or other family issues. All the students of color combined here do not equal the Caucasian student population. The church that sponsors Encore is almost 100 percent Caucasian, despite the fact that it is located on the edge of a large Hispanic community.

I asked the school secretary at the hosting Garlough School for statistics to illustrate the diversity of this student population. She sent me a collation of the responses of parents to an inquiry concerning the primary language spoken in the home. The results are shown below.

Amharic (1)

Cebuano, Philippines (1)

Hindi (1)

Russian (1)

Swahili (1)

Spanish (175)

English (206)

Chinese, Mandarin (2)

English-Creolized (2)

Somali (4)

Arabic (2)

Other Non English (15)

All Non English (205)

All school communications, especially those for the Encore program, are sent home in English and Spanish. By the way, both my assistant and I struggled to learn phrases in Spanish, to the great delight of our students and parents. They were eager to help us learn their language. When I asked the music teachers in the schools in which I was teaching, all of them Euro-American, how diversity statistics are reflected in their teaching and their students, their responses included the following:

"Even though I think I am a better teacher, I work harder
than ever."
"Motivating students at earlier ages is more difficult."
"It is hard to get and hold my students' attention."
"Evaluating individuals is difficult in the time I'm given. I have less prep."
"I hope I have a full-time job next year–at the same school."

They spoke about the pressure caused by increased testing, and the tensions that arise within their faculties because of it. Nearly all felt pressure and distance from their administrators, although they felt no direct lack of support. The number of students needing free lunch continues to rise, which reflects increased economic hardships. Fewer parents attend conferences due to work schedules. More homes depend upon the students to translate the smallest communications. It is difficult now to separate issues of color from the economics of the communities.

Though specific to my Minnesota location, I suggest that the above information is relevant to much, if not all, of the United States today. Both urban and rural areas now include new immigrant populations from cultures very different from the longtime residents. In order to feel "at home," immigrants need to establish communities that speak the same language. Their country of origin is likely considered the real "home" for the first generation that arrives here. How we as teachers and community members live is now highly influenced by how these people have lived in distant communities, often on other continents.

Teaching Philosophy

As seen in the learning task diagram at the beginning of this chapter, another important factor for curriculum planning is one's own teaching philosophy. Each of us, I suspect, has a primary teaching philosophy and/or method that figures strongly in how we teach. If we want to make changes, it will be helpful to first clarify our intentions. Keep this in mind as we refer to the work of two experts who clearly define their philosophies when expressing their views concerning multicultural music for American schools. First, I reviewed Patricia Shehan Campbell's writing because she teaches children in the Seattle area and adults at the University of Washington. My primary source was the book she co-authored with Carol Scott-Kassner, titled *Music in Childhood* (Campbell & Scott-Kassner, 2006). It was written for general music and elementary classroom teachers. Regarding the purpose for music teaching, they state, "If schools are the vehicles through which children are presented with the knowledge and values of a given nation, then the music program should offer children: (1) opportunities to experience a broad sampling of the world's musical traditions; (2) more thorough-going journeys into select musical traditions; and (3) multiple approaches to musical skills and understanding that appeal to their varied modes of learning" (Campbell & Scott-Kassner, 2006, p. 372).

Two approaches are suggested for meeting these goals: (1) *multiethnic music education*: children develop skills and understandings while the teachers address the cultural perspectives of the children and focus more narrowly and deeply on a specific culture; and (2) *world music in education*, which taught conceptually through a comparison of musical styles across the globe, "as products of a culturally diverse society, children must be led to listen and to respond to the aesthetic components and cultural meanings of more than a single musical tradition" (Campbell & Scott-Kassner, 2006, p. 375).

In her conclusion Campbell and Scott-Kassner (2006) state, "They may learn to take note of not only the *differences* among people and their musical expressions, but also the *similarities* that transcend all people" (p. 375). One of the particular goals that Campbell and Scott-Kassner suggest for U.S. school music is to build community, which is so necessary for binding students together into a school culture and for developing comfort and cooperation in the larger environment.

In his book *Music Matters: A New Philosophy of Music Education*, David Elliott (1995) takes a somewhat different approach. He begins in chapter one with the premise that music is a human activity—a statement perhaps all of us would accept as self-evident. He then develops the definition of musical activity as three separate components: the music maker, the music itself, and the music listener or receiver, all perhaps occurring simultaneously. The following chapters lead to the conclusion in chapter eight that *all* of music is multicultural at a micro and macro level. He follows his logic through and into the "Implications for Music Education": "If music listening and musical works are culturally informed and informative, what is the most appropriate way to develop students' understandings of them? My answer is: by teaching students to meet significant musical challenges in teaching/learning situations that are close approximations of real music culture" (p. 206). Elliott (1995) also posits the notion that:

> An effective way to increase students' attention to and awareness of the cultural-ideological dimension of musical works is to confront students with musically productive problems of performing, improvising, composing, arranging, and/or conducting. Active artistic-cultural problem finding and solving obliges students to 'live' a music culture's ways of thinking, believing, and valuing. (p. 207)

I found myself wondering how Elliott would teach in an elementary school or in a situation in which traditional performance is not the goal. He has an answer for this as well: "It is essential for self-growth and enjoyment that learners achieve a match between their novice level of musicianship and the first musical challenges they meet in the music education curricula" (p. 211).

In other words, he means to meet the students where they are. Later he says, "In short, musical breadth is not necessarily a virtue" (p. 211). Moreover, the curricula should build on a foundation of several closely related musical practices that spiral to meet the demands that build the students' musicianship—then move out toward the less familiar.

The experience of reading these authors' books again stimulated my own thought process. It is a given that my age and lifetime of experiences affected my teaching and my students' learning. However, in these recent classroom situations, I relished the opportunity to review my plans, with increased sensitivity to my processes and the choices I made to involve them in authentic music making. I could begin by learning songs to sing in Spanish that also fit the music skills of my students. This provided a common ground where students and I met as we shared music. It also addressed my challenge to increase my own skills and knowledge. Other resources became evident, e.g., I could invite parents to explain to the class how they played a childhood game or I could invest in some of the fine DVDs now available in most classroom music catalogs. And, along the way, I may discover that combining Orff Schulwerk with a multicultural attitude is easier than I suspicioned.

Teacher Training

A large component of my career has been teaching teachers in various contexts. Preparing this chapter has increased my desire to know how teachers in multicultural settings with strong training in specific methodologies are dealing with the relevance of their teaching. What are we teacher trainers doing to prepare them, not only in basic musicianship and methodologies, but also for being open to the change, which their individual settings will demand? What do we need to find out about how they are doing when they are actually in service? Not to know may drive us into irrelevancy! An encouraging trend I have noticed in my observations is that younger teachers find teaching music of other cultures to be much more acceptable and natural than previous generations.

I wonder about my influence on the teachers I have taught. How did I mentor them as I observed? Although student diversity was not always at the forefront of our concerns, I hope I modeled an openness to broadening our teaching skills, which in turn allows for interaction with more kinds of music. As many of us teach now in Schulwerk workshops and courses, how do we present the challenges of an increasingly multicultural teaching environment? One of these challenges may be the fluidity of the student population; school cultures can change very quickly. Music teachers are faced with the challenge of teaching in welcoming ways that capture the attention and participation of all students, whatever the diversity distribution.

If we are training teachers, what is our obligation to educate students regarding music traditions of other cultures? Certainly we will want to introduce material from a number of cultures and to make students aware of issues to consider and mistakes to avoid. But, for the most part, we will continue to rely on experts in each tradition to offer in-depth training and experience in specific traditions. Sometimes we are fortunate enough to encounter an individual who will provide us with one-on-one training, and workshops are available in many institutions throughout the country to provide more in-depth experiences.

My intent in this chapter is to bring into focus, by way of a Minnesota sampling, the diversity existing in today's classrooms in the USA, and to bring together ideas that may be useful as you consider how to address the cultural challenges in your own situations. It may be helpful to draw up your own bar graph, just to make visual the diversity profile in the school and community where you teach. Since everyone in attendance at the recent symposium in June 2011, *Global Connections in Orff Schulwerk: Reflections from Kentucky*, supports Orff Schulwerk as a particularly effective approach to active music making, you likely are doing it already in combination with music of various cultures. I encourage all of us to consider how the Schulwerk can be used most appropriately with the material from each culture we present in our classrooms and also how it fits into the cultural mix of students that we teach. We recognize it as being singularly valuable in helping us reach our goals in a way that we can all enjoy together.

Nota Bene: *At the time of the Symposium, Steen was still doing some teaching in the programs mentioned. She has now retired from all but occasional guest classroom teaching.*

References

Campbell, P. S., & Scott-Kassner, C. (2006). *Music in childhood: From preschool through the elementary grades* (3rd Ed.). Boston, MA: Schirmer Cengage Learning.

Elliott, D. J. (1995). *Music matters: A new philosophy of music education.* New York: Oxford University Press.

Steen, A. (1992). *Exploring Orff: A teacher's guide.* New York: Schott.

Chapter 8

THOUGHTS ABOUT ORFF SCHULWERK AND "CULTURE" IN TODAY'S CLASSROOMS

Mary Shamrock

In discussions of applying the Schulwerk pedagogy in the classroom, the relationship to "culture" often arises. We know that Carl Orff wanted the resources for spoken texts and songs to originate from the tradition of the students involved, with examples that have endured through time and still are expressions familiar to members of the culture. This chapter contains an examination about how that premise relates to today's classrooms, primarily in the USA but likely in many other countries as well.

Carl Orff grew up and lived his life in the German province of Bavaria. Along with familiarity with local traditions, he developed a fascination for the roots of the broader West European civilization—the classical heritage from Greece and the Roman Empire, especially the languages involved. In the initial Schulwerk phase at the Güntherschule in Munich, these sources provided strong motivation for the development of music, movement, and drama. Musical development was based upon the "elemental"—what he considered to be the basic components of the Western musical system. Orff and his colleague Gunild Keetman composed model pieces to introduce students to the rhythmic and tonal structures that were to serve as materials for improvising; the goal was to bring students to the point of using these elements with comfort and competence. The drone/*ostinato* texture served this purpose well, as accompaniment to melody and as reinforcement to the internalization of rhythmic and tonal elements through much repetition.

In the second phase, intended for children, song material came into consideration:

> the Güntherschule we had not allowed the word or the singing voice its fully rightful place. The natural starting point for work with children is the children's rhyme, the whole riches of the old, appropriate children's songs. The recognition of this fact gave me the key for the new educational work. (Orff, 1978, p. 214)

Being "old" complemented the idea of "elemental"—springing from the roots of culture, passed down through generations, and suitable to the world of the child of that place and time. The time was the late 1940s and 1950s, the place was Orff's own culture—Bavaria and western Austria, with the connection developing to the Mozarteum in Salzburg. The population in that area would have been decidedly homogeneous, by today's standards. The proverbs, rhymes, and songs chosen would have been familiar to many, if not most, of the children. The examples selected were organized in a way that would build familiarity and expand vocabulary with rhythmic and tonal elements. Small, composed instrumental forms provided additional material for solidifying the usable vocabulary. As in the Güntherschule phase, the purpose was to lead students into improvisation with these elements.

It is relevant to note here that, even though the initial songs were drawn from the indigenous culture, combining them with instruments playing drone/ *ostinato* settings was *not* part of traditional culture—it was a pedagogical device. The songs with their elemental accompaniments provided a joyful, playful music-making experience and at the same time developed the vocabulary that could be applied in improvising. We see the initial building blocks in Volume I of *Orff-Schulwerk: Musik für Kinder*. In the subsequent volumes, II-V, the indigenous songs and the additional composed material lead the student through layers of expansion, going as far as was considered "elemental." Although inspired by models from other cultures, the barred Orff instruments were developed specifically to provide an accessible, entry-level experience with "elemental" music making and the means for learning to improvise. They may be associated with Germany/Austria since that is where they were first used, but they are essentially "a-cultural," available for pedagogical purposes by any culture. Also, we acknowledge that they are often used to good effect for performance purposes, as a result of the pedagogy.

How does all of this transfer to cultures beyond the original just described? Some of the early attempts to adopt and adapt the Schulwerk in other countries simply translated the German material into other languages, removing even the song models from cultural relevance. For cultures that include practice of a Western musical tradition, the Schulwerk pedagogical model can be adopted with many features and objectives intact. However, to carry out the original intent, speech and song models should come from the indigenous cultural tradition. In time this notion was recognized and has been implemented in many cultures throughout the world. Instruction at the Orff Institute in Salzburg was and is intended to prepare students to develop frameworks that are relevant to the students they will teach. Orff foresaw and endorsed this trend; in 1975, the year of his eightieth birthday, he said:

> If you want to [do Schulwerk] in foreign countries, then you must begin again completely from the basis of what these children experience. And, those in Africa experience something other than those in Hamburg or in Stralsund, something other than in Paris—and in Tokyo again something else. (cited in Regner, 1984)

Let's fast forward to today's situation. In many classrooms—definitely in the United States—a common culture of origin is rare. Public school students typically represent a variety of cultures, and may be familiar with folk repertoire from their specific backgrounds. The repertoire that could be considered "common," that most will relate to, comes from what is popular in current media presentation. Hermann Regner, director of the Orff Institute for many years, acknowledged this change. In an article "Thoughts on Globalization and Cultural Identity," he (2005) suggests that from the beginning we should consider the cultural factor from both sides: acquainting students with their own culture(s), and introducing them to what is beyond. For ease of discussion, let's address the musical and the cultural dimensions of Schulwerk teaching in the United States separately, even though they will likely be interwoven in classroom presentations.

Musical Goals

A) Developing music practitioners—students who can make music themselves, in a group, with confidence, skill, and awareness of what they are doing.

B) Building vocabulary—starting from the simplest elements of the Western musical system and expanding the scope of what is familiar; and

C) Improvisation—developing the ability of individuals to create new material based on what is familiar. As speakers of a given language, we do this continually throughout our lifetimes, adding new elements and dropping old ones along the way. To use a language, first we have to experience enough of it to speak and understand at a very basic level. What we hear from parents and others is far beyond where we can join in, but through continual immersion in this *soundscape,* we develop recognition of familiar patterns that take on meaning. We begin to use the sounds that relate to what is close and important to us—mama, doggie, blanket, etc. The most natural development of musical vocabulary also happens through modeling. Even though what we hear is beyond what we can produce, we develop an internal repertoire of pitch and rhythm patterns from which we can draw as we learn to make musical sounds. Left on their own, young children will experiment with joy and interest, both vocally and with simple instruments; unfortunately this is often considered to be noise. As music teachers, we want to lead children into participating with meaning in this language—therefore, we must provide the mama/doggie/blanket examples, with much repetition, and expand the models as the child progresses into a fuller use of the language.

Recently, I heard an announcer on the local public radio station introduce a children's song, something composed and performed by an adult that was for children. It was quite a lovely song, which the announcer said was not the "annoying repetitive stuff." I smiled, assuming he had heard some Schulwerk music making and, perhaps as with many listeners, does not understand the purpose of this repetition. The children are learning to control elements of a specific musical language that subsequently can be expanded into more complex forms and can be combined in different ways—improvisation! For Orff teachers, a main principle that guides repertoire choices is the need to provide models. Some must be simple enough that students can jump into using the elements right away, and others will imprint into memory elements that later become part of identified vocabulary and are usable in improvisation.

Cultural Goals

The romantic notion that music is a universal language doesn't play out in reality. A group of students from many cultures all playing a Vivaldi concerto together just means they have all learned to express themselves musically through a specific example of a particular musical language that originated several centuries ago in Western Europe. From a broader knowledge of this musical language, we know that it is possible and appropriate to improvise with various dialects of this language. Maybe these same performers can demonstrate that skill as well—maybe not. Building on Regner's statement cited above, we can consider two objectives for the cultural dimension of our musical models:

A) To acquaint/confirm students in their own culture(s).

First the diversity factor: The students in today's classrooms likely come from a variety of ethnic backgrounds; they may have experience and/or skills in their original culture's musical language. Keeping in mind that Orff instruments do not belong to *any* traditional culture, we are open to choosing repertoire from various cultures that offer models using elements of the Western musical tradition and that do not impinge upon sensitive religious or cultural practices. Most cultures today have adopted some elements of Western music making into their artistic profile; sometimes Western elements are integrated into traditional genres, and sometimes the Western strands are practiced separately in Western form—e.g., a symphony orchestra in Korea or a bluegrass band in Japan. In the article cited earlier, Regner strongly urges us to present songs in as authentic a form as possible, definitely in the original language. He supports the idea that it is far better to learn one song in this other language than several in translation, knowing that translations often miss meanings that are evident only with cultural knowledge. Other than the languages, what gives music—vocal or instrumental—its cultural identity? To a great extent, it is *timbre*. The musical element we tend to identify most quickly with any genre of music is its immediate tonal color. We can experience this by moving the tuning knob across the radio dial—within seconds we can identify genres and styles simply by the *sound* we are experiencing, and recognize that there are some we have not learned to identify. The specific instruments, vocal production, and textures involved create the timbre. Dr. Regner long ago suggested expanding the instrumentarium with instruments from the appropriate cultural traditions:

> The instrumentarium ... results from the wish to make available for music education basic types whose diffusion is not limited to certain countries or continents. For this reason it is only necessary to think of expansion of the instrumentarium and this can be accomplished by the addition of folk derived instruments of varying tonal color. (Regner, 1965)

This may be done with relative ease in some cases—e.g., accompanying many Spanish-language songs with guitar. Locating culture-specific instruments and finding out how to use them can become a project in itself (recommendation: enlist the help of your students and your teaching colleagues!). In most cases, the immediate purpose will be to supply a timbre associated with a particular culture. The instrument might play a drone, simple *ostinato*, and/or interlude for the song. A valuable extension would be to invite a guest to the classroom who can demonstrate a traditional use of the instrument.

LESSON 1
Appalachian Traditional Song with Appalachian (Plucked) Dulcimer

The culturally appropriate addition here is the plucked dulcimer typical of the Appalachian mountain region (basic 3-strings but could be more). Have someone who knows show you (or find a book) how to hold it, tune it, and strum it. The strum pattern suggested below will supply a basic drone, which can be supplemented with any or all of the instrumentarium patterns suggested. You could also add a banjo pattern using the drone tones, and have a capable student play the melody on a fiddle (violin). Also appropriate: a percussion pattern for the spoons. (Note: the traditional elements here reflect Appalachian "Old Timey" music—bluegrass developed from it, but this isn't bluegrass!)

What'll I Do with the Baby-O?

Jean Ritchie

Figure 1.

"What'll I Do with the Baby-O?"

Song Source: Jean Ritchie, *The Dulcimer Book*. Oak Publications: New York, 1974. p. 33

Many students are likely to understand the situation expressed here: the frustration of a babysitter or older sibling who has been left with the task of putting the baby to sleep and is having no success. There are many more verses, all starting at bar nine; the traditional ones need cultural explanation. One is "Tell his daddy when he comes home (3X), and I'll give Old Blue [the dog] your chicken bone! [likely served the purpose of a pacifier]" The students can make up more up-to-date verses based on this model.

A caution here: there may be cultural constraints attached to some instruments that should be considered before using them in the classroom—this should be investigated beforehand. Also, teachers need *not* feel responsible for including material from each and every culture! The musical and social selection factors need to be balanced with the cultural. A song or game from a trusted source that fits into the curriculum framework musically and that both teacher and students will enjoy—this trusted source may be enough to acknowledge a particular culture. Beyond that, teachers are advised to expand within specific traditions that have become familiar to themselves through experience and study.

As for the classroom: take a bit of time to locate a culture on a map, name its main features (cities, oceans, mountains, etc.), and show a few photos. Classroom teachers can be very helpful in this regard. It is important to convey the purpose of the song—for celebration, just for fun, for a holiday, for sadness, whatever it is. We can ask students from a particular culture to share something about the culture (only if they agree to, and be sure to ask in advance). The various genres of music from specific populations and parts of the USA belong within this mix, since they will be unfamiliar to many students—e.g., bluegrass, Cajun, blues, etc. And, don't forget that the students whose families have lived in the school area for generations need cultural recognition as much as those who are very new. Most of them probably have little or no identification with their own ancestral cultures.

LESSON 2
Indonesian Game Song, as Played in Central Java

"Hom Pila Hom" is a game song for choosing "it" [it may also be used for selecting someone for any needed task]. All stand in a circle to sing the song, waving their hands rhythmically in front. At the end of the song, each puts out one hand, with palm up or down according to choice. Whichever hand is in the majority—palm up or down—is no longer in competition for being "it." (If it comes out even, play again). This competition continues until only two players remain. Then these two players extend only a finger: the thumb, the index, or the pinkie. The thumb ranks higher than the index, and the index higher than the pinkie. Whoever ends up with the lower value is "it." (Again, a tie means play again.)

Hom Pila Hom

Figure 2.

These rhythms are not a required piece of playing the game, but make it more fun and interesting.

Combining as speech:	Pattern 1:	pim		pim		pim	pah		
	Pattern 2:		pah		pah		pah	pah	pah

Body percussion:	Pattern 1:	clap		clap		clap	patch		
	Pattern 2:		snap		snap		snap	clap	snap

Combining body percussion:	Pattern 1 (feet):	stamp		stamp		stamp	stamp		
	Pattern 2 (hands):		clap		clap		clap	clap	clap

Possible Teaching Sequence: Have students play the game; teacher sings the song and explains what comes next. Early on, teach students the first phrase and have them join in singing it. Later teach and add the second phrase.

Teach rhythm patterns through speech, then combine them using two groups. Repeat this process with body percussion. Divide into three groups: two perform the body percussion while the third sings the song. (Work toward having each student able to sing the song and perform the combined rhythms.) Suggestion: start each time with the rhythm patterns going through once, then add the song. Since the song is so short, it may be better to sing it twice before ending (end with just two claps, not three).

Source: As sung by Tri Sutrisno from Surakarta, Java. The rhythmic accompaniment is added by Joko Sutrisno, also from Surakarta, a specialist in Javanese gamelan drumming; he excerpted this brief pattern from a longer drumming pattern. Joko (gamelan) and Tri (dance) currently direct these activities for Sumunar Indonesian Music and Dance, a non-profit in Minneapolis/St. Paul, Minnesota.

*Pronunciation: "Haum peela haum, pim pah, ah-lah-ee-kuhm, gahm-breng."

Meaning: None—these are "vocables"—just singable syllables.

Then there's the unity factor— students and teachers can all celebrate being members of American culture. This likely will involve repertoire learned through media, and participation perhaps by singing, movement, and the simplest of instruments. Also, there are songs that are considered "American," since they have circulated over a long time span and the specific origin likely is uncertain—e.g., *Old MacDonald* and *Polly Wolly Doodle*. These songs can be acknowledged as a common American heritage. (Suggestion: Google song titles to see what might be known about their origins—it may be a surprise, even for well-known songs.)

B) To Go Beyond

By experiencing repertoire from various cultures most students have already gone beyond the familiar into a more global perspective of musical expression. There's also the possibility of using Orff pedagogy and resources to "go beyond" the Western musical system and explore elements of other systems. The rhythmic, tonal, and formal components of Indonesian gamelan music and certain African xylophone traditions come immediately to mind. A guest expert and/or a teacher with specialized knowledge about the tradition will be required for this experience. Once again, the most identifiable element—*timbre*—is missing, and it must be made clear that the experience is indeed a learning experiment, not an authentic performance. Ideally, such experiences should include viewing DVDs that offer the authentic sounds and visual images of the music making being explored.

A caution: resist the temptation to improvise with elements learned from another musical system. Improvisation may be part of the unfamiliar system, and if it is, the application may be quite different. Proceeding as if all traditions have the same parameters is misrepresentation. It certainly is the case that current groups in the "worldpop" category borrow elements from each other constantly, with or without consideration of how it fits into the original tradition. But in an educational setting we have the opportunity to imbue students with an attitude of respect toward all traditions we introduce, recognizing that each has its own "rules" regarding how its elements are to be used.

The above discussion can only confirm that Schulwerk teachers have much to offer in today's culturally diverse classrooms. The musical dimension is built on the principles established in the original Orff-Schulwerk repertoire and pedagogy, but the cultural dimension has expanded greatly since those origins. The Schulwerk pedagogy incorporates tools for actively exploring repertoire and elements from many cultures, thus making the student an active participant in global learning—a significant piece of twenty-first-century education.

Nota Bene: The author's presentation at the "Global Connections in Orff Schulwerk: Reflections from Kentucky" Symposium consisted of a retrospective of her doctoral research in Japan, Taiwan and Thailand, surveying the development of the Schulwerk in those countries as of the year 1987. A summary of those findings is available in the monograph entitled Orff Schulwerk: Brief History, Description, and Issues in Global Dispersal, *published by and available from AOSA.*

References

Orff, C. (1978). *The Schulwerk* (English Ed.). Translated by M. Murray. New York: Schott.

Regner, H. (1965). The Orff Schulwerk abroad. *International Music Educator, 12,* 392-398.

Regner, H. (1984). Music for children: Observations on the reception and adaptation of Orff Schulwerk in other countries. Translated by M. Shamrock. *Musik und Bildung: Zeitschrift fur Musikerziehung, 16,* 784-791.

Regner, H. (2005). Thoughts on globalization and cultural identity. Translated by B. Haselbach. *Orff Schulwerk Informationen #74* (pp. 6-9), Salzburg: Mozarteum.

SECTION TWO
REFLECTIONS

Chapter 9

ORFF-SCHULWERK RESEARCH: WHERE ARE WE?

Cecilia Wang and David W. Sogin

The purpose of this chapter is to present an overview of research in Orff Schulwerk. We chose studies deemed important in understanding the impact of Orff Schulwerk on music education. This chapter is comprised of three parts. Part I is a report presented at the Orff 100 International Conference of Music and Dance at Monash University, Melbourne, Australia, in 1995. This report covers the research completed up to that time. Part II continues in the same strain, covering research studies completed up to the current time. Part III is a bibliography of the research studies according to research categories related to the Orff Schulwerk. This list includes all the studies discussed in Part I and II; also included are additional research entries that contribute meaningfully to the Schulwerk literature, but are beyond the scope of discussion in this chapter. Although this chapter includes only studies selected by the authors, we hope that readers can use these resources to gain a perspective of Orff-Schulwerk literature, and that the information will inspire further reading and projects in Orff Schulwerk.

PART I

A Research Perspective of Orff Schulwerk in the Classroom

There is no doubt that music educators have felt the impact of the Orff-Schulwerk movement. As we gather to celebrate the Orff 100, it is difficult to mention all the areas in which Carl Orff has been influential. As a composer, Carl Orff is known for his many compositions, which were greatly influenced by his own teaching. His most famous work, the 1936 *Carmina Burana*, is performed regularly worldwide. Another area of interest that began early on in his career is the area of dance. He and dancer Dorothee Günther founded the Güntherschule, where improvisation was a major part of the program. Finally, Carl Orff was known as a pedagogue and writer, all of which culminate in his five-volume work titled *Music for Children*. His accomplishments in these areas and others are reflected in numerous articles about Orff and Orff Schulwerk as well as the body of research called "Orff." The purpose of this section is to critically discuss those studies that relate specifically to Orff Schulwerk in the classroom through the year 1995. Data for this article come from journals, dissertations and theses, computer databases, and conference papers. Looking at research reports *per se*, we find that all methods of empirical research have been employed to study Orff. That is to say, there are articles and dissertations that are historical, philosophical, descriptive (including case studies), and experimental in nature that relate to some aspect of Carl Orff's influence.

The historical studies usually trace Orff Schulwerk comparatively against other important changes within a fixed period of time. The work by Patricia Osterby, *Orff Schulwerk in North America 1955–1969*, and De Lois Wimmer, *The Organization of American Orff-Schulwerk Association from 1968–1980 and its Influence upon Music Education in America*, are but two examples of this type of research. Philosophical research studies that explicitly deal with or relate to Orff Schulwerk are few, however, one of the most valuable dissertations reflecting this mode of inquiry is the work by Coralie Anderson Snell from the University of Southern California, *The Philosophical Basis for Orff Schulwerk*. The main purpose of her study was to determine if the approach of Orff Schulwerk demonstrates a coherent and systematic philosophy of education. We find that the majority of Orff research can be classified as either descriptive or experimental in methodology.

When consulting computer databases searching for "Orff," readers will likely see all kinds of research papers and topics from performance programs of doctoral choral students who performed a piece by Carl Orff on one of their recitals to other related topics such as Philip Tacka's work *Denise Bacon: Musician and Educator: Contributions to the Adaptation of the Kodály Concept in the United States*. Even when we narrow our search to focus on Orff Schulwerk in the classroom, it is obvious that the Orff approach is seldom employed alone but often in conjunction with other types of curricula such as Dalcroze and Kodály. More will be said about this at the conclusion of this chapter and in conjunction with our recommendations. Please note that the studies here represent early research efforts of Orff Schulwerk in North America by music educators. The description of studies below is arranged in alphabetical order of the authors. Here we want to call special attention to the study by Dolloff. We recommend readers to read her writing first, because the content provides the philosophical and psychological foundations on which Orff Schulwerk is anchored.

Critical Analysis of Studies Related to Orff Schulwerk in the Classroom

Barker, C. S. (1981). *Using Orff Schulwerk as a Method to Enhance Self-Concept in Children with Learning Disabilities.*

The purpose of this study was to determine if using Orff Schulwerk by children with learning disabilities would enhance their self-concept. The author used a quasi-experimental design with two groups, an experimental group and a control group. Subjects ($N = 42$) were randomly placed in these two groups. The investigator used the *Piers–Harris Children's Self-Concept Scale* as a way of measuring the dependent variable. A Mann-Whitney U Test was used to analyze the data. Significant differences were found at the $p \leq .05$ level of the testing on the *Piers–Harris Children's Self Concept Scale*. In addition, differences were found with regard to the children's self-concept of school status and intelligence.

This study was 145 pages in length and one of the few that reported significant results. The study was concise and well written, but the sample size may be considered quite small. However, the greater concern is for the validity of the study; it is not clear whether the results are due to the effect of the Orff treatment or due to the Hawthorne effect.

Dolloff, L. A. (1993). *Das Schulwerk: A Foundation for the Cognitive, Musical and Artistic Development of Children.*

There are few theoretical studies relating to Orff Schulwerk, and the study by Lori-Anne Dolloff (1993) is an excellent representative of such a theoretical study. In her thesis, she argues that the Schulwerk, as presented by Carl Orff, was congruent with several cognitive and developmental theories of the nineteenth century. In the first chapter, she identifies the Schulwerk with the developmental writings of Herder, Goethe, and Pestalozzi. Dolloff systematically describes each of these educational reformists and articulates their ideas and similarities to Orff Schulwerk. Johann G. Herder espoused the idea of language development and a poetic age of language to which Orff incorporated in his Schulwerk. Goethe stressed the necessity of participating in the experience, or as John Dewey would say—learning by doing. Finally, Pestalozzi maintained that a framework of development begins first with the kinesthetic or sensory experience and moving to the analytic or conceptual. In the second chapter, there is a discussion of three different theories of cognitive psychology that have educational implications. These theories include: schema theory; play theory; music as intelligence and music as a cognitive process. Building schemata requires the types of activities associated with Orff Schulwerk: learning through experience. Other cognitive psychologists consider music as intelligence. Howard Gardner, who believes in music intelligence, states that early exposure to music is a necessity to promote certain skills. Finally, Mary Louise Serafine posits that music is a set of cognitive processes and that the Orff Schulwerk includes those activities that are part of a child's development. To conclude, Dolloff states "that the Orff approach allows for musical and artistic development through its multiplicity of musical activities and opportunities for practicing artistic behaviours" (p. 44). This approach appears to be an excellent way to advance the development of children in music education limited perhaps by active listening to music that is composed and performed by others.

Grant, T. W. (1990). *The Effect of Orff-Schulwerk Instruction on Memory Development in Children Ages Ten and Eleven.*

This study was an investigation of fifth graders and the effect of Orff Schulwerk on memory development. There were basically two groups, a control group and an experimental group, with four classrooms participating. The experimental group received Orff-Schulwerk instruction and the control group received the traditional method. The *Visual Aural Digital Span Test* was used as the dependent measure. Multiple *t* tests were used to analyze the data. There were no significant results found in this study.

This study, sixty-six pages in length, was poorly designed in terms of research integrity. The investigator did not randomize her sample nor was there an attempt to define her population, such as from the middle class or inner city. In addition, description of methodology was minimal, and the improper use of the Student *t* in statistical analysis was employed. The most telling aspect of this study was the lack of definition of independent variables. Orff Schulwerk and what was considered the traditional method were not well defined.

Hensley, S. E. (1981). *A Study of the Musical Achievement of Elementary Students Taught by the Memphis City Curriculum Guide and Students Taught by the Traditional Approach.*

In this study, the author analyzed musical achievement by elementary students taught either by the *Memphis City Curriculum Guide* and students taught by the traditional method. The subjects ($N = 237$) in this study were four classes of fourth and fifth graders either placed in the experimental group, which received lessons from the *Memphis City Curriculum Guide*, or the control group, which received a traditional teaching method. The *Music Achievement Test*, developed by Richard Colwell in 1969, was used as the dependent measure. An analysis of variance and *t* test were used to analyze the data. Significant differences were found between the fourth grade experimental groups on the tonal memory and melody recognition subtests. However, all groups tended to score lower than the standardized norms.

Here again is a fairly well written document (160 pages), which includes good, supporting material in the appendices. The author does not make it clear, however, why she chose the MAT in this instance as her measure of achievement. Her description of the Orff Schulwerk in the Memphis curriculum is quite good, but her description of the traditional method was inferior. Furthermore, the author also describes the Kodály method as a component of the Memphis curriculum. In this regard what can truly be said about the Orff approach here?

Kelly, L. L. (1981). *A Combined Experimental and Descriptive Study of the Effect of Music on Reading and Language.*

This study is somewhat unusual, combining both an experimental approach as well as a descriptive approach in determining the effect of music on reading and language. First grade children were randomly placed in one of three groups: Orff-Schulwerk (music) group; visual arts group; and a control group. Subjects were both pre- and post-tested on the following: *Metropolitan Reading Readiness, The California Test of Basic Skills, Botel–Milestones Criterion-Referenced Reading Test*, and the *"Draw a Person"* test. An analysis of variance set at $p \leq .10$ was used to analyze differences between groups while field notes, observations, and interviews with both the children and teachers, in addition to work samples, were all used as descriptors. Results indicated no significant differences. However, the author makes the following observation: the meta-linguistic awareness results showed the greatest growth for the music group, demonstrated in phonics activity, oral reading, spelling, and language expression.

This study seems well organized and well written. However, there were no significant results, even at the $p \leq .10$ level, which may not be considered rigorous enough for this type of study. In addition, part of the problem with the research may have been too few subjects; no overall N was given to make this determination. Finally, the Orff/music group treatment seems to be vaguely defined.

Moore, J. L. (1984). *Rhythm and Movement: An Objective Analysis of Their Association with Music Aptitude.*

The purpose of this study was to look objectively at rhythm and movement and their association with music aptitude. Subjects were comprised of second and third graders (N = 260) randomly placed in one of three treatment groups: Orff/Weikart, traditional music, and no formal music instruction. To measure rhythmic aptitude, the investigator used Gordon's *Primary Measures of Music Audiation.* A music aptitude test was also administered, though the specific content of this test was unclear. Results indicate that there was no significant change found regarding music aptitude of the experimental group compared to that of the control groups. However, the experimental group was significantly higher in rhythmic aptitude.

This study is well organized and is carefully written, however, the researcher does not go into great depth about many of her decisions such as her choice for using the *PMMA* or the basis for her significant results. In addition, her use of Orff/Weikart versus traditional does not seem to be clear.

Munsen, S. C. (1986). *A Description and Analysis of an Orff- Schulwerk Program of Music Education.*

This project was an attempt to describe and to analyze an Orff-Schulwerk program of music education. This investigation represents a case study of a single school focusing on grades one, three, and five. To collect the data, the author used a *Modified Flanders System of Instructional Analysis,* narrative descriptors, an author-developed musical activity record, an opinionnaire, and an *Orff-Improve Rating Scale.* The results of this study are as follows: (1) teacher talk was higher for grade one and five than for grade three; (2) time spent singing decreased from first through fifth grade more than fifty percent; (3) third and fifth grade students spent almost thirty-three percent more time participating in playing activities than first grade students; and (4) there was little difference in the amount of time devoted to listening and moving activities among the three grade levels.

This study is thorough and well written. It also provides for a special model that can be replicated in other areas. Munsen is able to present a clear snapshot of an Orff-Schulwerk program taught by a master teacher. What is important to note about these results is that one cannot generalize them to other situations.

Osterby, P. M. (1988). *Orff Schulwerk in North America 1955–1969.*

The primary purpose of this study was to trace the spread of Orff Schulwerk in North America from its introduction in 1955 at the Royal Conservatory of Music at the University of Toronto through the first year of the AOSA. Data collected for this study include primary sources, journal articles, and interviews of charter members of the AOSA organization. Results of this paper established a clear connection between the Orff Schulwerk in North America and the philosophy of the progressive movement. It is clear that this paper is well researched and organized, and it provides a meaningful model for those interested in historical research.

Price, H. E. (1990). *Elementary School Music Teachers' Comparative Use of Classroom Time: Teachers Who Are Versus those Who are Not Orff Schulwerk Certified.*

The purpose of this study was to develop an observation instrument to document activities in the elementary music classroom and to identify those activities as Orff process and those termed traditional. The researchers audio-taped fourth grade classes taught by twelve school music specialists, six of whom had at least Level One of Orff-Schulwerk training. Two independent observers coded the time spent in different activities in each twenty- to thirty-minute class with good agreement (ninety-six percent average). Activities include these categories: Pitched (instrumental or vocal), Rhythm (verbal or nonverbal), Movement, Improvisation/Creativity, Discussion, and Listening.

Time was classified either as Orff or non-Orff activities. No significant difference in activities was found between the two groups of teachers. The authors explained that (1) only three Orff teachers had Orff instruments, whereas some non-Orff certified teachers had them; (2) having or not having Orff training does not translate directly into using Orff activities in the classroom; (3) types of activities alone do not define the operation of the

Orff-Schulwerk process, which include other pedagogic variables; and finally (4) the sample may be too small to show any meaningful difference. The authors rightfully suggest that much needs to be done to operationally define the Orff-Schulwerk process.

Shamrock, M. E. (1988). *Applications and Adaptations of Orff Schulwerk in Japan, Taiwan, and Thailand.*

Mary Shamrock's dissertation is a great example of the study of cultural diversity and musical traditions on site in various countries. Even though the three countries (Japan, Taiwan, and Thailand) are all Asian countries, her personal observations in the schools and interviews with teachers indicate that each culture has its own indigenous music and language that present special problems in adapting Orff Schulwerk. Furthermore, the style of singing, tuning of instruments, stylized body movement in each culture, and especially values given to different objectives and activity types must all be considered. Her ethnographic research provides first-hand data concerning music teaching and learning and resulted in several guidelines for cross-cultural adaptation of the Schulwerk model. She suggested that first and foremost, the pedagogy must be designed for active participation by all learners with an aim to incorporate improvisation and originality in the classroom. The linguistic characteristics must be understood when used for speech pieces. The Western tonal system that is comprised of *sol mi,* and *sol mi la* could serve well as starting points, although bi-musical goals using diatonic scales and scales of the culture should be applied later. Basic singing and movement should be expressive and natural with children. In sum, it would take a person who intimately knows the language and music of a specific culture to design the best practice in Orff Schulwerk for that culture. A good understanding of the Schulwerk approach and a positive attitude are a must as well. She described the current status of Orff Schulwerk in these three countries as of 1987 and suggested that future research track the progress of transplantation of the European model of Orff Schulwerk in these countries.

Siemens, M. T. (1969). *A Comparison Of Orff and Traditional Instructional Methods in Music.*

This investigation sought to reveal differences between the Orff approach of teaching and a traditional method with respect to music achievement as well as differences in interest, attitude, and success feelings in musical participation. Subjects in this study were fifth grade children ($N = 458$) selected from three similar schools. Comparisons were made through the use of eighteen variables collected for each subject, using the *Knuth Achievement Test in Music*, a student interest questionnaire, and the *Kwalwasser–Ruch Test of Musical Accomplishment.*

There were two main significant results from this study. The group that received the Orff approach as treatment performed at a significantly higher level in interest and attitude, and they reported higher choices of music as a favorite subject and higher enjoyment of rhythmic activities. Those students who received the traditional method performed significantly better on the *Knuth Achievement Test* and in the *Kwalwasser–Ruch* subtest one, in discrimination of better types of music, and in recordings of fine classical music.

Sogin, D. W. & Wang, C. C. (1990). *An Analysis of the Perceptions of Orff-Trained Teachers on an Elementary Music Lesson.*

The purpose of this study was to examine the perceptions of teachers in different levels of Orff training on an individual elementary music lesson and to identify those elements that were considered generally good teaching technique, the music instruction, and those elements that they considered Orff specific. Subjects for this study were participants and instructors of a summer Orff-Schulwerk Training Course. Subjects were asked to view a twenty-minute videotaped music lesson of a second grade music class and respond on two separate response sheets.

The differences in the study did not occur between the different levels of Orff-Schulwerk training, but between the perception of music as subject matter and the non-musical events in this teacher's lesson. That is, all three groups rated the time spent on musical activity consistently lower than those events that are considered general teaching techniques. In addition, the perceived amount of time on creativity was rated lowest by all the Orff participants.

Conclusions and Recommendations

1. The analysis of the research studies on Orff Schulwerk in the classroom suggest that much greater care must be taken in defining the variables used in conducting the research, specifically "Orff Schulwerk." Also, different researchers use a variety of definitions when using Orff Schulwerk as an independent variable. Comparisons cannot be made across studies when this is the case. For example, some researchers use the criterion that a student merely has to play a barred instrument to define this variable as Orff Schulwerk, while others define "Schulwerk" as Carl Orff describes it, and still others explain it some place in between. If researchers can better define "Schulwerk," then clearer patterns will evolve from the literature and research, and better information can be used in the decision-making process.

2. Another outcome of this study that relates closely to the first issue is that many researchers tend to use Orff in conjunction with other curricula such that it is difficult to say what the effect (if any) of Orff instruction has on the dependent variable when there is such cross pollination of curricular ideas. As mentioned earlier in this chapter, researchers often lump together different curricula and refer to it collectively as "Orff" or by some other name. If knowledge about Schulwerk and its effect in the classroom are important, then careful consideration must be given to the Orff curriculum.

3. The most striking conclusion that we found is the lack of research in the classroom regarding the role and use of improvisation. The hallmark of Carl Orff's ideas is that improvisation must be introduced at the child's level before the skill can be developed to its mature form. Very little has been done to investigate the use of improvisation in the classroom.

Although, in the larger picture, improvisation falls under creativity, and research in this area may help to better define those processes in Orff Schulwerk during child development. Since the Schulwerk has a progressive curriculum and a working definition of creativity/improvisation, it seems that research about Orff Schulwerk can open new vistas in this area.

4. Our final conclusion of this analysis is that more research should focus on teaching skills and the success of the institute teachers who are the ones that teach level classes during the summer months. Skills that every successful teacher needs, such as the pacing of a lesson, use of classroom time, and the type and effect of feedback that should be given, need investigation. These variables, along with musical skill levels, can provide a rich source of information that has not yet been tapped.

Recommendations

The following are recommendations as a way of pointing to the future regarding research *apropos* to the nature, purpose, effectiveness, and outcomes of Orff-Schulwerk education. First, we recommend an international consensus by those involved in research to use an operational definition of Orff Schulwerk when conducting their research. This clarity of definition would help the community at large to compare and contrast many future findings. Second, we recommend that when investigating Orff Schulwerk in the classroom, all variables be clearly defined, and that unless the study is comparative, researchers should not muddy the resultant data with other curricula. Finally, we recommend that researchers take a broader view of Orff Schulwerk and begin to investigate creativity, as well as good teaching techniques besides those musical skills and knowledge that Orff teachers possess.

Part II

The interest of researching Orff Schulwerk seems to have expanded in the last two decades—i.e., the turn of the twenty-first century. Not only did the number of studies increase, but also the use of research methods became wider. Furthermore, the operative definition of Orff Schulwerk in recent studies became clearer, and the Orff-Schulwerk process was focused instead on being part of the "eclectic approach" in research studies. More studies appeared to address the important issues such as improvisation and student outcomes. Some studies continued to be philosophical or historical in nature. More studies using qualitative methods emerged while descriptive research and experimental research remained.

Part I of this chapter serves to reflect the history of early Orff-Schulwerk research in music education, mainly in the United States in the second half of the twentieth century, whereas Part II here reveals how such research efforts have advanced both in diversity and in techniques. In Part III of this chapter, these studies and more are classified in different categories so that readers can get a panoramic perspective of Orff research at a glance, along with a listing of the bibliography. The research studies discussed below are again selected by the authors of this chapter who deem the studies to be significant and should be read first. There are other sources of good information related to Orff-Schulwerk research. The Webliography in the Research section of the American Orff-Schulwerk Association (AOSA) Web site offers a great place to start searching for research abstracts by authors or key words. The AOSA Web site also includes links to research resources such as the Orff Centrum, the Orff Institute in Germany, and the Isabell Carley Library at the Eastman School of Music where the AOSA writings are archived.

Critical Analysis of Recent Studies Related to Orff Schulwerk in the Classroom

Beegle, A. (2006). *Children at Work in Their Musical Expression: A Classroom-based Study of Small Group Improvisation.*

Amy Beegle's dissertation is an excellent example of a study that included an examination and description of children's musical improvisations, including their processes and products as well as the interactions that occurred within small groups. This study qualitatively looked at children's improvisational activity within an elementary school music classroom in which the investigator was also the music teacher. The participants in the study were drawn from three fifth-grade classrooms and videotaped. Forty-six students were videotaped during their weekly music class meetings. Children were assigned to groups of four so that there were six groups of four per class. The integrity of the groups was maintained throughout the twelve weeks of study.

Several prompts were developed and used in the study—a poem, a painting, and a section of a professional musical composition. These were presented to students in each class at least once at the beginning of the lesson. Lessons began with the entire group gathering for an introduction to or review of the prompt, followed by the teacher's description of the improvisational task as well as facilitating the children's group brainstorming session. Children listened to and evaluated each group's performance within a four-lesson format. The researcher also established student focus groups that were interviewed separately after every four lessons. Data were generated through a written pre-observational questionnaire, transcribed audio and video recorded observations, and field notes, as well as repeated individual and small group formal field interviews.

Several important themes emerged from this study. Social roles became defined, as leaders and followers as well as friendships appeared congruent to musical roles of lead player and support player. An established four-part non-sequential planning process appeared in the focus groups while the children were able to demonstrate expressed strategies for planning and evaluating improvisation performances. The children's musical product did vary, depending upon the prompt, and finally, the children's music was embedded with material inherent in the musical and technical knowledge relating to the Orff-Schulwerk experiences.

Boras, C. (1998). *The Orff Schulwerk and Traditional Music Education A Comparison of Approach.*

The following experimental study, a master's thesis by Carol Boras (1988), compared the benefits of the Orff approach with a more traditional approach to teaching music. She investigated the following three hypotheses:

(1) Orff students would demonstrate greater gross motor skills than non-Orff students; (2) Orff students would demonstrate more positive attitudes toward music than non-Orff students; and finally, (3) Orff students would demonstrate greater music skill acquisition than their non-Orff counterparts. There were fifty-two participants in the study randomly assigned to three groups. The dependent variables consisted of the Glasgow & Hamreus (1968) *Music Test*, the *M-P Pupil Attitude Scale* and the Ulrich (1985) *Test of Gross Motor Development*. This study occurred over a twelve-week period for thirty-minute sessions per week. Data were collected and analyzed using analysis of variance techniques and descriptive statistics. The results indicate no statistical differences between the Orff and non-Orff students regarding motor skills nor the acquisition of musical skills; and the Orff group did not perform more positively than the traditional groups. Further data were collected through interviews with the teachers and the students.

Champion, S. M. (2006). *The Musical Activities Found in Selected Orff-Schulwerk Elementary Music Classrooms.*

Susan Michele Champion's (2006) dissertation was an examination of musical activities in selected Orff-Schulwerk elementary music classrooms by measuring class time engaged in those activities. Similar to the Wang and Sogin (1997) study found in the *Journal of Research in Music Education*, Champion identified eight musical activities occurring on a frequent and regular basis. The eight musical activities were speech activities, instrumental improvisation, vocal improvisation, body percussion, simple compositions, movement/dance, use of ostinato, and performing on instruments. Seven highly trained Orff teachers were identified and videotaped teaching third and fourth grade classes. Data were analyzed using the SCRIBE computer software for observational behavior. Six of the eight musical activities occurred across all teachers and grade levels with both movement/dance and performing on instruments occurring most frequently. Both vocal improvisation and simple compositions were not observed at all across teachers or classes.

Chang, L. (2010). *A Comparison of the Orff-Schulwerk Music Education Approach in the United States and Taiwan.*

Ling-Yao Chang's master's thesis (2010) was an attempt to study the implementation of and attitudes about Orff Schulwerk in the United States and Taiwan. There were eight research questions posed in this study, although the most important were as follows: (1) What are the teachers' and students' attitudes and thoughts about the Orff Schulwerk approach? (2) Do American and Taiwanese teachers teach students in different ways, and what are those differences? Finally, (3) Does culture influence the teachers' teaching style when they teach using the Orff-Schulwerk approach? To answer these questions seventeen teachers, both in the United States and in Taiwan, were sent questionnaires, which were also sent to the students in both countries. In addition, videotapes were made of both the United States and Taiwan classes for *post hoc* evaluations in order to look at differences in student behavior in the United States and Taiwan.

The results from the initial questionnaire indicated that Taiwanese students in grades two to four performed more than students in grade five. However, American students felt more confident and active in performing and answering questions in music class. Secondly, American students appeared to sing and play instruments the most compared to their Taiwanese counterparts. In general, the American students liked to "show off" and be the center of attention in the class while the Taiwanese students were more reticent and shy. The music classes in the United States, according to Chang, were generally smaller than in Taiwan, and the researcher observed that the American students were given greater opportunity for individual responses. Finally, the researcher points out that the American students appeared more creative in class than the Taiwanese students. When the Taiwanese teachers asked questions of their students or had them create their own music, the students were not able to produce their own ideas.

Mason, E. J. (2008). *Kodály or Orff: Pre-Service Teachers' Perceptions of and Preference for Two Different Methodologies Used in Teaching Elementary General Music.*

Emily J. Mason's dissertation incorporates an investigation of pre-service teachers' abilities to identify the approach as either Orff or Kodály when viewing teaching episodes in general music classes. The participants in this study were 134 undergraduate music education majors in their sophomore, junior, or senior year, across eight different universities. All the participants viewed five teaching excerpts containing music lessons using either Kodály or Orff in which they had to decide which method was being used. They had several choices to choose from—Orff, Kodály, Dalcroze, Suzuki, or "don't know." The results indicated that pre-service teachers were more able to identify the Kodály method when viewing the stimuli tapes using Tonic Sol-fa and the Orff method when viewing the excerpt with Orff instruments. Those excerpts that contained the use of Orff body percussion and speech chant as well as a Kodály game showed low percentages of correct responses. The elementary majors, however, did have the most correct answers across all five teaching episodes. The conclusions of the study suggest that there is a lack of recognition of these well-versed methodologies, particularly from pre-service teachers as they prepare to enter the teaching profession.

Mason, N. F. (2012). *The Effects of Orff-Schulwerk Instruction on Rhythmic Achievement in Beginning Band.*

Nicola Mason's research dealt with the effects of applying Orff-Schulwerk pedagogy in teaching middle school bands. She confined her student outcomes to rhythmic achievement, including listening, notating, and performing rhythm on band instruments. She used the pre-posttest control group design and randomly assigned students to the experimental group receiving Orff pedagogy ($n = 44$), taught by the researcher, and to the control group receiving regular instruction ($n = 44$), using a band method book, which was taught by the regular teacher, over ten weeks. Prior to the treatment, she had her lesson plans scrutinized by several Orff-Schulwerk teacher trainers to ascertain the validity of the Schulwerk process. In addition, other Orff-trained teachers observed her actual teaching in real time and from video recordings. Her researcher-designed *Rhythmic Skills for Beginning Band Test* indicated good reliability (r values of .80 and .88), and data analysis using ANOVA revealed significant difference ($p \leq .05$) in rhythmic achievement favoring the Orff group. This experimental study represents, hopefully, the beginning of a trend of expanding the application of Orff Schulwerk not only for older children, but also for instrumental ensemble settings. The results are encouraging and further studies should follow.

Sanborn, R. J. (2005). *The Contribution of Doreen Hall to the Development of Orff-Schulwerk in Canada, 1954-1986.*

This dissertation is an historical study of the career and life of Doreen Hall and her efforts to introduce the work of Carl Orff and his Schulwerk to North America. The first chapter frames the time period of the post-WWII era and the new ideas that were beginning to emerge from Europe. Sanborn goes on to explain that Hall was a student at the Royal Conservatory of Music (Toronto) from 1951 to 1954 and pursued a career in music education. She studied in Salzburg and then in 1956, she began offering courses for teachers consistent with Orff's underlying pedagogical and musical ideas. This study goes on to show how Doreen Hall almost single-handedly worked at helping Orff establish his ideas and educational methodology in Canada and the United States. By the 1960s, Doreen Hall was considered one of the most authoritative and influential individuals to offer course work in Orff during the summers in North America and, by the 1970s, Orff was considered prominently in the curriculum across almost every province throughout Canada. Sanborn points out that Doreen Hall was a first-class musician and that to teach teachers the value of the Orff Schulwerk, she did not simply lecture to them, but engaged them in a pragmatic approach that emphasized the experience of those key elements of the Orff Schulwerk through actively engaging in music making. Sanborn finishes by arguing that it took people such as Hall and her actions and specific events that helped to promulgate Orff's ideas.

Scott, J. K. (2010). *Orff-Schulwerk Teacher Educators' Beliefs About Singing.*

Julia Kay Scott's dissertation is a study of Orff-Schulwerk teacher educators' views and values about singing. Her investigation addressed the following issues: (1) pedagogical and curricular priority beliefs; (2) self-concept beliefs; (3) efficacy beliefs; and finally (4) a larger belief systems. Data were collected through open-ended interviews conducted with eight AOSA-approved Orff-Schulwerk teacher educators from the United States. Transcripts of the interviews were coded to discern the most important words and phrases during the interview process. Categorizations of the words were intended to discover trends in the data in order to answer the research questions. Additional quotes from selected interviews were cited to support those claims. The results from the study indicate that singing in the context of the Orff Schulwerk is not only important to the approach, but also incorporated and prioritized according to the ability level of the students. The participants of the study believed that not all of them had adequate singing voices, yet they were able to overcome those feelings of vocal inadequacy and arrive at a value center that everyone should be able to participate in the act of singing. These values and the orientation toward singing were fundamentally influenced through the participants' early experiences with family singing and their initial collegiate involvement with the Orff-Schulwerk approach. One of the more interesting correlates that was made, unlike the Sogin and Wang (2008) study, which reported that teachers thought that singing was the most important component in the elementary music experience, was that Scott reports that teacher educators believed that with beginning students, singing in Orff Schulwerk is balanced with playing instruments and engaging in movement.

Sogin, D. W. & Wang, C. C. (2008). *Music Activity Reports by Music Teachers With Varying Training in Orff Schulwerk.*

Sogin and Wang have observed many music teachers receiving Orff teacher training over the years. In general, they noticed that most teachers completing Level One became overwhelmed with the many new ideas to bring back to their teaching. Some continued for Levels Two and Three, proclaiming at each level that they now understood further how the real Orff process works. The question was related to how the teachers change with each level of training. The authors attempted to determine some answers by giving a survey to teachers completing varying levels of training at the end of a summer training course. Forty-nine teachers, including seventeen at Level One (L1), twelve at Level Two (L2), and twenty at Level Three (L3), with an average of 5.39 years of elementary music teaching, completed a survey form used in an earlier research study (1997). This survey was used to obtain teacher's self-report of an estimate of the percentages of time these teachers typically spend in various activities in their classroom. Results indicated similarities in the time devoted to reading, listening, and singing among teachers of all three levels, with singing scoring the highest time spent—sixty-five percent or more. The impact of Orff-Schulwerk training appears in the amount of time spent playing instruments, creating, and moving during activities, with an increase of each of these activities at each level of training. Additionally, the increase is larger between L1 and L2, and smaller between L2 and L3. Teachers with more Orff training also reported more opportunity for students to make decisions and expansion of active student participation. These results suggest that advanced training in Orff Schulwerk provides the teachers not only with further skills in the Schulwerk process, but also increases confidence to empower their students to create and express themselves.

Taranto, A. S. (2010). *Orff Schulwerk Levels Course Instructors and Their Teachers: Determining Pedagogical Lineages and Influences.*

Albert Steven Taranto, in his dissertation, traces the pedagogical lines of the current generation of American Orff-Schulwerk levels course instructors and their teachers to better understand the ideals and philosophies established by both Carl Orff and Gunild Keetman that have been passed down from Orff-Schulwerk teachers to their students. The primary source data were collected through a researcher survey of 2010 Orff-Schulwerk levels course instructors. Secondary sources included the writings by and about Carl Orff and Gunild Keetman, doctoral dissertations, online postings through AOSA and the Orff Institute of Salzburg, and finally, several journal articles. Besides a family tree of Orff-Schulwerk teachers and students, the following list of influences were named by the participants: (1) Orff Schulwerk (OS) is a child-centered approach; (2) OS activities are open ended; (3) OS is a multi-faceted approach integrating speech, singing, movement, drama and the playing of instruments; (4) improvisation is at the core of the OS; (5) OS involves process teaching; (6) the *Music für Kinder* volumes are primary source material; (7) OS develops musicianship; (8) OS improves teaching ability; (9) OS improves such skills as composition, arranging and orchestration, and; (10) music making in OS leads to community building. Additionally, this study is an excellent historical account of both the history of the Orff Schulwerk and the selected level courses here in the United States. Such studies as this can provide a dialogue among Orff-Schulwerk practitioners to look at those pedagogical elements that remain consistent with the teachings of Carl Orff and Gunild Keetman and those that do not.

Taylor, D. M. (2004). *Beating Time: Refining Learned Repertoire for Percussion Instruments in an Orff Ensemble Setting.*

Donald M. Taylor examined the teaching practices of eight Orff-Schulwerk instructors with their upper elementary students working to refine learned repertoire for percussion instruments. Videotapes were made of four group rehearsals. The results from analyzing the teaching episodes indicated that teachers taught with fast pacing and a predominance of instructional directives that were mostly procedural as opposed to musical. Taylor reported that students performed twenty-nine percent of all performance trials successfully, regardless of the targets identified by the instructors. Most of the performance problems were associated with precision brought on by rushing the basic pulse. In addition, in about half of all student trials, teachers were able to identify those targets prior to initiating student performance. When students were given verbal prompts prior to performance trials, they appeared successful sixty–three percent of the time, however, they were seventy-four percent successful during performance trials when teachers verbalized the targets while students were actually playing. Taylor concludes that students were most successful when teachers employed clear, explicit directives and positive modeling.

Wang, C. C. & Sogin, D. W. (1997). *A Comparative Study of Self-Reported Versus Observed Classroom Activities in Elementary General Music.*

The purpose of this study was to compare general music teachers, who have an expressed interest in Orff Schulwerk, on time usage activities in their general music classes with actual observations. Specifically, teachers were asked to rank order and estimate their time spent on specific types of activities such as instruction, singing, playing instruments, reading, creating, moving, and describing music that they include in their teaching. Subsequently, videotapes were made and analyzed to assess observed behaviors of these same teachers, comparing the observed data with the self-report. It was found that teachers generally overestimate the time they spend in all activities when compared to actual time spent observed from their teaching.

Wang, C. C. & Sogin, D. W. (2004). *An Examination of the Teacher-Student Interaction in the Orff-Schulwerk Process.*

Wang and Sogin believe that a major weakness in previous Orff-Schulwerk research studies has been the lack of a common operative definition of the Orff process across the studies. They reasoned that the best way to define the Orff process was to examine the teaching of expert Orff teachers and to identify what they actually do in delivering their lessons. Five nationally known expert Orff teachers with an average of teaching 16.2 years using the Orff approach, who had been active as teacher trainers, participated in the study. Twenty-four second and fifth grade music lessons with a minimum of twenty-five minutes of instruction time were videotaped for this study. Each teacher was specifically told to use the Orff process as they regularly do in their teaching. Time analysis, using the fifteen-second "observe" and five-second "record" protocol, was applied to the videos according to teacher and student activities in the Orff approach. Time spent by the teacher averaged as follows: teacher talking/giving directives (77%); teacher modeling (49%); and teacher giving approval (4.9%). The student activity revealed as follows: playing pitched instruments (21%); student talking (18%); using notation

(18%); singing (12%); body percussion (12%); moving/dancing (9%); rhythmic speech (8%); playing unpitched instruments (7%), creating (4%), listening (1%), and improvising (16%). The common characteristics among teachers can be observed readily when the data are displayed in graphic form. From observation of these exemplary teachers, the Orff process is one that is filled with multiple activities occurring simultaneously, with the teacher providing short, verbal directives and/or gesturing throughout the lesson while students participate in multimodal fashion—e.g., clapping and chanting, in an intensive and efficient manner. In fact, an average of 2.5 events occurred at all times. With such total music participation, verbal approval is not really necessary, because the students are rewarded by engaging and enjoying the activities. The classroom atmosphere is one of joy and eagerness with no discipline problems observed. It seems that more time for improvisation should be recorded here. An explanation is that improvisation usually takes place near the end of learning a certain musical concept and the lessons observed were only snap shots of many beginning lessons. The expert teachers in this study delivered the learning process seamlessly with much interaction with the students, and provided them with optimal learning opportunities through music making together.

Part III

For the purpose of building a body of professional knowledge in Orff Schulwerk (OS), we propose to use the themes or categories below to classify research studies related to OS. This systematic procedure was inspired by the example provided by Radocy (1998). Some studies can be classified into more than one category, but each study is listed here only once. The decisions belong to the authors and may be reclassified by others. Existing research articles and writing (in English) from journals, dissertations, theses, and conferences papers were grouped into fifteen categories identified to cover all areas related to research in Orff Schulwerk. Important findings are described in Part I and Part II of this chapter, to provide an overall perspective of Orff-Schulwerk research. The list below is not exhaustive but rather a representative sample to denote the topics related to Orff Schulwerk that attracted music-education researchers. As apparent to readers, the majority of the studies were completed in the last two decades, attesting to the fact that the interest of Orff Schulwerk has accelerated in recent years. This trend will most likely continue as more music educators receive advanced training in Orff Schulwerk and as more teachers and musicians attempt to extend the Orff process to new student populations.

A Listing of Orff Research Studies

1. Curriculum/Assessment: Addo (1990), Calusel (1998), Daigneault (1993), Lyne (1991), Madden (1984), Roberts (1981), Tsisserev (1993), Woody and Fredrickson (2000)

2. Effect of OS on Music Knowledge/Skills: Bellflower Study (1968), Flohr (1981), Glasgow & Hamreus (1968), Hensley (1981), Hill (2008), Hudgens (1987), N. Mason (2012), Muse (1994), Olson (1964), Shank and Rashley (2001), Siemens (1969)

3. Teacher/Student Characteristics: Hamilton (1999), Martin (1992), Munsen (1986), Taylor (2004), Wang and Sogin (1997)

4. Attitudes/Preferences/Feelings: Barker (1981), Bondurant-Koehler (1995), Cose-Giallella (2010), Mishenhelter (2001)

5. Contributions of Organization/Individual: Orrell (1995), Osterby (1988), Sanborn (2005), Weisert-Peatow (2002), Wimmer (1993)

6. Creativity/Improvisation: Amchin (1995), Beegle (2001), Beegle (2006), Brophy (1998), Fairfield (2010), Flohr (1980, 1981), Reese (2006)

7. Pedagogic Process/Settings: Champion (2006), Pedell (2005), Price (1988), Sogin and Wang (1990), Taranto (2010), Wang and Sogin (2004)

8. OS Teacher Education: Bugos (2011), Brophy (2002), E. Mason (2008), McDowell, Abril, & Frego (2003), Robbins (1994), Scott (2010), Williamson (2011), Sogin & Wang (2008)

9. Relating OS to Language/Other Curricula Subjects: Kelley (1981), Kennedy (2007),Whitehead (2001)

10. OS and Theoretic/Philosophical Inquiries: Dolloff (1993), Jaccard (1995), Jacobus (2009), Snell (1980)

11. Learning and Development/Diverse Learners: Boras (1988), Grant, (1991), Halliday (2012), Persellin (1999)

12. Instruments/Recorders in OS: Sogin & Wang (2002), Velasquez (1990)

13. Relating OS to Movement/Arts: Moore (1984)

14. OS Research/Research Methods: Wang & Sogin (1995), Wang & Sogin (current chapter)

15. Cross-Cultural Education: H. Chang (1991), L. Chang (2010), Chin (1993), Kubitsky (1998), Mckoy (1998), Shamrock (1988)

References

Addo, A. O. (1990). *A survey of music teaching strategies in Ghanaian elementary schools as a basis for curriculum development.* (Unpublished master's thesis). The University of British Columbia, Vancouver, Canada.

Amchin, R. A. (1995). *Creative musical response: The effects of teacher-student interaction on the improvisation abilities of fourth- and fifth-grade students.* (Unpublished doctoral dissertation). The University of Michigan, Ann Arbor.

Barker, C. S. (1981). *Using Orff-Schulwerk as a method to enhance self concept in children with learning disabilities.* (Doctoral dissertation). Retrieved from ProQuest Digital Dissertations & Theses. (UMI No. 8124776).

Beegle, A. C. (2001). *An examination of Orff-trained general music teachers' use of improvisation with elementary school children.* (Unpublished master's thesis). University of St. Thomas, St. Paul, Minnesota.

Beegle, A. C. (2006). *Children at work in their musical expression: A classroom-based study of small group improvisation.* (Doctoral dissertation). Retrieved from ProQuest Digital Dissertations & Theses. (UMI No. 3224185).

Bellflower Symposium. (1968). Orff Schulwerk: Design for creativity: A report of the project "creativity and participation in music education." (EASA Title 3 Report). Bellflower, California: Bellflower Unified School District. (ERIC ED 053 153).

Bondurant-Koehler, S. (1995). *The effect of selected modes of music instruction on children's music preference.* (Unpublished doctoral dissertation). Indiana University, Bloomington, IN.

Boras, C. (1998). *The Orff Schulwerk and traditional music education a comparison of approach.* (Master's thesis). Retrieved from ProQuest Digital Dissertations & Theses. (ML45438).

Brophy, T. S. (1988). *The melodic improvisations of children ages six through twelve: a developmental perspective.* (Doctoral dissertation). Retrieved from ProQuest Digital Dissertations & Theses. (UMI No. 9906615).

Brophy, T. S. (2002). Teacher reflection on undergraduate music education. *Journal of Music Teacher Education, 12*(1), e19-e25.

Bugos, K. M. (2011). *New York State early-career teachers' selection and use of pedagogical approaches in elementary general music.* (Doctoral dissertation). Retrieved from ProQuest Digital Dissertations & Theses. (UMI No. 3475296).

Champion, S. M. (2006). *The musical activities found in selected Orff-Schulwerk elementary music classrooms.* (Doctoral dissertation). Retrieved from ProQuest Dissertations and Theses. (UMI No. 3259401).

Chang, H. (1991). *A status report and suggestions for improving elementary music education in the Republic of China.* (Unpublished doctoral dissertation). University Of Oregon, Eugene Oregon.

Chang, L. (2010). *A comparison of the Orff-Schulwerk music education approach in the United States and Taiwan.* (Doctoral dissertation). Retrieved from ProQuest Digital Dissertations & Theses. (UMI No. 1477396).

Chin, J. (1993). *Curriculum for introducing Chinese instruments in grades four through six.* (Master's thesis). Retrieved from ProQuest Digital Dissertations & Theses. (UMI No. 1352631).

Clausel, S. L. S. (1998). *Applications of Cambourne's model of literacy learning and the Orff-Schulwerk music method to the development of a curriculum model for Mississippi music education, K-1.* (Doctoral dissertation). Retrieved from ProQuest Digital Dissertations & Theses. (UMI No. 9908513).

Cose-Giallella, C. D. (2010). *Children's perceptions of and feelings about their musical performance.* (Doctoral dissertation). Retrieved from ProQuest Digital Dissertations & Theses. (UMI No. 3410530).

Daigneault, D. J. (1993). *A survey of recommended procedures and teaching methods for building and maintaining a wind and percussion instrumental music education program grades six through twelve.* (Doctoral dissertation). Retrieved from ProQuest Digital Dissertations & Theses. (UMI No. 9406640).

Dolloff, L. A. (1993). *Das Schulwerk: A foundation for the cognitive, musical, and artistic development of children.* Research Perspectives in Music Education, Monograph Number 1, Bartel, L. (Ed). University of Toronto, Canada.

Fairfield, S. M. (2010). *Creative thinking in elementary general music: A survey of teachers' perceptions and practices.* (Doctoral dissertation). Retrieved from ProQuest Digital Dissertations & Theses. (UMI No. 3439183).

Flohr, J. W. (1980). *Musical improvisation behavior of young children.* (Doctoral dissertation). Retrieved from ProQuest Digital Dissertations & Theses. (UMI No. 8009033).

Flohr, J. W. (1981). Short-term music instruction and young children's developmental music aptitude. *Journal of Research in Music Education, 29,* 219-223.

Glasgow, R. B. and Hamreus, D. G. (1968). Study to determine the feasibility of adapting the Carl Orff approach to elementary schools in America. (Final Report). Monmouth, Oregon: Oregon College of education. (ERIC ED 020 804).

Grant, T. W. (1991). *The effect of Orff Schulwerk instruction on memory development in children ages ten to eleven.* (Doctoral dissertation). Retrieved from ProQuest Digital Dissertations & Theses. (UMI No.9127644).

Halliday, A. R. B. (2012). *Interpretations of student engagement in the context of the Orff Schulwerk music classroom at the Dubard School for Language Disorders.* (Doctoral dissertation). Retrieved from ProQuest Digital Dissertations & Theses. (UMI No. 3530729).

Hamilton, H. J. (1999). *Music learning through composition, improvisation and peer interaction in the context of three sixth grade music classes.* (Doctoral dissertation). Retrieved from ProQuest Digital Dissertations & Theses. (UMI No. 9937857).

Hensley, S. E. (1981). *A study of the musical achievement of elementary students taught by the Memphis City Curriculum Guide and students taught by the traditional approach.* (Doctoral dissertation.). Retrieved from ProQuest Digital Dissertations & Theses. (UMI No. 8207825).

Hill, G. L. (2008). *Teaching rhythm to beginning piano students: An analysis of various counting systems and the integration of Kodály and Orff rhythm strategies.* (Doctoral dissertation). Retrieved from ProQuest Dissertations and Theses. (UMI No. 3361149).

Hudgens, C. K. K. (1987). *A study of the Kodály approach to music teaching and an investigation of four approaches to the teaching of selected skills in first grade music classes.* (Doctoral dissertation). Retrieved from ProQuest Dissertations and Theses. (UMI No. 8713951).

Jaccard, J. L. (1995). *A conceptual model for literature-based musical education.* (Doctoral dissertation). Retrieved from ProQuest Dissertations and Theses. (UMI No. 9606520).

Jacobus, C. L. (2009). *Urban Orff: The music and philosophy of Carl Orff as it relates to No Child Left Behind in urban schools.* (Master's thesis). ProQuest Dissertations and Theses. (UMI No. 1472176).

Kelley, L. L. (1981). *A combined experimental and descriptive study of the effect of music on reading and language.* (Doctoral dissertation). Retrieved from ProQuest Dissertations and Theses. (UMI No. 8117801).

Kennedy, L. C. (2007). *A short term study of the effects of the Orff-Schulwerk musical approach on reading fluency and reading comprehension in second grade students.* (Master's thesis). Retrieved from ProQuest Dissertations and Theses. (UMI No. 1444503).

Kubitsky, I. (1998). *Ewe children's music from Ghana, West Africa, in the classroom.* (Master's thesis). Retrieved from ProQuest Dissertations and Theses. (UMI No. 1389656).

Lyne, J. K. (1991). *Beginning strings class instruction: Practice and theory.* (Doctoral dissertation). Retrieved from ProQuest Dissertations and Theses. (UMI No. 9134876).

McDowell, C.; Abril, C.; and Frego, D. (2003). Attending summer courses: Why we do it. *The Orff Echo. 36,* 20 – 23.

Mckoy, C. L. (1998). *The effect of two instructional approaches on fourth-grade students' preferences for indigenous folk music of Ghana.* (Doctoral dissertation). Retrieved from ProQuest Dissertations and Theses. (UMI No. 9919185).

Madden, J. A., Jr. (1984). *Zoltan Kodály and Carl Orff: Implications for program development in elementary instrumental music education.* (Doctoral dissertation). Retrieved from ProQuest Dissertations and Theses. (UMI No. 8410135).

Martin, M. A. (1992). *An examination of the Orff-Schulwerk approach to music education in a public elementary school: a replication study.* (Doctoral dissertation). Retrieved from ProQuest Dissertations and Theses. (UMI No. 9234992).

Mason, E. J. (2008). *Kodály or Orff: Pre-service teachers' perceptions of and preference for two different methodologies used in teaching elementary general music.* (Doctoral dissertation). Retrieved from ProQuest Dissertations and Theses. (UMI NO. 3340738).

Mason, N. F. (2012). *The effects of Orff-Schulwerk instruction on rhythmic achievement in beginning band.* (Unpublished doctoral dissertation). University of Kentucky, Lexington, KY.

Mishenhelter, D. (2001). An investigation of university students' perceptions of personal teaching ability and anxiety before and after an Orff-Schulwerk workshop. Paper presented at the 2001 national convention of the American Orff-Schulwerk Association, Cincinnati, OH.

Moore, J. L.S. (1984). *Rhythm and movement: An objective analysis of their association with music aptitude (Orff Schulwerk, Weikart movement).* (Doctoral dissertation). Retrieved from ProQuest Dissertations and Theses. (UMI No. 8417898).

Munsen, S. C. (1986). *A description and analysis of an Orff-Schulwerk program of music education.* (Doctoral dissertation). Retrieved from ProQuest Dissertations and Theses. (UMI No. 8701575).

Muse, M. B. (1994). *A comparison of two methods of teaching singing to primary children an attempt to determine which of two approaches to teaching singing is more effective.* (Master's thesis). Retrieved from ProQuest Dissertations and Theses. (UMI No. 1358052).

Olson, R. G. (1964). *A comparison of two pedagogical approaches adapted to the acquisition of melodic sensitivity in sixth grade children: The Orff method and the traditional method.* (Doctoral dissertation). Retrieved from ProQuest Dissertations and Theses. (UMI No. 6503508).

Orrell, M. S. (1995). *The work of Grace C. Nash in music education in The United States, 1960 – 1990, and her influence upon members of the American Orff-Schulwerk Association in the states of Arizona and Colorado.* (Doctoral dissertation). Retrieved from ProQuest Dissertations and Theses. (UMI No. 9611456).

Osterby, P. M. (1988). *Orff Schulwerk in North America, 1955-1969 (United States, Canada).* (Doctoral dissertation). Retrieved from ProQuest Dissertations and Theses. (UMI No. 8823221).

Pedell, K. A. (2005). *Activities in elementary general music classrooms: Current practices in Pennsylvania.* (Doctoral dissertation). Retrieved from ProQuest Dissertations and Theses. (UMI No. 3198132).

Persellin, D. (1999). The effect of Orff-based music instruction on spatial-temporal task performance of young children. *Texas Music Educators Association Research.*

Price, H. E. (1990). Elementary school music teachers' comparative use of classroom time: Teachers who are and are not Orff-Schulwerk certified. *Missouri Journal of Research in Music Education, 27,* 30 – 49.

Radocy, R. (1998). Personal perspectives on research: Past, present, and future. *Journal of Research in Music Education*, 46, 342-350.

Reese, J. W. (2006). *Definitions of improvisation: Perspective of three elementary general music teachers.* (Master's thesis, University of Michigan). ProQuest Dissertations and Theses. (UMI No. 1440086).

Robbins, J. (1994). Levels of learning in Orff SPIEL. *Bulletin for the Council for Research in Music Education*, *123*, 47-53.

Roberts, C. (1981). *A sequential series of beginning Orff-Schulwerk arrangements for use in the middle school.* (Master's thesis). Retrieved from ProQuest Dissertations and Theses. (UMI No. 1316268).

Sanborn, R. J. (2005). *The contribution of Doreen Hall to the development of Orff Schulwerk in Canada, 1954-1986.* (Master's thesis). Retrieved from ProQuest Dissertations and Theses. (MR02316).

Scott, J. K. (2010). *Orff Schulwerk teacher educators beliefs about singing.* (Doctoral dissertation). Retrieved from ProQuest Dissertations and Theses. (UMI No. 34116011).

Shamrock, M. E. (1988). *Applications and adaptations of Orff-Schulwerk in Japan, Taiwan and Thailand.* (Doctoral dissertation). Retrieved from ProQuest Dissertations and Theses. (UMI No. 8822884).

Siemens, M. T. (1969). A comparison of Orff and traditional instructional methods in music. *Journal of Research in Music Education*, 17, 272-285.

Snell, C. A. (1980). *The philosophical basis of Orff-Schulwerk.* (Doctoral dissertation). Retrieved from ProQuest Dissertations and Theses. (UMI No. 0533880).

Shank, J., and Rashley, B. (2001). The effect of musicing on recognition of music concepts by college students. Paper presented at the 2001 national convention of the American Orff-Schulwerk Association, Cincinnati, OH.

Sogin, D. W. and Wang. C. C. (1990). An analysis of the perceptions of Orff-trained teachers on an elementary music lesson. Paper presented at the World Congress of the International Society for Music Education, Helsinki, Finland.

Sogin, D. W. and Wang, C. C. (2002). A descriptive analysis of the recorder component of an Orff-Schulwerk teacher-training course. Paper presented at the National Conference of the American Orff-Schulwerk Association, Las Vegas.

Sogin, D. W. & Wang, C. C. (2008). Music activity reports by music teachers with varying training in Orff Schulwerk. *International Journal of Music Education: Research*, 26(3), 269-278.

Spurgeon, A. & Barber, C. (1995). What is actually taught by Orff and Kodály-trained teachers? Perception vs. reality. *Kodály Envoy, 21*(2), 2-8.

Taranto, A. S. (2010). *Orff-Schulwerk levels course instructors and their teachers: Determining pedagogical lineages and influences.* (Doctoral dissertation). Retrieved from ProQuest Dissertations and Theses. (UMI No. 3463456).

Taylor, D. M. (2004). *Beating time: Refining learned repertoire for percussion instruments in an Orff ensemble setting.* (Doctoral dissertation). Retrieved from Dissertations and Theses. (UMI No. 3143477).

Tsisserev, A. (1993). *An analysis of the music education methodology of Dmitry Kabalevsky and a comparison with those of Zoltan Kodály and Carl Orff.* (Master's thesis). Retrieved from Dissertations and Theses. (UMI No. MM13537).

Velasquez, V. (1990). Tuned idiophones in the music education of children: The history of Orff instruments. *The Bulletin of Historical Research in Music Education, 11*, 93-109.

Wang, C. C. and Sogin, D.W. (1995). A research perspective of Orff Schulwerk in the classroom. Paper presented at the *Orff 100* International Conference of Music and Dance, Melbourne, Australia.

Wang, C. C. and Sogin, D.W. (1997). A comparative study of self-reported versus observed classroom activities in elementary general music. *Journal of Research in Music Education, 45*, 444 – 456.

Wang, C. & Sogin, D. (2004). An examination of the teacher-student interaction in the Orff-Schulwerk process. *Research Perspectives in Music Education, 8*, 6 – 14.

Weisert-Peatow, H. S. (2002). *Leadership in the American Orff-Schulwerk Association, 1968-1998.* (Doctoral dissertation). Retrieved from Dissertations and Theses. (UMI No. 3053466).

Whitehead, B. J. (2001). *The effect of music-intensive intervention on mathematics scores of middle and high school students.* (Doctoral dissertation). Retrieved from ProQuest Dissertations and Theses. (UMI No. 3023878).

Williamson, C. P. (2011). *Elementary music educators' perceptions of effectiveness after Orff-Schulwerk training.* (Doctoral dissertation). Retrieved from ProQuest Dissertations and Theses. (UMI No. 3459853).

Wimmer, D. L. (1993). *The organization of the American Orff-Schulwerk Association from 1968-1980 and its influence upon music education in America.* (Doctoral dissertation). Retrieved from ProQuest Dissertations and Theses. (UMI No. 9320328).

Woody, R., and Fredrickson, J. (2000). A partnership project integrating computer technology and Orff Schulwerk. *General Music Today, 13,* 8-11.

Nota Bene: *The content of Chapters 10 and 11 reflects the studies of young teachers who begin to do research. It is of utmost importance to encourage and empower music teachers to engage in research and contribute to the knowledge of the field of music education. It is with this spirit that this Symposium included a session for budding researchers to demonstrate their work and work in progress. Teaching using the Orff-Schulwerk approach is not an isolated discipline, rather it benefits from the knowledge of all research pertaining to music teaching. By the same token, research studies in Orff Schulwerk should inspire teachers using others' approaches.*

Chapter 10

ORFF IN BAND:
RESEARCH AND IMPLEMENTATION
Nicola F. Mason and K. Michelle Lewis

As Orff-Schulwerk certified teachers and band directors, we attended the 2011 Curriculum Development Teacher Training course at the University of Kentucky, which was instructed by Jay Broeker. Being the only two band directors in the class, we began talking and brainstorming about expanding the principles and instructional activities of the Orff Schulwerk to the band room. Our motivation was the fact that, as performers, we had rarely been given the opportunity to improvise or perform independently from our scores. And, despite the many hours we spent in the practice room rehearsing for recitals, band performances, and orchestra performances, some of our most musical moments occurred in Orff settings. We desperately wanted to share this experience with students and knew that the Orff Schulwerk would provide the ideal platform.

As we began to research and share our discoveries, we developed a plan for implementing an Orff-Schulwerk curriculum in a middle school band setting. We received our primary motivation from the pedagogy of the Orff Schulwerk based upon the learning process of imitation, exploration, literacy, and improvisation (Frazee, 1987, p. 26) and the National Standards for Music Education, specifically composition, improvisation, listening, and analyzing. We also researched the concepts and curriculum brought forward by the Comprehensive Musicianship Movement. The Comprehensive Musicianship

Project, a nationwide program launched by the Music Educators National Conference in 1968, was designed to bring about conditions favorable to the creation, study, and performance of contemporary music to develop comprehensive musical understanding (Beglarian, 1967). Comprehensive musicianship is a term still used today to describe the interdisciplinary study of music (Heavner, 1995). Studies by Birdwhistell (1998), Gage (1994), and Heavner (1995) found that several beginning band method books included the principles of Comprehensive Musicianship, including *Essential Elements: A Comprehensive Band Method* (Rhodes, Bierschenk, Lautzenheiser, & Wiggins, 1991), *Standard of Excellence Band Method* (Pearson, 1993), and *Belwin 21ˢᵗ Century Band Method* (Bullock & Maiello, 1996).

Although traditional Orff-Schulwerk instruction is found in the elementary general music classroom, there is documented research and literature that supports and guides the successful inclusion of Orff Schulwerk in the upper grades and in various instrumental settings. In her discussion about target age groups for future Orff-Schulwerk study, Haselbach (1993) includes a range of ages from toddlers to adults. In an interview with several junior high teachers, Stewart (1988) observed that Orff Schulwerk could be "used more intellectually" beyond the sixth grade. Madden (1984) suggested that band instruments be introduced into the Orff-Schulwerk general music classroom in his study about the implications for program development in elementary instrumental music education. In Daigneault's (1993) survey of recommended procedures and teaching methods for building and maintaining a wind and percussion instrumental music education program in grades six through twelve, he concluded that applying the principles of the Orff-Schulwerk approach to the instrumental music setting could prove beneficial to wind and percussion players.

Previous research documents the collaborative efforts of various instructional approaches in band that include teaching approaches such as the Orff Schulwerk (Daigneault, 1993; Madden, 1984). Glasgow and Hamreus's (1968) study about the adaptability of the Orff approach to elementary school music found significant gains by Orff-instructed elementary students in their ability to perform rhythm patterns. The purpose of this study was to examine the effects of incorporating Orff-Schulwerk instruction, traditionally used in the elementary general music classroom, on the rhythmic achievement skills of seventh- and eighth-grade instrumental band students ($N = 52$).

Procedures

The implementation of Orff Schulwerk in band for the purposes of this study included a curriculum design and a research design to study the effectiveness of the curriculum. The curriculum design was guided by previous studies that identified specific musical activities of Orff Schulwerk. Martin's (1992) replication study of Munson's (1986) study identified six musical activities typically used in an Orff-Schulwerk classroom including singing, playing, moving, creating, listening, and reading. Wang and Sogin (1997) determined that the activities and instructional tools most frequently used in an Orff-Schulwerk classroom were performing on instruments and movement, and Champion (2006) identified speech activities, improvisations, body percussion, movement, echo activities, and listening as prominent instructional activities. Orff-Schulwerk instructional activities used in the curriculum design of this study included:

1. rhythmic exploration—students use both locomotor and non-locomotor movements and body percussion to explore, improvise, and imitate various rhythmic patterns and ostinati without their band instruments;
2. imitation—students imitate the teacher in various activities, including movement, body percussion, and performance of rhythmic patterns on their band instruments;
3. composition/notation/literacy—students compose, notate, and discuss each other's rhythmic examples;
4. improvisation—students improvise short phrases using student compositions;
5. performance of speech to rhythm associations; and
6. Creation station—weekly reflection, class discussion, and journal writing.

The research design included a pre- and post-test quasi-experimental design that documented students' rhythmic achievement before and after a twelve-week curriculum that included either traditional band instruction or the researcher-designed curriculum of Orff-Schulwerk instruction. A cluster sampling of two intact classes from two southern school bands consisting of combined seventh- and eighth-grade students was used. One band served as the control group ($N = 24$) and received traditional band instruction using the method book *Accent on Achievement* (O'Reilly & Williams, 2006) with no Orff-Schulwerk instruction, while the other band served as the experimental group ($N = 28$) and received the researcher-designed curriculum of Orff-Schulwerk instruction in band.

A researcher-designed test (*Rhythmic Skills for Performance in Band Test*), which incorporated listening, notating, and performance of rhythmic elements, was used to determine significant differences in rhythmic achievement between the control and experimental groups at the pre- and post-test. The tests consisted of two parts. Part A was designed for administration in a group setting as a paper-pencil test. Part B consisted of individual student performance of rhythmic patterns, audio recorded for inter-judge reliability scoring. Two judges who had Orff-Schulwerk training and had taught middle-school bands served as independent raters for Part B of the *Rhythmic Skills for Performance in Band Test*. An average Pearson correlation coefficient of $r = .91$ for pre-test and post-test scores indicated strong inter-judge reliability.

The level of significance for statistical testing for this study was set at alpha = .05. Results of the *t*-tests indicated that there was no significant difference between the groups in rhythmic achievement at pre-test, therefore suggesting that both bands were homogenous before treatment. At post-test, the experiment group scored significantly higher in the performance of rhythms, Part B of *Rhythmic Skills for Performance in Band Test*, $t(48) = 4.76$, $p < .001$.

Discussion

Carl Orff did not provide a fixed curriculum or exact procedures for the implementation of his approach. By incorporating what Goodkin (2002) refers to as the fundamental principles, clear models, and basic processes, teachers and students are able to expand on the pedagogy of the approach to meet their own lesson objectives. Orff considered the primary purpose of the Schulwerk to be the development of a child's creative abilities (Roberts, 1981). The creative element of the Orff Schulwerk lies at the root of its philosophy and applies to both the student and the teacher. Snyder's description of Orff Schulwerk includes "an umbrella term for process, sequence, concepts, and classroom management strategies" (Snyder, 1990, p. 8). But, at the heart of the Orff-Schulwerk process is the development and comprehension of rhythms and its focus on rhythmic and melodic motifs as the foundations of music in the Western tradition.

Students in the experimental group's first experience with Orff Schulwerk in band began with simple body percussion. In small groups, students explored rhythms, rhythmic ostinati, and timbres away from their instruments. Reflection became a routine component of the curriculum. Journal entries included the completion of statements that began with " I notice...", "I wonder...", and "I value...". A "creation station" was scheduled for group discussion and exploration of creative concepts through the realization of student ideas into musical motives and melodies.

Using the basis of a narrative, students pooled their ideas to tell a story. Students considered questions such as, "How do you know when a story begins?" "How do you know when a story ends?" "Who are the characters?" "What emotions are evoked?" "How do the elements of a story relate to the music?" The student answers were collected and placed on a melody worksheet on which they connected the story with musical elements.

In groups, students improvised, composed, and later notated a simple melodic line and accompaniment. Students were guided to begin their improvisations in B-flat pentatonic, exploring simple time signatures in various forms such as theme and variation and call-and-response. Students' initial concern: their composition did not sound like a "traditional melody," but they found solace after listening to music of other composers who did not conform to predictable melodies and accompaniments. The instructors took the opportunity to expose students to twentieth-century sounds found in the music of Varese's *Ionisation* and Penderecki's *Threnody for the Victims of*

Hiroshima to validate their musical selections and encourage their creativity. As their collaborative composition began to develop, the students decided that the music should have two distinct sections, with the "A" section comprised of an exploration of sounds seemingly random and chaotic. The "B" section consisted of a steady beat with imitation between solo and tutti instruments through traditional melody and accompaniments. Thinking ahead to their performance, students considered the acoustic setup of the performance space and how they could use the space within their composition. They decided that their composition would be more impactful if their sounds were in close proximity to the audience. They spaced themselves in the aisles of the hall with the percussion at the front of the hall. Students voted on a title for their group composition. They considered the theme of Memorial Day, the current war, and the sounds of their composition, and decided on the title *Aftershock*.

Aftershock is a programmatic work in binary form and was performed at a school music concert in May 2010. Dedicated to the veterans and soldiers who serve the United States, it is the product of students' work throughout the school year. Students explored twentieth-century techniques such as flutter-tonguing and nontraditional means of sound production on their individual instruments. The piece began with a snare drum solo. The rest of the band joined in with indeterminate sounds and chaotic accompaniment. A warm clarinet ostinato brings the ensemble together, and a flowing tutti melody remains. A call-and-response technique between woodwinds and brass with lower brass chordal accompaniment diminishes to silence before the solo trumpet, standing alone on the stage, performs *Taps*.

In addition to the measurable benefits of the approach, we also documented qualitative components of the curriculum. These included the collaboration between students, between students and teacher, and between teachers' reflection that gave way to divergent thinking; intrinsic motivation brought about through student-directed activities; alignment of the band curriculum with contemporary philosophies; validation of the curriculum through performance of student-directed composition; and the connection of rhythmic skills learned in elementary general music to those required in band through Orff Schulwerk.

Conclusion

The results of this study suggest the successful introduction of an Orff-Schulwerk curriculum in beginning band by providing instructional activities that complement current curricula and increase rhythmic achievement. More important, the activities provide ample opportunities for creative thinking, which has been largely missing in band. This study led to multiple investigations into the effects of Orff-Schulwerk instruction on rhythmic achievement in band. The most recent study culminated in the completion of the first author's PhD dissertation, "The Effects of Orff-Schulwerk Instruction on Rhythmic Achievement in Beginning Band" (Mason, 2012) that included a larger sample size, longer treatment period, descriptive data, revised test items, student attitude survey, observation and treatment validity records, and a detailed curriculum that included daily lesson plans. The results of Mason's study, which occurred after this presentation, were consistent with the results of this first study.

Our vision to further implement an Orff-Schulwerk curriculum in band includes (1) the promotion of the approach as a means of empowering teachers to allow more student-directed and teacher-guided activities; (2) an incorporation of more movement in the exploration stages; (3) an incorporation of more technology-based design into student performance; (4) the publishing of student compositions; and (5) a continuation of further research regarding the effects of Orff Schulwerk in band.

References

Beglarian, G. (1967). The contemporary music project: Origin and objective. *College Music Symposium, 7, 29.*

Birdwhistell, E. H. (1998). *Content analysis of five beginning band method books.* (Master thesis, University of Louisville). ProQuest Dissertations and Theses. (UMI No. 1391751).

Bondurant-Koehler, S. (1998). Orff Schulwerk and Kodály in beginning group and private string education. *American String Teacher, 48*(1), 65-68.

Bullock, J. & Maiello, A. (1996). *Belwin 21st Century Band Method.* Van Nuys, CA: Alfred Publishing Co.

Champion, S. M. (2006). *The musical activities found in selected Orff-Schulwerk elementary music classrooms.* (Doctoral dissertation, University of Mississippi). ProQuest Dissertations and Theses. (UMI No. 3259401).

Daigneault, D. J. (1993). A survey of recommended procedures and teaching methods for building and maintaining a wind and percussion instrumental music education program grades six through twelve. (Doctoral dissertation, University of Mississippi). *Dissertation Abstracts International, 54-09A, 3362.*

Erwin, J. (1995). Beyond the page. *Teaching Music, 3*(3), 28-30.

Frazee, J. (1987). *Discovering Orff: A curriculum for music teachers.* New York: Schott.

Gage, S. (1994). *An analysis and comparison of rhythm instructional materials and techniques for beginning instrumental music students.* ProQuest Dissertations and Theses. (UMI No. 9512364).

Glasgow, R. B. & Hamreus, D. G., (1968). *Study to determine the feasibility of adapting the Carl Orff approach to elementary schools in America.* (Washington, D.C.: Office of Education).

Goodkin, D. (2002). *Play, Sing, and Dance: An introduction to Orff Schulwerk.* New York: Scott.

Haselbach, B. (1993). Orff Schulwerk: Past, present, and future. *The Orff Echo, 25*(4). 6-10.

Heavner, T. L. (1995). *An analysis of beginning band method books for principles of comprehensive musicianship.* (Doctoral dissertation, University of Northern Colorado). ProQuest Dissertations and Theses. (UMI No. 9542099).

Madden, J. A. (1984). Zoltan Kodály and Carl Orff: Implications for program development in elementary instrumental music education (Doctoral dissertation, Temple University). ProQuest Dissertations and Theses. (UMI No. 8410153).

Martin, M.A. (1992). *An examination of the Orff-Schulwerk approach to music education in a public elementary school: A replication study.* (Doctoral dissertation, University of North Carolina at Greensboro). Dissertation Abstract International, 53, 2728A.

Misenhelter, D. (2004). Orff technique to freshen up. *Teaching Music, 12*(2), 56-60.

Munsen. S.C. (1986). A description and analysis of an Orff Schulwerk program of music education (Doctoral dissertation, University of Illinois). *Dissertation Abstracts International, 47*(09), 3351A.

Mason, N. F. (2012). The effects of Orff-Schulwerk instruction on rhythmic achievement in beginning band. (Unpublished doctoral dissertation, University of Kentucky).

O'Reilly, J., & Williams, M. (2006). *Accent on achievement.* Van Nuys, CA: Alfred Publishing.

Pearson, B. (1993). *Standard of excellence.* San Diego, CA: Neil A. Kjos Music Company.

Rhodes, T. C., Bierschenk, D., Lautzenheiser, T. & Higgins, J. (1991). *Essential elements: A comprehensive band method.* Milwaukee: Hal Leonard Corporation.

Roberts, C. J (1981). *A sequential series of beginning Orff-Schulwerk arrangements for use in the middle school.* (Doctoral dissertation, Stephen F. Austin State University). ProQuest Dissertations and Theses. (UMI No.1316268).

Riley, P. 2006. Including composition in middle school band: Effects on achievement, performance, and attitude. *Update: Applications of Research in Music Education, 25*(1), 28-38.

Scott, J. (2007). Me? Teach improvisation to children? *General Music Today, 20*(2), 6-13.

Snyder, S. (1990). Question upon question: A quest for Orff Schulwerk. *Orff Echo, 22(4)*, 8.

Stewart, C. (1988). Beyond Sixth Grade. *Orff Echo, 20*(3), 3-5.

Walker, R. (1984). Innovation in the music classroom II: The Manhattanville Music Curriculum Project. *Psychology of Music, 12*(1), 25-33.

Wang, C. C. & Sogin, D. W. (1997). A comparative study of self-reported versus observed classroom activities in elementary general music. *Journal of Research in Music Education, 45*, 444 – 456.

Chapter 11

MUSIC EDUCATION PHILOSOPHIES AND PRACTICES OF EARLY CHILDHOOD EDUCATORS

Terri Brown Lenzo

Background and Purpose

Over the last thirty years, numerous survey research studies have focused on the music teaching practices of early childhood classroom or generalist teachers. Nardo, Custodero, Persellin, and Fox (2006) conducted a national study and investigated music education in accredited American preschools. Results of that study suggest that the consistency of several factors over a period of several years include: (1) a majority of classroom teachers, rather than music specialists, were responsible for the music education of their students; (2) respondents described singing as the most commonly used musical activity and creative opportunities related to composing as the least used; (3) teacher philosophies and practices often indicated that music skill development and the teaching of musical concepts received a low priority in the curriculum; and (4) teachers did not feel prepared to deliver meaningful music instruction (Nardo et al., 2006).

The purpose of this chapter is to present an examination of the music education practices of early childhood classroom teachers working at two child care centers located in northeast Ohio, to compare results with those reported by Nardo et al. (2006), and to make recommendations for the design of future music education professional development opportunities. Three questions were investigated: (1) what musical activities are early childhood classroom teachers most comfortable including in their classrooms? (2) what types of musical training in terms of content and format have early childhood teachers experienced, and what types would they be most interested in pursuing? and (3) what are the attitudes and opinions of early childhood generalists toward music education?

Method

This investigation was conducted according to the guidelines of descriptive research, which employed purposeful sampling and a cross-sectional survey design. The study was carried forward at two independently owned childcare centers located in northeast Ohio. These centers offer childcare for infants and toddlers as well as preschool classes for three- to five-year-olds. Participants were classroom teachers who taught infants to five-year-olds.

The instrument was specifically designed for this study by the researcher based upon information gleaned from extant research and literature. A structured item questionnaire with options for open-ended responses was administered to the subjects. In order to determine content validity, a copy of the survey was sent to one early childhood music educator, one early childhood generalist teacher, one center administrator, and one K-12 music educator with experience in survey development. The instrument was revised based upon recommendations from the panel.

The final version of the survey contained twelve questions and was divided into two parts. Part I (Musical Activities and Curriculum) pertained to the musical activities teachers included in their curriculum, types of early childhood music education training received, and participant opinions regarding the format and content of future professional development in music. Part II (Your Experiences) sought to determine general teaching experience, ages of children taught, and the personal musical experiences of the participants.

Upon completion of the revised survey, the study was submitted to the Institutional Review Board (IRB) at Kent State University. After approval was granted, site permission was obtained from the administrator of the two childcare centers. Materials were prepared for distribution, and appointments were made with each center director in order to discuss the administration of the survey.

During the site meetings, the researcher explained the purpose of the study, its potential benefits, reviewed the survey materials, and discussed the nature of the survey distribution. A request was made that all teachers be afforded the opportunity to complete the survey, and it was emphasized that they were not required to participate due to IRB protocol. The directors distributed the surveys on the day of our meeting, and the researcher returned three days later to collect them.

After gathering the surveys, a data specialist at Kent State University provided coding suggestions. The coded responses were entered into an Excel file and then returned to the specialist who exported it to Statistics Package for Social Sciences (IBM SPSS) software. The results were analyzed using the frequency tables generated from SPSS.

Results

Twenty-one teachers responded to the survey. One blank survey was returned in a sealed envelope, and three surveys were returned without consent forms, resulting in a smaller sample ($N = 17$). Participants included teachers of infants through five-year-olds, and responses showed that several teachers taught children in more than one age category. Three teachers taught children ages newborn to eleven months, four teachers taught children ages twelve to eighteen months, two teachers taught children nineteen months to twenty-four months, nine teachers taught three-year-olds, eight teachers taught four-year-olds, and eight teachers taught five-year-olds.

Part II of the survey (Your Experiences) served to gather information about the teachers' teaching experience and previous musical experiences. Teaching experience ranged from one to ten years. Two teachers were in their first year of teaching, five teachers had between one and three years of experience, five teachers had taught from four to six years, one teacher had six to ten years of experience, and four teachers indicated that they had taught for ten years or more. In regard to previous musical experiences, almost half of the participants—forty-seven percent—had one or more years of school band experience, and the same percentage indicated they had been members of a school choir for at least one year. One respondent had five years of string experience, and two respondents indicated that they had studied piano for one year.

In Part I of the research instrument, teachers were questioned about the musical activities used in their classrooms. More than half of the respondents, sixty-five percent, selected singing as the most frequently used activity. Infrequently used activities were creating music (12%) and playing instruments (6%). Respondents also ranked objectives for including musical activities in the classroom. The majority (52%) ranked development of physical coordination or listening skills as most important followed by 41% who chose listening to music as most important. An equal number of respondents (29%) ranked development of music skills and enjoyment and relaxation as most important. Using music as a tool to assist with learning in other subject areas was chosen by 17.6% as the most important objective for musical instruction. Four teachers described how they used music to accomplish other objectives: (1) "Sing the ABCs or days of the week"; (2) "It might keep them more interested"; (3) "World studies/days of the week/ months, etc."; and (4) "Subject content/months of the year."

Respondents were asked to indicate all types of early childhood music training they had experienced. Five choices were given: half-day workshop, full-day workshop, music methods courses completed for an associate degree, music methods course completed for a bachelor's degree, or none. Given those choices, sixty-four percent responded that they had received no training in early childhood music education. Space was provided for teachers to describe any other training they had received. One response was received: "Learned lots of kid songs at camp."

Teachers were permitted to indicate areas in which they would like to receive additional training. Choices included singing, moving to music, creating music, playing instruments, teaching musical concepts, and integrating music with other subject areas. Seventy-seven percent desired additional training in integrating music with other subject areas. Regarding training format, seventy-three percent of the subjects were most interested in attending a group workshop held at their school. The second most popular choice was in-class mentorship training, described as "individualized training provided by a music specialist working with you in your classroom over a period of two-to-four weeks."

Discussion

The purpose of this study was to account for the music education practices of early childhood classroom teachers working at two child-care centers located in northeast Ohio, to compare results with those reported by Nardo et al. (2006), and to make recommendations for the design of future music education professional development opportunities. Results of this investigation suggest that responses to the three research questions were consistent with the findings of Nardo et al. (2006).

In response to the first research question ("What types of musical activities are early childhood generalists most comfortable including in their classrooms?"), teachers indicated that singing was the most frequent activity and creating music and playing instruments were the least-used activities. Replies to the second research question ("What types of musical training in terms of content and format have early childhood teachers experienced, and which types would they be most interested in pursuing?") indicated that a large majority of teachers had received no preparation in early childhood music education. Concerning the format and content of future training, participants indicated a clear preference for on-site group workshops designed to increase skills for integrating music with other subject areas. Regarding the third question ("What are the attitudes and opinions of early childhood generalists toward music education?"), teachers again expressed preferences for integrating music with other subject areas and using music to develop physical coordination or listening skills.

When considering the musical development of young students, the most salient findings may be that early childhood generalists are responsible for the music education of their students, lack sufficient musical training, but are interested in professional development opportunities. These results agree with those of Nardo et al. (2006) and provide implications for the state of affairs in early childhood music education. Five years after a national study was conducted (Nardo et al., 2006), this small study replicated the findings for teacher training. The replication appeared to indicate consistent and widespread prevalence of the conditions. Due to the fact that early childhood is a critical period for musical development, future studies should investigate feasible training options for teachers who serve young children.

A secondary aim of this study was to offer recommendations for the format and content of early childhood music education professional development opportunities. Nardo et al. (2006) encouraged course designers to plan for the specific needs of those who would be enrolled in the training. Participants in this study indicated a strong preference for professional development opportunities presented at their own school in a group workshop format. Learning how to integrate music with other subject areas was the topic requested by over three-quarters of the survey respondents. Therefore, a professional development workshop designed for this sample should account for these needs.

One way to meet the desire for training in music integration might involve the use of Orff techniques. Course designers could consider training teachers to use expressive speech activities in their lessons. Such activities would allow teachers to integrate music with other subjects through the use of published or created stories, poems, and texts. Expressive speech activities might be a comfortable starting point for non-singers and could nurture the vocal development of teachers and their students. Having met the training objectives identified by the teachers, instructors might then be able to encourage professional development in other areas of music teaching.

Results of this study contain implications for the design of music education professional development opportunities for early childhood teachers. A pre-training survey is suggested in order to inform course designers of the needs of the teachers. Training providers should use that information to make decisions about course curricula. Considerations might include the personal musical experiences of those enrolled in the course, their music education philosophies and practices, prior music educational training, and format and content preferences. The Orff process shows promise for the music education professional development of early childhood classroom teachers.

Reference

Nardo, R. L., Custodero, L., Persellin, D., & Fox, D. (2006). Looking back, looking forward: A report on early childhood music education in accredited American Preschools. *Journal of Research in Music Education, 54*(4), 278-292.

Chapter 12

ORFF SCHULWERK IN UNDERGRADUATE MUSIC EDUCATION:
PROMISE AND POSSIBILITY

Judith W. Bond

Orff teacher training in the U.S. has traditionally been conceived as a course for practicing general music teachers who already possess a college degree and a teaching license, and have some experience working with children in the classroom. As the Orff movement has evolved and grown through summer courses taken by general music teachers, there has been simultaneous growth in other major active music-making approaches, primarily those of Zoltan Kodály and Edwin Gordon, and to a lesser extent that of Jaques-Dalcroze. The tremendous success of this post-graduate teacher education across the U.S. has resulted in a growing number of teachers in higher education, professors at colleges and universities who are committed to teaching undergraduate music education students through Orff Schulwerk or one of the other active music-making approaches based upon the Kodály philosophy, the Eurhythmics of Jaques-Dalcroze, the Music Learning Theory activities of Edwin Gordon, or some combination of these and other approaches. We see a proliferation of PhDs and other terminal degrees attained by teachers who have also taken the Orff levels courses or comparable courses in Kodály, Dalcroze, or Music Learning Theory. These teachers of undergraduate general music education methods classes have found that learning about teaching through experiences with one or more of these active music-making approaches can help prepare their students—the next generation of music teachers—for greater success in their early years of teaching music. Indications are that this trend will keep growing. For example, the 2011 Mountain Lake Colloquium for Teachers of General Music included a presentation by three doctoral students who had just completed Level 1 Orff. Only one of the three had previous classroom experience, but they were all convinced that Orff Schulwerk would enhance their future careers in music education, and it's likely that all three will soon be teaching at the undergraduate and graduate level, ideally after a few years of experience in elementary music classrooms.

As a starting point for thinking about Orff Schulwerk and other active music-making approaches in undergraduate music education today, consider the following example of music teacher preparation the way this author experienced it as an undergraduate. Although the example is personal, indications are that this model of undergraduate teacher preparation in music education was typical for most teachers in the past, and may still be typical for many today.

As with many music education students in my generation, I finished my undergraduate degree with no knowledge of Orff, Kodály, or Dalcroze, and Gordon's Music Learning Theory had not been developed. I was a "happy camper" who loved practicing and making music in every way possible: singing, dancing, playing, and learning more about music was exciting for me. Adding the "teacher certification" component to my music degree meant primarily that I took classes in which we read educational philosophy, starting with Plato and Aristotle and continuing through John Dewey. I'm glad I was introduced to the ideas of these philosophers, but when I entered the classroom, I was really clueless about teaching, although I certainly didn't know it. I did know about directing choirs, so that part went very well, but general music was a big challenge. Looking back, I think my self-confidence and love for music, plus the combination of having had good teachers and being a solid musician, enabled me to complete that first year of general music teaching. Some years later, hearing teachers express their gratitude for what they learned in Level 1 Orff, I remembered my inadequacies as a first year general music teacher. Although we've come a long way since that time, there are still teachers who finish their undergraduate music education training and enter the classroom with little or no meaningful experience with Orff Schulwerk, Dalcroze Eurhythmics, the Kodály Method, or Gordon's Music Learning Theory. How shall we define "meaningful experience"? It involves more than reading a chapter in a textbook, listening to a lecture, or writing a paper. At the very least, it has to be an experience in making music, followed by some reflection on that experience.

What kind of progress are we making in this vitally important component of music education? A short introduction to the Alliance for Active Music Making provides some background. In 1998, the American Orff-Schulwerk Association (AOSA) President Linda Ahlstedt had completed three levels of Orff training, taught elementary general music, and began to mentor student teacher candidates. She wondered why these emerging music teachers came to her with so little knowledge of Orff Schulwerk. Linda's curiosity and concern led her to explore her questions about Orff at the undergraduate level with Ann Kay, who at that time was president of the Organization of American Kodály Educators (OAKE), and then with proponents of other active music-making approaches.

As discussions continued, leaders from OAKE, the Dalcroze Society of America (DSA), and the Gordon Institute for Music Learning (GIML) were invited to meet at an AOSA conference. Formation of a committee was the next step. Twenty people were asked to join the Undergraduate Curriculum Reform Committee, an ad hoc committee of AOSA. Marilyn Davidson, a past president of AOSA, was named chair, and under her leadership members of the group, with representatives from each organization, contributed ideas for an undergraduate music teacher education curriculum based upon the National Standards for Music Education. The curriculum, described by Davidson as "a work in progress," was presented at conferences of AOSA, OAKE, and the National Association of Schools of Music (NASM). Those who attended the presentation at NASM were supportive and encouraged continuation of the work, especially because it showed collaboration instead of competition between proponents of the four approaches mentioned above. Although this meeting concluded the work of the original committee, their work resulted in the formation of the Alliance for Active Music Making, with members from AOSA, OAKE, DSA, and GIML. Each organization provided a letter of support for the concept of collaboration. In a statement requesting approval as a special interest group of MENC's Society for Music Teacher Education (SMTE), Alliance members stated their mission as follows: "the study and promotion of active music-making approaches as foundational to the teaching of undergraduate courses for students preparing for licensure in general music" (Bond, n.d.). More details about the history, mission, and goals of the Alliance can be found on the group's Web site, www.allianceamm. org. The original curriculum, which does not attribute ideas to any specific approach, is available upon request by contacting the AAMM.

Continuing this spirit of collaboration, members of the Alliance began attending and presenting sessions at the national conferences of each group, the symposia of the Society for Music Teacher Education (SMTE), and the Mountain Lake Colloquium for Teachers of General Music Methods. The very first collaborative conference session was at the AOSA Conference in Louisville, Kentucky, in 2003, with the title "Preparing the Next Generation of Music Teachers: Four Variations On A Theme." There were four presenters representing the approaches of Dalcroze, Gordon, Kodály, and Orff. This session became the model for later presentations. Panel discussions and session presentations at national, state, and regional conferences followed, to promote the Alliance's goal of increasing awareness, understanding, and support for the inclusion of Orff, Kodály, Dalcroze, and Music Learning Theory in music teacher education programs at the undergraduate level.

During more than twenty years of working with undergraduate music education teacher candidates, this author's commitment to the inclusion of Orff Schulwerk in teacher preparation has continued to grow. Orff Schulwerk is foundational to each undergraduate class taught, whether for music education majors or general classroom education students. Due to the influence of the AAMM, it is also compelling to introduce students to the principles and elements of Dalcroze Eurhythmics, the Kodály Method, and Gordon's Music Learning Theory. The desired outcome is an open and curious attitude about exploring a variety of approaches. Perhaps the results can best be summed up by the following words from students. From the final reflection of one student: "This class takes an exceptional and pluralist look at the importance of music in the school, not just in the music classroom, but in each and every classroom. Singing, speaking, dancing, playing, listening, improvising, teaching, and learning—this class covered all aspects of what music means in elementary school education. I have become enlightened and prepared to teach music in my future classroom." A student preparing to become a classroom teacher said: "When I first walked in and you said we would sing, dance, and play the recorder, I thought you were crazy. Well, I was wrong. Now I know the importance of making music with my students every day." These students preparing for careers in teaching have experienced the joy of making music and learning how to teach music through Orff Schulwerk and other active music-making approaches. The evidence indicates that experience with the Schulwerk and other active music-making approaches in the general music methods class for music majors can give beginning music teachers what they need for early success in the classroom. Ideally, this experience will also lead to participation in continued in-depth study of one or more of the major approaches to teaching general music.

In conclusion, it must be acknowledged that the comments and ideas in this chapter are based upon the author's background, perceptions, and thinking. There is a great need for research and documentation of information about the inclusion of Orff Schulwerk and other active music-making approaches at the undergraduate level. Where is it happening? Why was it implemented? Who is responsible? How is it taught? Will this change the nature of summer courses as they are presently taught? Will new courses be developed to serve the needs of the changing population?

Many other questions about this effort remain. Some of the issues, questions, and challenges (Bond, n.d.) are listed below.

- Will collaboration between proponents of different approaches lead to eclecticism and loss of identity or watering down the special qualities of each approach?
- How much time can we rely on Orff music making, or any active music-making approach in a methods class in which there are so many other requirements?

- How can we avoid a narrow approach that causes the opinion that she/he "does Orff," or a surface approach that may result in misunderstanding and misuse?
- How can college and university professors of general music methods who have not had courses in these approaches be expected to give their students an in-depth understanding?
- What about those who object to labels such as Orff or Kodály but who use terms such as "constructivist" or "generative" to describe their teaching?

What is next for Orff Schulwerk in the world of undergraduate music education? In 2011, AOSA President Julie Scott appointed the AAMM/AOSA committee, a standing committee of the AOSA National Board of Trustees, to continue the study, development, and promotion of active music-making approaches in undergraduate music education. The spirit of collaboration continues with this committee, comprised of members representing each of the organizations supported by the AAMM. Promise and possibility: stay tuned!

Nota Bene: *Members of the Alliance who participated in the "Global Reflections in Orff Schulwerk: Reflections from Kentucky" symposium at the University of Kentucky include Carlos Abril, Rob Amchin, June Grice, Mary Shamrock, Kim McCord, and the conference chair, Cecilia Wang. All have made significant contributions to the improvement of undergraduate music education through the inclusion of Orff Schulwerk and other active music-making approaches in methods classes for general music.*

Reference

Bond, J. W. (n.d.). Preparing the next generation of music teachers: Four variations on a theme of best practice. Retrieved from http://www.allianceamm.org/history.htm

Chapter 13

ORFF SCHULWERK TEACHER EDUCATION:
REFLECTIONS AND DIRECTIONS
FOR THE TWENTY-FIRST CENTURY
Cindy Hall and Jay Broeker

Orff Schulwerk at the University of Kentucky (UK) began with a vision of Dr. Cecilia Wang in 1987. She invited Arvida Steen to develop the course, initially committing to continue for five years. Arvida invited colleague Nancy Miller (Dancy Nancy) and co-author of this chapter, Cindy Hall, to join her for this adventure. In 1988, Jay Broeker joined our merry band. Guest Level III teachers during these years included Jane Frazee and Judy Bond. In 1999, Brian Crisp joined us to teach recorder and then Level I, and in 2002, Brian Burnett became our movement instructor. Other guests who have been part of our family history include Angie Broeker, Jo Ella Hug, Sarah Richardson, and Martha Riley.

Why is this course still here after twenty-five years? There are at least five reasons. The first and most obvious reason is, of course, Cecilia Wang. What tenacity it has taken to assure funding for this course, to convince colleagues and administrators of its value, to assure in-state tuition for out-of-state students, and to keep the cost of the course so much lower than courses in other, similar programs. What organization it has taken to manage publicity, hire wonderful assistants and student helpers, and to find teaching spaces during band camp and building renovations! And, what a time commitment it has taken to take care of our personal needs by helping us to find housing and child care, cooking us lovely meals, and showing up with such mundane needs as blankets and coat hangers! Cecilia, we are all recipients of your dedication to this work and we thank you.

The second reason this course thrives is the students. The warmth and generosity that prevail here promote easy community and respectful collaboration. The musical heritage of our "locals" and the added gifts of our Asian students give the course a singular flavor. The state Orff chapter is remarkably active, and with its many course alumni, nurtures growth and communication during the year. The UK graduate and undergraduate students add their newly gained theoretical knowledge to the course, while the many seasoned teachers in schools with well-established Orff programs keep us practical and grounded.

The third reason that this course is still here is the Kentucky Education Reform Act, which, for a while at least, ensured that music programs would continue amid drastic budget cuts. I remember the multiple phone calls from teachers who, thanks to one of our former students working at the state level, had "textbook" money to spend for instruments: "I have $10,000 dollars to spend. What should I buy?" Many music rooms were well equipped by this funding, with administrators requiring Orff training of new hires.

The fourth reason is our curriculum. In a wise decision encouraged by Arvida Steen many years ago, we "spiraled" our Level II and III content to assure that students had two years to assimilate both modes and functional harmony. We retained the Hamline/Saint Thomas ideal of having the students practice what they were learning through the levels, with small group teaching in Level I, paired planning and teaching in Level II, and solo teaching in Level III. Over the years, we have tried to balance the use of historical Orff and Keetman resources, folk music, and integrated arts materials. We have included lessons that promote artistry for the classroom and others purely for the students' personal musical growth. We have learned to trust our individual styles and choices, understanding that different models in the course show students multiple interpretations and applications of this large and inclusive philosophy.

The fifth reason that this course is still here, and we are still here, is because we like it here. We have "tithed" to the Kentucky economy with purchases of quilts, dulcimers, and Shaker brooms. We have eaten our fill of fried green tomatoes, country ham, and key lime pie ("key lahm pa"). We have worn our hats to the races, paddle-wheeled down the Kentucky River, and experienced the life of Stephen Foster. We have spent humid summer evenings mesmerized by Jean Ritchie's singing of "Froggie Went a'Courtin" along with Ron Pen, and listened to "real" bluegrass music in Berea. We have shared lovely evenings together passing plates at A La Lucie, driving through horse farm country, and watching falling stars in Shaker Village. When Cecilia says, "same time next year" we inevitably say yes, because we can't imagine not being here in our "old Kentucky home." We know that our experiences teaching here have been special, but what do the students have to say about Orff at UK?

According to one:

> The world of Orff Schulwerk has opened up a new world of teaching for me: one of imagination, creativity, excitement, and wonderment. My years of the UK Orff workshops (all three levels plus master classes) have been quite beneficial in my teaching and in the giving of my gift of music to children. The workshops have definitely changed the way that I teach and the way I view teaching children.

Another shares:

> The Orff process grew slowly in me, changing the way I viewed my role as a teacher, and freeing up the little girl in me who had forgotten how to play. Learning to improvise, playing recorder, moving and dancing in new ways—it was scary and exhilarating all at the same time! As I learned to change my lessons from teacher-centered to child-centered, making music with children became a joyous, creative expression of who *they* were.

And a third:

> The UK Orff courses have completely revolutionized my teaching. Level II taught me about effective teaching process and how to incorporate exploration, imitation, improvisation, and creation in a lesson. Level III showed me how to take a simple idea and transform it into a work

of beauty through play and imagination. Curriculum development opened my eyes to the importance of sequencing lessons in a way that ensures student mastery of elemental music concepts. My overall experiences at UK these past summers have shown me that music teachers are some of the most dedicated people in the world and that the art of teaching music using the Orff-Schulwerk [approach] is truly a magical thing.

We have reflected briefly on our past, and we turn to you, our esteemed colleagues and dear friends, to help us chart a path for the future. It seems a pivotal time for Orff Schulwerk in this country, a time to look for common threads rather than divisions and to emphasize the central themes of this work that have perhaps gotten lost in its multiple wildflower hybrids. We would like for you to help us grapple with three questions.

The first question, the one to which we return yearly in late-night discussions (which have gotten much earlier!), is "What is the essence of this work?" What do we really want our students to "get" about Orff Schulwerk? For the past several years, many conferences and workshops have caused me to question the larger organization's understanding of what this work is about. I have been asked to help determine a final form, create a movement to show a phrase, choose a sound effect, or decide how a character will act. Only rarely have I been asked to improvise an original melody or rhythm, alter an existing one, or work with a poetic text to create something that might be recognized as music. I think often about Brian Burnett's comment that it's not Schulwerk until the students do the "werk" and Jay's mantra that "It's all about the music." So, is it working with the elements of music? Is it about building student compositions? Is it about making musical decisions? Is it about creating "understandings?" What part should folk music play in this work? Is teaching music in "elemental style" the end goal or a means to a larger musical world?

The second question is perhaps even more difficult. How do we affect the transfer of learning from what we model to what students can create for themselves in their classrooms? One research study by Wang and Sogin suggests that time spent on musical tasks is greater for Orff-trained teachers. (See Chapter 9). Is there more transfer when we make the levels courses more "practical," or is it the artistic experience that students have in the two weeks (six weeks over three summers) that inspires them to create in their classrooms? What systems would ideally be in place to assure mentoring throughout the years between and after levels training?

Third: with globalization and social media, how should what we teach change? Should our folk-music examples, if we use them, come from many different cultures? How can we use the Internet to bring authentic music into our classrooms? How can we collaborate with other teachers and their students through technology? Is there a danger that technology and an emphasis on the visual could diminish the humanizing effect of singing and dancing together in a circle?

Closing Session

The closing session of the symposium returned to the three questions proposed in the opening session:

1. Based upon your experience as a learner and teacher, what is the essence of the Orff Schulwerk? Are there elements of this work that are essential for it to be considered Schulwerk?
2. How can we, as Levels instructors, music teachers, administrators, and students, strengthen the transfer between Orff training and classroom practice?
3. How do globalization, technology, and social media impact our Orff-Schulwerk teaching? What are the benefits and risks associated with these changes?

In response to the first question, participants believed that Orff Schulwerk is essentially using quality sources of music and literature to "sing, say, dance, and play" with the primary focus of making music together. Essential elements in the approach include movement, creativity, process-based learning, collaboration, and play.

Discussions about strengthening the connection between training and practice revealed goals in multiple areas. First, teacher trainers should include time for reflection and discussion of the teaching process. Second, strong mentorship programs should be implemented by connecting beginning Schulwerk teachers with more experienced ones in either the course or a local chapter. Third, students and teachers should have a forum, either in person or online, for collaboration and dialogue as they experiment with the Orff approach.

The third question, a focus of the symposium, promoted the most lively debate and discussion. It was proposed that the idea that "globalization" must not mean homogenization, but rather the study and appreciation of multiple, diverse, and rich cultural musical traditions. Participants agreed that technology provides increased availability of cultural and pedagogical resources, but others cautioned that the visual nature of technology could interfere with aural attention or the human contact so essential to the Schulwerk. Some proposed that facility with technology and awareness of how our students are currently using technology outside our classrooms would enhance our instructional practice.

Proposed action plans suggested by conference attendees included the publication of the symposium proceedings, continued dialogue among participants, and personal reading and reflection related to symposium topics. Participants felt a need to share more information about current practice in Orff Schulwerk with the college and research community and to develop programs for educating and mentoring pre-service and new music teachers.

In the closing discussion, participants reflected on their experience at the symposium. Several commented on the strong sense of community created by the participants who represented diverse cultures and multiple visions of this work. There were words of appreciation for the probing questions of Carlos Abril about the educational foundations of our work, for the insight of Ana Lucia Frega about the practice of Orff Schulwerk in South America, and for Jane Frazee's enlightening description of the artistic background out of which Orff Schulwerk developed. Others expressed their impression that the link between research and practice had been strengthened through the symposium and that the dialogue might continue as Orff Schulwerk evolves.

SECTION THREE

DIRECTIONS FOR THE TWENTY-FIRST CENTURY

Chapter 14

CREATIVE THINKING IN ORFF SCHULWERK

D. Gregory Springer[1]

Few educational goals are more important than developing students' creative thinking skills. Indeed, some view creativity as a necessary quality for ensured success in the twenty-first century. Bloom's Taxonomy (Bloom et al., 1956), which has guided educators since the 1950s, was revised in 2001 to identify "creating" as the outcome associated with the highest level of knowledge (Hanna, 2007). Some authors have supported a focus on creativity as a determinant of future achievement. Gardner (2007), for example, describes the "creating mind" as one of the five capacities necessary for success in the future. In addition, Sawyer (2012) claims that creativity and innovation are essential for economic success and that their importance will continue to increase.

Despite these supporting rationales, creativity is sometimes undervalued and underappreciated in certain settings, including schools (Sternberg & Lubart, 1995). Furthermore, some teachers and other school personnel do not know practical ways of designing instructional activities that encourage their students to be creative. In an effort to address this need, the purpose of this chapter is to describe the concepts of creativity and creative thinking, to discuss the principles of Orff Schulwerk as they relate to a model of creative thinking in music, and to describe strategies and classroom environments that are most conducive to creative thinking in a music classroom.

Creativity and Creative Thinking

In spite of many attempts by psychologists and educators, there is little agreement about a common definition of creativity. The word "creativity" is used regularly in everyday life with a variety of meanings, and there are a multitude of published definitions of the term. These definitions vary in scope, ranging from the scientific— "[t]he capacity to generate ideas that are simultaneously original and adaptive" (Simonton, 2003, p. 214)—to the evocative—"[l]istening for smells" (Karl Anderson, as cited in Torrance, 1988, p. 50). Given the sheer number of definitions available to readers, the varied scope of these definitions, and the ubiquitous use of the word throughout a variety of situations, the definition of creativity is problematic.

Adding to the complexity of defining creativity is a fact that it exists at different levels. "Little c" creativity refers to the small-scale creative contributions that many individuals demonstrate every day. Examples of this "everyday creativity" include preparing a tasty meal with a special ingredient or discovering a new functional use for a coffee filter. "Big C" Creativity, on the other hand, refers to the large-scale creative outcomes that are associated with geniuses or with creative eminence. This is the type of creativity that is of the highest magnitude that significantly impacts people and large social groups (Sawyer, 2012). In his book *Creating Minds*, Gardner (1993) examines the "Big C" creative work of Sigmund Freud, Albert Einstein, Pablo Picasso, Igor Stravinsky, T. S. Eliot, Martha Graham, and Mahatma Gandhi.

Some authors have suggested alternatives to the term creativity. Hargreaves, MacDonald, and Miell (2012) claim that *imagination* is a more useful label because it focuses on internal mental processes and is a broader, more inclusive term. Lehmann, Sloboda, and Woody (2007) use the term *generative* to stress the generation of creative products or outcomes, which is at the heart of creativity.

Webster (1990, 2002) maintains that the term *creative thinking* is a better way to describe the processes underlying creative thought. His model of creative thinking in music (Webster, 2002), first published in 1987 and subsequently revised, describes creative thinking as a dynamic mental process that occurs between a product intention and a creative product.

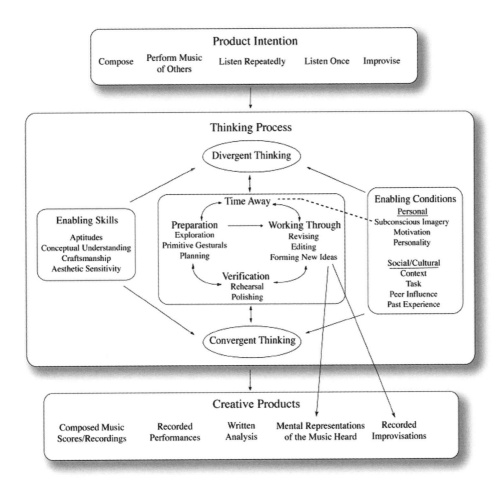

Illustration 1. *Model of Creative Thinking in Music* (Webster, 2002)

Product Intention. According to this model, creative thinking begins with some product intention; these intentions are expressed in verb form in the model. In a music setting, creative thinking can be sparked with intentions to compose, perform, listen, and improvise. All these intentions reflect valid learning outcomes for music classes, and they support the National Standards for Music Education.

Thinking Process. What occurs between the product intention and creative product is a lively, chaotic process in which creative thought actually takes place. This process is composed of two types of thinking. Divergent thinking, as introduced by Guilford (1967), is a thinking process that can generate multiple solutions. This type of thinking is most often associated with creativity because it is involved in imaginative thought and with the production of original, novel outcomes. Open-ended tasks such as story writing, painting, and music composition require individuals to think divergently. Convergent thinking, on the other hand, refers to a thinking process that results in only one correct or acceptable solution. Multiple-choice tests, for example, require students to choose the single best answer for each item, which requires them to think in a convergent manner. Certain tasks involve students' thinking in both convergent and divergent ways, and these are the types of tasks that typically encourage creative thinking. Divergent thinking alone is not sufficient for creative thinking to take place; rather, it is the interplay of both divergent and convergent thinking that occurs during the creative thinking process.

Although individuals toggle between divergent and convergent thinking, the thinking process is influenced by various enabling skills and enabling conditions. Enabling skills are those skills that give individuals a creative advantage, such as conceptual understanding and aptitudes. Certainly, those with a higher conceptual understanding of music and a higher musical aptitude are more likely to achieve creative success in music. Enabling conditions, both personal and social, also affect individuals' creative thinking. Motivation, particularly intrinsic motivation, is one enabling condition that positively influences individuals' creative thinking and encourages creative achievement (Amabile, 1989; Collins & Amabile, 1999). Other enabling conditions are social or cultural in nature, including peer influence, context, and past experience (Webster, 2002).

At the center of Webster's model of creative thinking is a circular process composed of the following steps: (1) preparation, (2) time away, (3) working through, and (4) verification. These steps are based upon one of the earliest models of the creative process (Wallas, 1926), which described the process according to the phases of preparation, incubation, illumination, and verification. Webster's terms are certainly related to those introduced by Wallas, and they reflect perhaps the most essential components of Webster's creative thinking model. In the preparation phase, the emphasis is on exploration and planning. Primitive gesturals, which are essentially the artifacts of musical brainstorming, are prevalent, and they guide musicians throughout the preparation phase. During the working through and verification phases, musicians refine their ideas through a process of revision and rehearsal. It is during these phases that primitive gesturals become more substantive musical ideas. Many music teachers commonly practice the working through and verification phases that are important parts of the creative thinking process.

The time away phase, called "incubation" in the creative thinking process presented by Wallas (1926), represents a particularly important stage in creative thinking. During this phase, individuals take time off from their task to divert their attention to other areas, allowing their unconscious mind to incubate on the former task while their conscious mind is focused on other areas. This time away positively influences creative thinking. Because learning involves structural changes to the brain at the cellular level (Sawyer, 2011; Schlaug, 2003), students need adequate time away and multiple experiences with a task to totally develop their creative thinking. Other research (Simmons & Duke, 2006) has shown that certain motor skills, such as performing a keyboard melody, improve when individuals sleep in a process of sleep-based memory consolidation. Therefore, this time away or "incubation" period is necessary for secure learning in music, and it affects the development of both creative thinking and musical skills.

Creative Products. As shown in Webster's model, the creative thinking process concludes with a creative product, which can include music compositions, performances, analyses, mental representations of the music heard, and improvisations. It is important to note that not all of these products—e.g., compositions or musical performances—are necessarily creative, however. Two criteria are necessary for products to be recognized as creative—novelty and appropriateness (Hickey, 2012; Hickey & Webster, 2001; Sawyer, 2012; Simonton, 2003; Sternberg & Lubart, 1999). Without doubt, novelty or originality is needed for a product to be considered creative, but without some amount of appropriateness, the product cannot be considered creative (Hickey & Webster, 2001).

Orff Schulwerk as Creative Thinking in Action

The philosophy and pedagogy of Orff Schulwerk are intimately related to creative thinking because the Orff approach naturally emphasizes activities that promote creative thought (Anderson & Lawrence, 2010; Webster, 1990). In fact, several features of the Orff-Schulwerk approach neatly align with Webster's (2002) model of creative thinking in music, and these features are discussed below.

Product Intentions & Creative Products

Improvisations and compositions are perhaps the most conspicuous products of creative thinking, and they are prominent in Orff-Schulwerk instruction. Students' ability to spontaneously generate musical material represents the highest level of musical understanding, and as a result, improvisation is particularly emphasized in Orff Schulwerk. In fact, improvisation is often used to conclude learning sequences and can be viewed as the final outcome of instruction (Frazee, 1987). Orff teachers are responsible for setting up environments and designing tasks for students that encourage creative thinking, beginning with creative intentions and concluding with creative products. Additionally, Orff teachers must ascertain that these products are musically appropriate for their students in terms of difficulty, based upon their students' current musical knowledge and skills. When students improvise short musical answers to teachers' rhythmic questions using body percussion, for example, they demonstrate not only observable music skills but also a product of their creative thinking.

Thinking Process

Orff teachers are not only concerned about musical products; they are also interested in an experiential learning process—a multimodal, hands-on process that engages students in various ways. In fact, many Orff teachers deliberately amplify the process of learning over the products. This emphasis on process is a key element of Orff Schulwerk, and through this active learning process, students are given opportunities to stimulate their own creative thinking.

Orff-Schulwerk pedagogy is focused on a process that includes the phases of imitation, exploration, and improvisation (Frazee, 1987). Imitation allows the teacher to present musical material in various ways to ensure student success and to develop their aural musicianship (Burgess, 2012). Through exploration, students extend their knowledge and experiences by experimenting with sounds and movements (Shamrock, n.d.). The Orff process usually concludes with improvisation, which is one of the only opportunities where students create music independent from their teacher (Frazee, 1987). Because composition and improvisation experiences require students to produce and manipulate sounds in a purposeful manner, students should be given numerous opportunities to experiment with sounds—both on instruments and on any other sound sources found in the classroom (Hickey, 2012). Given the seemingly endless variety of timbres and sonorities available to students in the Orff instrumentarium, including corresponding non-pitched percussion instruments, sound exploration is easily accomplished.

When adhering to this Orff process, teachers should make certain that students are given sufficient time for exploration and planning at the beginning of the process and time for revision and polishing later in the process. Also, teachers need to challenge the students as they fully develop their ideas, put these ideas into practice, and prepare for their next intended product. Thus, as teachers follow this traditional Orff process, they guide students through the core stages of preparation, time away, working through, and verification that are at the center of Webster's creative thinking model.

The processes of divergent and convergent thinking interact with the core thinking process outlined above during Orff instruction as well. For example, when students compose a xylophone melody within the constraints of a particular scale—e.g., pentatonic, hexatonic, diatonic, blues, etc.—and a given rhythm pattern—e.g., "Bow, wow, wow. Whose dog art thou?", they simultaneously demonstrate divergent and convergent thinking processes. The open-ended nature of the composition task allows for multiple solutions (divergent thinking), but given the constraints in terms of rhythm and tonality, students are also focused on a given standard of appropriateness (convergent thinking). This interplay between divergent and convergent thinking is one of the chief characteristics of the creative thinking process, and it frequently occurs during the Orff process.

Enabling Skills & Conditions

The Orff-Schulwerk approach offers accessible instruction to all students, regardless of prior experience, musical ability, or understanding. Music in Orff Schulwerk is elemental, which is meant to be unsophisticated, natural, and adaptive to the children's current level of achievement. Orff teachers work to include high quality music that is accessible to students of all levels (Purdum, 2012).

As illustrated in Webster's model, enabling skills and enabling conditions play a significant role in the creative thinking process. Because musical materials in Orff Schulwerk can be used with students of varied aptitude and achievement levels, it is a flexible approach that works for all students, even those who are lacking in certain enabling skills. Due to this flexibility, all students can be challenged to think creatively during Orff activities (Shamrock, n.d.). Because the Orff instruments are designed with removable bars, all children are set up for meaningful participation as they compose and improvise with success.

Enabling conditions, such as peer influence and environment, also influence creative thinking (Webster, 2002). Many Orff activities are collaborative and social in nature, involving students in small groups as they sing, move, and play instruments. As a result of these experiences in an Orff classroom setting, which often includes product sharing, peer evaluation, ensemble work, and activities involving poetry, drama, and movement, students are typically engaged in a learning environment whose enabling conditions naturally promote creative thinking.

Fostering Creative Thinking in the Music Classroom

Music teachers can establish learning environments and design instructional activities in various ways to promote their students' creative thinking. First, music teachers should create learning environments that are satisfying, musically rich, psychologically safe, and socially rewarding—a place in which students are comfortable taking risks (Hickey & Webster, 2001; Wang, 2008; Webster & Hickey, 1995). Without this type of positive environment, students are unlikely to completely engage in exploration, and they are also unlikely to fully develop their musical ideas. Second, teachers should also give students frequent opportunities to imagine and manipulate sounds, because these activities lead toward creative thinking and aesthetic decision- making, which are key components of composition and improvisation activities (Hickey & Webster, 2001). Orff instruments function as only a part of a larger pedagogical approach, but the use of the instruments truly enhances the development of creative thinking by providing numerous opportunities for sound exploration. Cooper (2005) also suggests that teachers should refrain from applying adult expectations to children's products because these expectations can restrict students' creative production.

Music teachers are charged with the responsibility for stimulating their students' creative thinking skills, and as noted above, Orff teachers seem particularly well suited for this task. As stated by psychologist and creativity scholar Mihalyi Csikszentmihalyi (1996),

> Each of us is born with two contradictory sets of instructions: a conservative tendency, made up of instincts for self-preservation, self-aggrandizement, and saving energy, and an expansive tendency made up of instincts for exploring, for enjoying novelty and risk—the curiosity that leads to creativity belongs to this set. We need both of these programs. But, whereas the first tendency requires little encouragement or support from outside to motivate behavior, the second can wilt if it is not cultivated. If too few opportunities for curiosity are available, if too many obstacles are placed in the way of risk and exploration, the motivation to engage in creative behavior is easily extinguished. (p. 11)

Experiences that encourage exploration and discovery, such as those active music-making experiences associated with the Orff-Schulwerk approach, are those that stir instincts related to Csikszentmihalyi's second tendency and initiate creative thinking. That these experiences hone students' creative thinking skills and motivate creative behaviors is one of the most compelling features of the Orff-Schulwerk approach.

As a means of critically reflecting upon teaching and learning processes, Orff teachers should engage in unequivocal discussions about the natural connections between Orff Schulwerk and creative thinking. Through this type of dialogue, music educators will strengthen their own philosophy as well as their practice. In an effort to stimulate this type of discussion, an application of Webster's model of creative thinking as applied to Orff Schulwerk is provided in Illustration Two. This application represents a modest first draft, and because it is only an early attempt, it is certainly subject to revision. Readers are encouraged to contact the author with ideas or suggestions for improving this application of the model as it relates to Orff Schulwerk. Given enough incubation time, revision, and enthusiasm from Orff teachers, this early application of Webster's creative-thinking model to Orff-Schulwerk pedagogy will hopefully generate productive dialogue among music educators as they continue to chart their new directions for the twenty-first century.

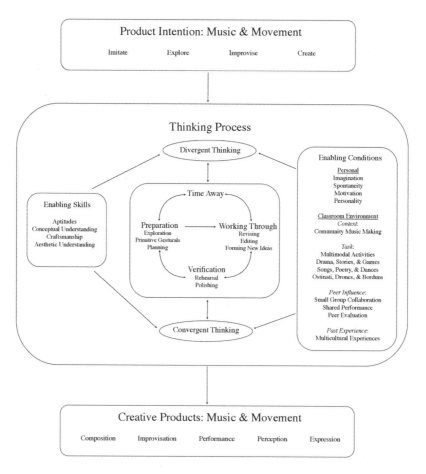

Illustration 2. A Preliminary Application of Webster's (2002) Model Proposed by D. G. Springer: Creative Thinking in Orff Schulwerk

References

Amabile, T. M. (1989). *Growing up creative: Nurturing a lifetime of creativity*. New York: Crown Publishers.

Anderson, W. M., & Lawrence, J. E. (2010). *Integrating music into the elementary classroom* (8th Ed.). Boston, MA: Schirmer Cengage Learning.

Bloom, B. S., Englehart, M. D., Furst, E. J., Hill, W. H., & Krathwohl, D. R. (1956). *Taxonomy of educational objectives, handbook I: Cognitive domain*. New York: McKay.

Burgess, S. (2012). An elemental approach to composition: Guiding student composers. *Orff Echo, 44*(2), 22-26.

Collins, M. A., & Amabile, T. M. (1999). Motivation and creativity. In R. J. Sternberg (Ed.), *Handbook of creativity* (pp. 297-312). Cambridge: Cambridge University Press.

Cooper, S. (2005). Cultivating composition and creativity. *General Music Today, 18*(3), 6-12.

Csikszentmihalyi, M. (1996). *Creativity: Flow and the psychology of discovery and invention*. New York: Harper Collins Publishers.

Frazee, J. (1987). *Discovering Orff*. New York: Schott.

Gardner, H. (1993). *Creating minds*. New York: Basic Books.

Gardner, H. (2007). *Five minds for the future*. Boston, MA: Harvard Business School Press.

Guilford, J. P. (1967). *The nature of human intelligence*. New York: McGraw-Hill.

Hanna, W. (2007). The new Bloom's taxonomy: Implications for music education. *Arts Education Policy Review, 108*(4), 7-16.

Hargreaves, D. J., MacDonald, R., & Miell, D. (2012). Explaining musical imaginations: Creativity, performance, and perception. In D. J. Hargreaves, D. E. Miell, & R. MacDonald (Eds.), *Musical imaginations: Multidisciplinary perspectives on creativity, performance, and perception* (pp. 1-16). Oxford: Oxford University Press.

Hickey, M. (2012). *Music outside the lines: Ideas for composing in K-12 music classrooms*. New York: Oxford University Press.

Hickey, M., & Webster, P. R. (2001). Creative thinking in music. *Music Educators Journal, 88*(1), 19-23.

Lehmann, A. C., Sloboda, J. A., & Woody, R. H. (2007). *Psychology for musicians: Understanding and acquiring the skills*. New York: Oxford University Press.

Purdum, T. (2012). Is it elemental? *Orff Echo, 44*(2), 27-30.

Sawyer, R. K. (2011). The cognitive neuroscience of creativity: A critical review. *Creativity Research Journal, 23*(2), 137-154.

Sawyer, R. K. (2012). *Explaining creativity: The science of human innovation (2nd Ed.).* New York: Oxford University Press.

Schlaug, G. (2003). The brain of musicians. In I. Peretz & R. Zatorre (Eds.), *The cognitive neuroscience of music* (pp. 366-381). Oxford: Oxford University Press.

Shamrock, M. (n.d.). *The Orff-Schulwerk approach.* Retrieved from http://www.allianceamm.org/resources_elem_Orff.html

Simmons, A. L., & Duke, R. A. (2006). Effects of sleep on performance of a keyboard melody. *Journal of Research in Music Education, 54*(3), 257-269.

Simonton, D. K. (2003). Expertise, competence, and creative ability: The perplexing complexities. In R. J. Sternberg & E. L. Grigorenko (Eds.), *The psychology of abilities, competencies, and expertise* (pp. 213-239). Cambridge: Cambridge University Press.

Sternberg, R. J., & Lubart, T. I. (1995). *Defying the crowd: Cultivating creativity in a culture of conformity.* New York: The Free Press.

Sternberg, R. J., & Lubart, T. I. (1999). The concept of creativity: Prospects and paradigms. In R. J. Sternberg (Ed.), *Handbook of creativity* (pp. 3-15). Cambridge: Cambridge University Press.

Torrance, E. P. (1988). The nature of creativity as manifest in its testing. In R. J. Sternberg (Ed.), *The nature of creativity: Contemporary psychological perspectives* (pp. 43-75). New York: Cambridge University Press.

Wallas, G. (1926). *The art of thought.* New York: Harcourt, Brace, and Co.

Wang, C. C. (2008). Reflections on issues related to assessment and creativity, and music education policies in the United States. In C. C. Leung, L. C. R. Yip, & T. Imada (Eds.), *Music education policy and implementation: International perspectives* (pp. 157-165). Hirosaki, Aomori, Japan: Hirosaki University Press.

Webster, P. R. (1987). Conceptual bases for creative thinking in music. In J. C. Peery, I. W. Peery, & T. W. Draper (Eds.), *Music and child development* (pp. 158-174). New York: Springer-Verlag.

Webster, P. R. (1990). Creativity as creative thinking. *Music Educators Journal, 76*(9), 22-28.

Webster, P. R. (2002). Creative thinking in music: Advancing a model. In T. Sullivan & L. Willingham (Eds.), *Creativity and music education* (pp. 16-34). Toronto: Britannia Printers.

Webster, P. R., & Hickey, M. (1995). Challenging children to think creatively. *General Music Today, 8*(3), 4-10.

End Notes

1   The author extends a sincere and enthusiastic "thank you" to Cindy Hall, Joanne Rojas, Joan Stansbury, and Cecilia Wang for reviewing an early draft of this chapter.

Chapter 15

ADAPTING ORFF TECHNIQUES FOR INDIVIDUALS WITH SPECIAL NEEDS

Lori F. Gooding

Orff educators inherently create an environment that sets the stage for success in children with and without disabilities. Yet, Orff educators, as with many other music educators, can often feel unprepared to deal with the practical demands of teaching students with disabilities. The purpose of this chapter is to provide practical applications for teaching children with disabilities in the music classroom. In particular, strategies, adaptations, and accommodations will be discussed. A list of helpful Web resources is also provided.

Current Teaching Environment

The number of children receiving special education services in the United States has changed tremendously since 1980. During the 1980-1981 academic, year approximately 4.1 million children, or ten percent of the student population, were served under the Individuals with Disabilities Education Act (IDEA). By 2008-2009, the number served had increased to approximately 6.5 million students, or thirteen percent of the student population (Aud et al., 2011). Not only has the number of students served changed over the past three decades, but also has the way in which services are delivered. Perhaps the most significant change is the push toward inclusion, with fifty-eight percent of the children enrolled in special education services spending at least eighty percent of their day in regular classroom settings in 2008-2009 as compared to only thirty three percent in 1990-1991 (Aud et al., 2011).

The increase of special learners in the regular classroom means that music educators are increasingly involved in the education of special learners. Music has been an important part of the educational process for individuals with disabilities since the early days of music education (Pontiff, 2004). Today, music classrooms are places in which children with varying abilities are routinely incorporated. In fact, a survey investigating music teachers' perceptions of inclusion found that nearly all the respondents reported teaching children with special needs (Wolery, 1998), yet many music educators state that they are inadequately trained to work with special learners (Pontiff, 2004). This admission may be due in part to the fact that music educators often find themselves teaching children with greater needs and more severe disabilities (McDowell, 2010).

Orff Schulwerk and Special Education: Common Principles

In order to adequately address the needs of students with disabilities, the American educational system has adopted an individualized approach in which a free and appropriate education must be provided in the least restrictive environment to all students with disabilities between the ages of three and twenty-one (Hammel & Hourigan, 2011). A significant part of this process is the individualized education plan (IEP); these plans, which focus on students' strengths and needs, are designed to facilitate student-specific educational goals. They are developed and implemented by a variety of professionals (teachers, therapists, etc.) across a range of media and disciplines.

Orff educators, as with special educators, inherently create an environment that sets the stage for success in children of all ability levels, including those with and without disabilities. As a result, many of the guiding principles of Orff Schulwerk are particularly well suited to teaching students with special needs. In particular, the principles of (a) inclusion, (b) individualization, (c) teaching to strengths, (d) adapting the curriculum as needed, (e) using a multisensory approach, and (f) focusing on developmentally appropriate learning are key to successful teaching and learning for children with disabilities (AOSA, 2011; McRae, 1982).

Even though the Orff-Schulwerk approach may be ideally suited to educating special learners, Orff educators often feel unprepared for the diverse aspects of teaching individuals with special needs. The purpose of this section of the chapter is to provide practical applications for teaching children with disabilities in the music classroom that can be used in conjunction with Orff-Schulwerk pedagogy.

Practical Applications for the Classroom

Concerns

Research suggests that music educators have concerns about the increased challenges faced when working with special learners. In particular, teachers often cite (a) behavior problems/classroom management, (b) large student numbers, (c) large course loads, (d) lack of information about students with disabilities, (e) adapting instruction, and (f) creating a successful learning environment for all students as major concerns (VanWeelden & Whipple, 2007; Wolery, 1998). In the current educational environment, some of the above areas—i.e., course loads—are difficult to address while others can be enhanced by incorporating a few, simple techniques. The following concepts can be easily incorporated into any music classroom to enhance the educational experience for all students.

Preparation

As is the case with any student, preparation and planning are essential when working with students with special needs. Being prepared permits teachers to focus on student behaviors, which allows them to prevent problems before they arise. Planning for special learners may involve speaking with special educators, consulting with a music therapist, or doing basic research on the Internet about disability characteristics. (See Table 1 for helpful Web sites.)

Table 1

Helpful Web sites

A Day's Work, LLC (Adaptive Equipment)	http://www.adaysworkmusiceducation.com/
American Music Therapy Association Center for Music Learning (Disabilities Information)	www.musictherapy.org http://cml.music.utexas.edu/online- resources/disabilities-information/introduction/
National Association for Music	http://www.nafme.org/Education
Exceptionailites SRIG	https://sites.google.com/site/exceptionalitiessrig/home (NAfME members only)
West Music	www.westmusic.com

Observing a veteran teacher or music therapist can also be a way to gain new ideas and strategies. Finally, seeking advice from veteran colleagues can help educators better plan for the particular challenges of individuals with special needs (Pontiff, 2004).

Strategies

In addition to being prepared, expanding the array of instructional strategies available for use in the classroom can also facilitate successful learning. When working with students with disabilities it is helpful to consider the following:

- *logistics*—Classroom space should be set up for success. Both physical setup and student placement are important issues. For example, a child with a disability may need to sit close to the teacher or next to a strong performing peer. Conversely, a child who has a tendency to wander may need to sit far away from the door.

Possible options for facilitating successful use of the space include the use of stations and a consistent layout;

- *modeling*—"Talk less and do more" is always the best approach for students with disabilities. Teachers should model as much as possible. In addition to teacher modeling, peer modeling can be an excellent way to provide enhanced instruction; peer modeling also has the added benefit of creating positive interactions between students with and without disabilities. *If instructions are used, keep them concise and clear;*

- *multimodal approach*—Orff-Schulwerk educators regularly combine auditory, visual, kinesthetic, and tactile presentations of class concepts, but it is important to remember that some students with disabilities may need adapted material in many of these modes. For example, a student may be able to "read" a passage using color-coded music that coincides with color-coding on the instrument —i.e., colored tape or stickers placed on individual bars on the Orff instruments. *As often as possible, present materials in more than one mode at a time to facilitate successful learning;*

- *pacing*—Students with disabilities often need slower pacing. On the other hand, gifted and talented students may work with faster spacing. Students with special needs also often need more time to respond. *Repetition is essential for students with disabilities. Repeat, Repeat, Repeat!;*

- *paraprofessionals*—Encourage paraprofessionals to participate. Convey your expectations for them while they are in your classroom. Keep in mind that they may not be comfortable with the musical elements, so you may need to support them musically. *Paraprofessionals are often your best source of information about individual students with disabilities;*

- *props/manipulatives*—Props can facilitate learning, especially for students who are highly concrete. *Key Point: Be aware that students with sensory difficulties may become overwhelmed with too much sensory input, or have sensitivities to particular sounds, textures, smells, etc. In the case of sensory overload, decreasing props may be necessary.*

- *structure*—Students with disabilities respond well to structure. Classroom rules should be consistent and posted in an obvious place. Class schedules can be posted on the board or individually posted for students with special needs. Hello and goodbye songs can be used to provide structure for younger students. *Picture Exchange Communication Systems (PECS) can be a great way to communicate schedule. Provide appropriate pictures for the special education staff that represent music classroom activities;* and

- *technology*—Technology can facilitate success for students with disabilities. For example, sounds can be recorded onto a "Bigmac" button or iPad for students with limited motor control so that they may play with the rest of the group using their head, one finger, etc. *SMART boards can be excellent tools to facilitate learning for students with disabilities.*

Adaptations

Using adaptive equipment and instruments can facilitate success for students with special needs. Music and educational companies design instruments and equipment specifically for use with students with special needs. Some items, such as instrument mounts and drum tables, can be costly. Others, such as wrist bells and adaptive picks, are relatively inexpensive. If you are considering purchasing adaptive equipment, buy items that will have the widest use; for example, wrist bells (available with tie and Velcro straps) and mallet cuffs are practical, cost-effective choices.

Keep in mind that you can also create your own adaptive equipment. For example, a mallet holder can be devised using a hair scrunchie to hold a mallet in place. Rubber doorstops can be used to strum instruments such as the autoharp. Velcro can be attached to instruments to hold them in place. Mallets can even be attached to instrument stands, chairs, etc., using string to ensure they are not lost or thrown.

In addition to adaptive equipment, playing instruments in non-traditional ways can facilitate learning. For example, step bells can help facilitate the concept of high and low through direction; the higher notes are literally "higher" spatially than the lower notes. Likewise, a buffalo drum, which has ropes on the back, may be easier to manipulate than a traditional frame drum for students with fine motor deficits.

Accommodations and Modifications

Consider that some students with disabilities may not be able to participate in classroom activities in the traditional manner, nor will they always be able to participate in traditional forms of assessment. It is important to recognize when it is necessary to provide accommodations—adapting the requirements when a child can learn at the same level as other students with increased support—or modifications, adaptations based upon different goals and the individual's level of functioning. Accommodations include increasing time, changing the assignment format, or changing the response format. Modifications include changing assignment content or requirements to reflect students' abilities (Adamek & Darrow, 2005).

Accommodations examples include (a) enlarging the font on musical materials for a student with visual impairments, (b) wearing a microphone for a student with hearing impairments, or (c) allowing a student to come in during lunch or after school so that they can have extra time to learn class concepts. Modification examples include: (a) creating simplified assignments using the same concepts that other class members are doing—i.e., a simpler rhythm part), (b) creating special parts that add musicality and allow students to participate using their strengths, and (c) creating a recorder part with notes that can be played with one hand so that a student with use of only one hand can participate.

Orff-Specific Adaptations

Many Orff-based activities will be easily accessible to students with a wide range of needs. Using movement to illustrate concepts, adding text to musical rhythms, and pairing music with other modalities are all common Orff elements that can help facilitate learning for students with special needs. However, it is important to adapt Orff-instruction techniques as needed to facilitate learning in students with specific disabilities. For example, some students such as those with hearing impairments may need to work from print while the rest of the class uses an auditory format. Other students with limited hand movement or strength may benefit from the use of adaptive mounts/holders when playing recorders and other two-handed instruments.

Finally, students may benefit from having a partner when playing an instrument. In particular, instruments that are large enough for two people to play, either side-by-side or facing each another, are especially applicable in partner activities.

Final Thoughts

The above strategies, adaptations, accommodations, and modifications become easier with practice, and the rewards are great for students with and without disabilities. As Hammel and Hourigan (2011) state, "the hallmark of a truly successful classroom is that all students can benefit from the strategies introduced to assist students with special needs" (p. 79). With a little "out of the box thinking," the music classroom can be a place in which all students succeed and develop an appreciation for music.

References

Adamek, M. S., & Darrow, A. A. (2005). *Music in special education.* Silver Spring, MD: American Music Therapy Association.

AOSA (2011). Rationale for the Orff Schulwerk learning model. Retrieved from http://www.aosa.org/documents/Guidelines/rationale.pdf

Aud, S., Hussar, W., Kena, G., Bianco, K., Frohlich, L., Kemp, J., Tahan, K. (2011). *The Condition of Education 2011* (NCES 2011-033). U.S. Department of Education, National Center for Education Statistics. Washington, DC: U.S. Government Printing Office.

Hammel, A. (2001). Preparation for teaching special learners: Twenty years of practice. *Journal of Music Teacher Education, 11(5),* 5-11.

Hammel, A. M., & Hourigan, R. M. (2011). *Teaching music to students with special needs: A label free approach.* New York: Oxford University Press.

McDowell, C. (2010). An adaption tool kit for teaching music. *Teaching Exceptional Children Plus, 6(3),* 1-20.

McRae, S. (1982). The Orff connection … Reaching the special child. *Music Educators Journal, 68,* 32-34.

Pontiff, E. (2004). Teaching special learners: Ideas from veteran teachers in the music classroom. *Teaching Music, 12(3),* 52-58.

VanWeelden, K., & Whipple, J. (2007). An exploratory study of the impact of field experiences on music education majors' attitudes and perceptions of music for secondary students with special needs. *Journal of Music Teacher Education, 16(2)*, 34-44.

Wolery, M. (1998). Teachers' perceptions of inclusion: Emphasis on art, music, and physical education teachers. *Research to Practice Summit*. Retrieved from http://ectacenter.org/topics/inclusion/research/rs_perception.asp

Chapter 16

JAZZ AND ORFF
Kimberly McCord

My first introduction to Orff was in 1980 at the National Association for Jazz Education Conference. Nancy Ferguson was presenting the one and only elementary session at the conference and was using a student group. I had never seen anything like it, little kids playing the blues and improvising on these very cool instruments. At the time, I was teaching high school instrumental music, but it was the beginning of what has turned out to be one of my real passions, jazz on Orff instruments.

Nancy kept after me to take the levels, and I was lucky enough to enroll in Level I with another great jazz Orff teacher, Vivian Murray. Both Nancy and Vivian were wonderful mentors. They helped me to figure out how to introduce jazz at the elementary level, and I hope this chapter might provide some ideas for you regarding integrating jazz into your curriculum.

In 1987, Congress passed a bill declaring jazz a "rare and valuable national treasure" worth preserving and celebrating (H.CON.RES 57, n.d.). How are you helping to preserve and share our national treasure? If you teach Orff, you already have the tools and basic knowledge to get started.

First Experiences

Jazz is tied to African-American culture. In African culture, movement and dance are almost always paired with music. As Orff teachers, we embrace this way of introducing music to children, because we know that a "doorway into music" is through movement.

I begin in kindergarten with a wonderful recording that five-year-olds all over the world respond to with joy, "Zip-a-dee-doo-dah" performed by Louis Armstrong. It is a good place to start; Armstrong is generally known as the father of jazz, and children love his playful, gravely voice. In the recording, one hears Armstrong sing and play the trumpet. The children should use locomotor movement when they hear Louis Armstrong sing and non-locomotor movement when they hear him play the trumpet. It is fun to pretend as if they are playing the trumpet during the trumpet solos. The tempo is slow enough that some children might show movement on the strong second and fourth beats. Whatever they do is fine; we mostly want them responding to what they hear in the music.

Feeling the accented second and fourth beat is essential to eventually getting children to where they feel swing, but it can't be rushed. If children aren't able to feel steady beat first, they won't be able to find beats two and four. It is better to focus on something other than two and four, such as locomotor and non-locomotor movement, until the children begin to master steady beat and feeling accented one and three.

Tempo is important. Teachers love to play Duke Ellington's recordings for movement activities, but tempos at 120 beats per minute and faster are too quick for children to easily find beats two and four. Start them out more slowly with *Summertime* recorded by Miles Davis—his version of *Porgy and Bess*. Then, once the children are secure with ninety beats per minute, you can gradually share some of the popular, faster recordings such as Ellington's *It Don't Mean a Thing if it Ain't Got That Swing, Take the A Train,* and *C Jam Blues*, which are typically faster at 120-140 beats per minute.

Feeling swing is important. Later on, as students begin to improvise and perform jazz, it is important that they have a swing feel to make the music sound right. Take plenty of time to teach the swing feel; it won't happen in one activity, in one week of classes, or maybe in one month of repeated experiences. Think of it as expecting children to match pitch, using a full chromatic scale before isolating *sol/mi* first. You can do all sorts of activities that focus on feeling beats two and four. Passing an F boomwhacker to

Summertime on beats two and four is a great way to experience swing feel. You should hear the F sound as the student passing the boomwhacker sets it on the floor in front of the next student. Miles Davis is very accessible for children; he is a very melodic improviser who doesn't play too fast. But, in my experience, most children are not developmentally ready to do this activity until late third grade or the beginning of fourth grade.

Speech and Singing

Transferring beats two and four to snaps or two-finger claps is great to use whenever children listen, sing, or move. Whenever they hear jazz it is good to get them accustomed to finding two and four and "putting it in their bodies." The hi-hat cymbals on a drum set are where the two and four usually live.

The drums are important, but the most important instrument in the jazz rhythm section is the bass. Keeping it simple, focus on the walking bass, which is the steady beat. You can have children chant something such as "walk-ing bass, um, walk-ing, bass, um" to turn it into an ostinato. See if you can get them to say the "ing" and "um" a little louder to accent the two and four. Put the walking bass on patschen. Add the two and four snaps and you are now starting to have a nice groove.

The other important ingredient is the ride cymbal. It is called the ride cymbal because it sits on the stand and takes a ride. Have the children slide their palms together and chant, "ride cym-bal, ride cym-bal" (long, short, short) with your walking bass and hi-hat parts. Drop the speech out and listen for a nice swing groove. You have a rhythm section!

You can do all sorts of chants over the rhythm section with a swing feel. In fact it is fun to compare chants and songs performed "straight" and "swung." Pick chants and songs you have already taught and then see if the students can switch to a swing style. For example, what would Liza Jane sound like swung? See if the students can work in small groups with their body percussion rhythm section and figure it out.

Improvisation

One of the great things about Orff Schulwerk is the emphasis on individual student creativity. Improvisation should be something students are quite comfortable with already from experiencing lots of Orff process, and changing to a jazz style of improvisation will be quite natural. An easy way to begin is to improvise using unpitched percussion such as rhythm sticks, hand drums, or boomwhackers. Get the body percussion rhythm section going, and let students take turns performing call-and-response improvisation with long and short C boomwhackers. The long C plays the call first and the short C answers when the first solo is done. The improvisation should be swinging and feel good with the body percussion rhythm section. You can use this same activity with the *Summertime* recording.

Scat singing is improvisation using the voice. Start students out simple; keep them on the root of the chord, and sing short phrases that swing. "Doo, bah, doo, bah, doo, dot" is an example. Most of the time, jazz phrases will end with a short note so "dot" or "bop" are good syllables to use at the end of a scat phrase. Longer syllables are generally doo, bah, dah, etc. Consider Duke Ellington's *C Jam Blues*, and turn the melody into scat phrases. The students can decide if notes are long or short and assign syllables. A melody can then be sung on syllables as a way to develop a scat vocabulary. Listening to great scat singers such as Ella Fitzgerald is another important way for students to develop a vocabulary of scat syllables they like. One of the greatest scat solos of all time is Ella Fitzgerald's recording of *How High the Moon*. Play one chorus (one time through the form of the song) of scat improvisation for students; listening to the whole song will be too long, and one chorus is plenty to get great ideas.

Gradually add the third, fifth, and seventh to the root when scat singing. It will help the students hear the harmony of chords. Try to keep it simple, and don't try to add too many notes too soon. *C Jam Blues* (also recorded with lyrics as *Duke's Place*) is a perfect example of a great swinging melody with very few pitches.

Transferring to the Instruments

If you have bass, alto, and soprano xylophones, you can perform a lot with jazz. You do need a ride cymbal, though, to really make the music sound jazzy. There really isn't a good substitute for the ride cymbal. You can create the hi-hat two and four feel on just about any pitched or unpitched instrument that doesn't sustain. I have used claves, a tambourine, or soprano xylophone played in octaves (long and short C in the key of C). If you have access to hi-hat cymbals, they sound the best and are really fun to play. Make sure they aren't open too wide and have children play sitting down pushing on the pedal with their toe to get a nice crisp click.

The walking-bass part should be on the bass xylophone. Use a dominant seventh chord or a sixth chord for the four notes going up and then back down. For example, a C6 chord would be played C, E, G, A, A, G, E, C. The 6th and 7th chords sound jazzier than triads or crossover borduns.

Add the ride cymbal part and you have a rhythm section on the instruments! Add improvisation by setting up an alto xylophone with the same bars as you use on the bass xylophone, either a sixth chord or a seventh chord. Students can play call-and-response solos over the rhythm section or "trade fours," which just means call-and-response in four measure phrases. You can trade fours on instruments, scatting, or a combination.

The Final Chorus

The two most important elements that should be present in jazz are swing feel and improvisation. The improvised solos should incorporate swing feel to be jazzy sounding. Children will sometimes get excited when soloing and try to do too much. If you keep them focused on being simple and swinging, they should be fine. Miles Davis and *C Jam Blues* will help children to remember that you can make great jazz without playing lots and lots of notes.

Teachers need to remember that jazz needs to be included in any general music curriculum. Choose quality recordings of musicians and composers who have stood the test of time; Louis Armstrong, Duke Ellington, Miles

Davis, and Ella Fitzgerald are a good place to start. College students may be shy about jazz improvisation, but encourage them to improvise in a jazz style and emphasize the importance of including jazz in their curriculum when they become teachers. For some reason, jazz improvisation has a reputation that it is only for the experienced jazz player. You can't get experience unless you perform it, so encourage your students to learn along with their peers. We all are beginners at some point!

Be playful with jazz. It is meant to be spontaneous. Bobby McFerrin embodies playful improvisation. He somehow manages to get entire concert halls of people singing and improvising with abandon. If you have fun with it, then so will the students.

I have included a blues Orff rhythm section piece in the lesson plans at the end of this volume that can be used with recorders for improvisation. The blues are more complex than what I have discussed in this chapter. There are three chords to listen for and certain notes will sound better in each chord. Often we think of the blues as the easiest entry point to jazz but it is actually fairly challenging for beginners. Teaching blues is best left until students are changing chords in other pieces. Use this piece when some of the basic skills are in place.

This has been just a little taste of Orff jazz: just an appetizer. Jazz is a pretty big menu, but you can be quite satisfied with this sample as an entry point into the larger jazz gumbo.

Reference

H.CON.RES 57. (n.d.). Retrieved from http://www.hr57.org/hconres57.html

Chapter 17

BALINESE GAMELAN ANGKLUNG ADAPTED FOR ORFF INSTRUMENTS

Han, Kuo-Huang

What is a *Gamelan Angklung*?

The word "gamelan" came from low Javanese *gamel*, meaning "hammer" (Lindsay, 1992). By extension, it can mean a hammered (percussion-dominated) orchestra. Probably the most popular Asian ensemble in the world, gamelan is found in Central Java, West Java (Sunda), Bali, and other localities in Indonesia. Each type of gamelan has its own instrumentation, function, and characteristics. There are many gamelans outside of Indonesia with 150 or more orchestra sets in the United States. On the island of Bali, there are some twenty different types of gamelans with *gamelan gong kebyar* being the biggest and most famous type. The medium-sized *gamelan angklung* is less familiar but not necessarily less numerous in Bali. It used to include four or eight bamboo *angklung* [rattles] from which comes the name of the ensemble.[1] Very often the Balinese simply refer to this ensemble as "*angklung,*" even though the bamboo rattles are rarely used with the ensemble now. Even in the 1930s when Colin McPhee, the Canadian-American composer and ethnomusicologist, organized a children's *gamelan angklung* group and "reintroduced" bamboo *angklung* rattles in Sayan Village, child musicians were skeptical about the "strange" instruments at first (McPhee, 1970).

As with most Balinese arts, *gamelan angklung* began as a musical offering for temple festivals and cremation. In a most comprehensive recording of *gamelan angklung* and its most informative accompanying notes on this subject to date, Ruby Ornstein (who also recorded the music) writes, "For a Balinese, playing gamelan is a pleasure and a contribution to the community, but fundamentally it is a religious offering" (*From Kuno to Kebyar*, 2010, notes, p. 12). Colin McPhee, who revived the *gamelan angklung*[2] (McPhee, 1944, 1966), reported in the 1930s that this ensemble's function was "purely ritualistic" and "rarely indeed is it employed to accompany dancers" (McPhee, 1937, p. 323). However, in practice, villages that could not afford a large set of instruments would use any ensemble they had for a given purpose, sacred or secular. This is precisely the situation with *gamelan angklung*. Japp Kunst even came across the use of *gamelan angklung* for a wedding in Blahbatoeh [Blahbatuh] Village in the 1920s. He described at length the archaic dumbbell [*reyong*], which has been replaced by inverted kettles sitting on a wooden frame (Kunst, 1924). The ensemble did accompany *kebyar* dances and even topeng, masked dance drama. (Ornstein, 1971). In 1985, the author came across a *gamelan angklung* performing for a tooth-filling ceremony along with a *gamelan gong kebyar* fifty-feet away one day, and on a different day, for a cremation. As time progressed, new compositions were created and new repertoire (especially inspired by *gamelan gong kebyar*) was borrowed for it. From the mid-twentieth century, independent pieces were created for concert performances and dance accompaniment as heard in the recordings by Ruby Ornstein recorded in the 1960s (*From Kuno to Kebyar*, 2010) and learned by the present author in the 1970s (under Pak I Wayan Suweca) and 1980s (under Pak I Wayan Sinti and others). *Gamelan angklung*, though still active in religious settings, has also stepped onto the modern concert stage now.

Unlike most other gamelans, *gamelan angklung* employs only four pitches (North Bali has a five-pitched *gamelan angklung*). Tuned to the *slendro* scale system, the pitches in Balinese names are *ndeng, ndung, ndang, nding*—roughly A-flat, B-flat, C, E-flat (sounding similar to *do, re, mi, sol* in Western *solfège*).[3] Despite its pitch limitation, *gamelan angklung's* mood is sentimental and bittersweet to the Balinese (Tanzer, 1991). The melody can be light-hearted or exuberant. The rapid *kotekan* [interlocking] can be very busy, and the rhythm can be just as complex as any standard Balinese gamelan music. The punctuation by the gong types and elaboration by keyed and kettle instruments are as familiar as other Balinese gamelan music. One interesting aspect of this ensemble: due to its smaller size and portability, the whole ensemble can be carried on bamboo poles for procession, itself a marching gamelan.

Instrumentation of a Gamelan Angklung

The instruments of a contemporary south Balinese *gamelan angklung* can be classified by eight categories (older style and five-tone style have some special instruments). Different villages may have different names for the metallophones. Below is a list of the most common instruments by categories. In the illustration, suggested Orff Schulwerk and other instruments are placed on the right side (Illustration 1 by Charlotte Rollman).

Illustration 1.

Instrumentation of a Balinese Gamelan Angklung (sketch by Charlotte Rollman) and Classification by Categories with Orff Substitutes

Balinese Gamelan Angklung & Orff Instruments

A. Metallophones

Kantil (small metallophones) 4 — soprano metallophones
Gangsa (medium metallophones) 4 — alto metallophones
Jegogan (larger metallophones) 2 — bass metallophones

B. Gong-Chimes

Reyong (kettles) — [not used]

C. Gongs

Gong ageng (large gong) 1 — large gong or tam-tam
Kempur (medium gong) 1 — medium gong or tam-tam
Kempli (primary time beater) 1 — cowbell
Kenelang (secondary time beater) 1 — used coffee can

D. Cymbals

Rincik 1 — cymbals (3 pairs)

E. Drums

Kendang (large drum) 1 or 2 — [not used]
Kendang angklung (small drums) 2 — bongo (played with sticks)

F. Flute

Suling (ring flute; optional) — alto recorder

G. Rattles

Angklung (bamboo rattles; optional) — [not used]

In general, the small and medium metallophones are used to play melody or *kotekan* [interlocking], while the large metallophones are used to play the bass (usually key notes of the melody). Gong-chimes play interlocking melody, accentuated at important points in "chords," or simply create non-pitched sound similar to the sound of cymbals. Large and medium hanging gongs play colotomic points, which divide the beats of a musical phrase at specific points, and smaller gongs act as primary and secondary time beaters. Flutes play melody, employing improvisation, including adding a fifth pitch as well as high or low octave pitches, and drums direct. If bamboo *angklung* rattles are used, they always play a melody in interlocking fashion.

Instrument Descriptions

1. Metallophones are bronze keyed instruments suspended over corresponding bamboo or aluminum tubes and supported by a wooden frame and come in eight to ten in three to four sizes.

2. Gong-chimes are inverted kettles resting on a wooden frame—four or eight. Each person plays two kettles. These are not used in adapting to Orff ensemble settings.

3. Gongs are individual gongs hanging on stands, horizontally mounted or hand held and come in four sizes. Traditional pieces use the medium gong; *kebyar* style pieces, the large gong. But, for newer compositions, there is no absolute rule. Two smaller hand-held gongs are needed as time beaters.

4. Cymbals are pairs of upturned small cymbals, usually mounted on the back of a carved turtle and struck from the top by a similar pair.

5. Drums are large and small-laced drums, one pair each. Traditional pieces use the small pair (with two sticks) and *kebyar* style pieces, large pair; large pair are played with bare hands except for special dance pieces.

6. Flutes are end-blown bamboo ring flutes; use one flute or two flutes in unison.

7. Rattles (bamboo *angklung*), four rattles in *do re mi sol*, or eight rattles doubling the same pitches, if used. They are not used in adapting to Orff ensembles.

The Orff Instruments and the Gamelan

In the "Carl Orff" entry of the *New Grove Dictionary of Musical Instruments*, one will read the following phrases describing why Orff invented instruments for students to improvise with after his experience in the school he and Dorothee Günther founded in Munich in the 1920s: "To enable them to do so without first acquiring advanced keyboard fluency, he introduced a great variety of percussion instruments. Some of these were already used in the orchestra and in jazz ensembles, but others were modeled on the melodic and heterophonic bar-instruments of the Indonesian gamelan" (Horton, 1984, p. 838). In general, the style of Orff Schulwerk is remarkably similar to gamelan music: it is percussion-dominated, rhythmically oriented, made up of short musical phrases and *ostinati,* learned by rote in groups, etc.

It is unlikely an elementary school would purchase a set of authentic gamelan instruments. However, since many schools own Orff instruments, it is an easy step to use them in teaching simple gamelan pieces. One should bear in mind that the gamelan is not tuned to the Western tempered system and that no two gamelans sound the same. Furthermore, the same pitches in the same octave of two identical instruments within the same gamelan are tuned differently in cents to create acoustic beats resulting in shimmering sound effects. Orff instruments, on the other hand, are tuned to the Western tempered system. So the adaptation of Orff instruments in playing gamelan music is just an idea to introduce a different culture through hands-on experience, not a one hundred percent reproduction.

Playing Techniques

All metallophones [keyed instruments] are played with one mallet, which is different from the common practice of using two mallets when playing Orff instruments. A right-hander (most Balinese) would strike a key with the mallet in the right hand and dampen the previously struck key that is still ringing with the left-hand fingers (usually the thumb on top and index finger below the key edge). In other words, one strikes the second key while simultaneously dampening the previous key. This is a technique that requires practice for some players. Orff metallophone instruments should be played similar to the above description. But, the smallest keyed (barred) instruments may have to be dampened with a single finger from above. Even in playing *reyong* kettles, which are struck by the same person with two long sticks, dampening the same kettle after striking the knob with the same stick is desirable. Playing *kotekan* (interlocking) on metallophones uses a different dampening technique, but it is not discussed here because it is employed for more advanced pieces. Gongs should continue to ring after playing them except for the primary time beater, which requires a muted sound achieved by placing the left palm on the surface of the gong. Two players can use the same Orff metallophone (high and low octaves), since only four pitches are required. Unused keys (bars) can be removed if necessary.

Cipher Notation

Traditionally, musicians in Indonesia learn music by listening and imitating. But, a cipher notation is in use now, especially in schools. The concept of using notation was due to Western, mainly Dutch, influence in the late nineteenth-century Java. This action "coincided with the movement of the Javanese priyayi [aristocrats], with the support of their sympathetic Dutch colleagues, to define Javanese gamelan as a classic work, in accord [sic] with the status of European music" (Sumarsam, 1995, p. 111). One of the systems, cipher notation, has become more widely used since then. Based upon the nineteenth-century French Galin-Paris-Chevé system (Rainbow, 2001), this cipher notation was introduced by the Dutch. The Chinese and Japanese used similar systems, also coming from the French source in the late nineteenth century. Following is a description of the Javanese practice.

The seven pitches of a diatonic scale are denoted by numbers, no matter what key it may be in: 1 = *do*, 2 = *re*, 3 = *mi*, 4 = *fa*, 5 = sol, 6 = la, and 7 = ti, basically the movable *do* system. A dot above the number denotes a higher octave and a dot below, a lower octave. Double dots above or below a number would denote even higher or lower octaves respectively. West Javanese practice just reverses them—i.e., a high dot equals a low pitch and a low dot, a high pitch. If a single number is a quarter note equivalent (for easy identification), a line above two connecting numbers equals two eighths. (The Chinese and Japanese counterparts place the lines underneath the numbers). Two lines above are two sixteenth notes. A dot after a number under a line represents a dotted-eighth note. So, the number immediately following it with two lines above it is a sixteenth note. However, a dot after a number, without a smaller valued note following it, indicates an extension of the previous note. In this case, it is a half note, if the previous note is a quarter. Bar lines and rests were once in use but not any more (See the author's modified examples in Appendix I). Almost all traditional gamelan compositions are in quadruple meter, so there is no need for time signatures. For easy reading, four notes are notated as a group, with a space separating it from the previous or following four-note group.

Traditionally, the Balinese hardly use any notation when teaching one to play the gamelan. If they do use notation, it is fragmented (just numbers as pitch references) or abbreviations of their *solfège*. For four-pitched *gamelan angklung*, the four notes are *ndeng*, *ndung*, *ndang*, and *nding*. Their abbreviations are "*e*", "*u*", "*a*", and "*i*" (the vowels), respectively. Sometimes, these tones would be notated as 1, 2, 3, and 4. As mentioned before, the four pitches of the *gamelan angklung* are approximately Western A-flat, B-flat, C, and E-flat (sounding *do, re, mi,* and *sol*). For the sake of easy learning, the present author has been using G, A, B, D as their equivalences. When these notes are written in cipher notation, they become 1, 2, 3, 5 (*do, re, mi,* and *sol*), the easiest way to match the pitches in the movable *do* system. Notice that this approach is different from the Balinese who use 4 as the fourth pitch.

Selected CDs that Only Pertain to Gamelan Angklung

Bali South - Gamelan Gong Kebyar and Gamelan Angklung. UCLA Ethnomusicology Archive Series, vol. 1. 2003. The first four *gamelan gong kebyar* pieces were recorded by Gertrude Robinson in 1970 [in LP format]. The remaining five *gamelan angklung* pieces came from UCLA Archive.

Gamelan Music of Bali: Gamelan Angklung and Gamelan Gong Kebjar. Lyrichord LYRCD 7179. Recorded by Ruby Ornstein in 1964. Originally issued in LP format. Includes several *gamelan angklung* compositions.

Gamelan of Bali: Angklung. Ricks Records. Performed by the gamelan group from Sidan Village, Gianyar, Bali; Wayan Japa, director (Indonesian label).

Gamelan of Bali: Angklung, vol. 2. Ricks Records. Performed by the gamelan group from Sidan Village, Gianyar, Bali; Wayan Japa, director (Indonesian label).

Gamelan Sekar Jaya: Balinese Music in America. GSJ-011. 1995. Produced by the most famous American gamelan group, Sekar Jaya (director: Wayne Vitale), "the finest Balinese gamelan outside of Indonesia according to Indonesian press" (Marc Perlman's liner note: 6); includes two newly composed compositions for *gamelan angklung* one of which features bamboo *angklung* (melodic rather than interlocking playing).

Gamelan Tunas Mekar: Music of Bali, Indonesia. Prolific Records, 1995. Traditional and new compositions for *gamelan angklung* performed by Denver, CO based Gamelan Tunas Mekar, I Made Lasmawan, artist-in-residence, Jill Fredericksen, music director.

From Kuno to Kebyar: Balinese Gamelan Angklung. 2010. Smithsonian Folkways Recordings SFW CD 50411. Recorded in 1960s and annotated by Ruby Ornstein. To this date, it is the most extensive recording of *gamelan angklung* and includes extremely informative liner notes.

Music from the Morning of the World. 2002. Elektra/Nonesuch Explorer series 9 79196-2. Originally 2 LPs released in 1967 and 1969 (H-72015; H-72028), this is a good sample of different types of Balinese music recorded by David Lewiston in the 1960s, including a long *kebyar* style *gamelan angklung* composition: *Margepati*.

The Roots of Gamelan (The First Recordings, Bali, 1928; New York, 1941). World Arbiter 2001. Annotated by Edward Herbst. Includes two traditional *gamelan angklung* pieces (numbers seventeen and eighteen) and Colin McPhee's transcriptions of Balinese music performed by McPhee, Benjamin Britten (both on piano) and Georges Barrère (flute).

West Meets East: Chinese and Balinese Music. Folkways Records, FSS 37455 (originally issued in LP in 1981). Includes five *gamelan angklung* pieces learned by the author in the 1970s under Pak I Wayan Suweca at the Center for World Music and performed by Northern Illinois University's Asian Music Ensemble (non-professional student performance).

Selected Web Sites

Gamelan Sekar Jaya: <www.gsj.org/angklung> (on *gamelan angklung*).

Gamelan Anak Swarasanti: http://www.anakswarasanti.com/instruments/
angklung.php.

Many examples can be found on You Tube by searching "Gamelan
angklung, Bali."

American Gamelan Institute: <www.gamelan.org> (everything you want to
know about gamelan).

References

Brinner, B. (2008). *Music in central Java: Experiencing music, expressing
culture*. New York: Oxford University Press. (Global Music series)
Highly recommended for beginners (with a CD).

Cole, J. (1997a). Sacred sounds from the morning of the world. *Orff Echo,
29*(3), 24-26.

Cole, J. (1997b). Beginning Javanese gamelan: A community of listeners.
Orff Echo, 29(3), 28-32.

Dibia, I. W., Ballinger, R., & Anello, B. (2004). *Balinese dance, drama and
music: A guide to the performing arts of Bali*. Singapore: Periplus
Editions. A dazzlingly beautiful and informative guide.

Gold, L. (2005). *Music in Bali: Experiencing music, expressing culture*.
New York: Oxford University Press. (Global music series) Highly
recommended for beginners to learn about music in Balinese society.
(with a CD that includes a brief *gamelan angklung* selection)

Harnish, D. (2004). Translating Balinese music from gamelan to Orff
ensemble. *Orff Echo, 37*(1), 20-26.

Holtfreter, L. (1996). *Flowing waters: Building a musical bridge between
your Orff-Schulwerk ensemble and the Javanese gamelan*. Danbury,
CT: World Music Press. (with one videocassette).

Horton, J. (1984). Orff, Carl. In S. Sadie (Ed.), *The New Grove dictionary
of musical instruments*, Vol. 2, 838.

Kunst, J., & Kunst-van Wely, C. J. A. (1924). De gamelan angkloeng. In *De
Toonkunst van Bali*, Deel 1. Weltevreden: Druk G. Kolf & Co., 95-
107. (In Dutch)

Lindsay, J. (1992). *Javanese Gamelan: Traditional orchestra of Indonesia*
(2nd ed). Singapore: Oxford University Press. (Images of Asia) Highly
recommended for beginners.

McPhee, C. (1937). Angkloeng Gamelans in Bali. *Djawa* (Java-Instituut, Jogjakrata, Java), vol. 17, 322-360.

McPhee, C. (1970). Children and music in Bali. In J. Belo (Ed.), *Traditional Balinese cultures* (pp. 212-239). New York: Columbia University Press.

McPhee, C. (2002). *A club of small men, a children's tale from Bali*. Hong Kong: Periplus Editions. Originally published in 1948; written for children; based upon his own experience in forming a children's *gamelan angklung* in the 1930s in Sayan Village, Bali.

McPhee, C. (1946). *A house in Bali*. New York: The John Day Company. Reprinted by Oxford-in-Asia, 1972.

McPhee, C. (1966). *Music in Bali: A study in form and instrumental organization in Balinese orchestral music*. New Haven, CT: Yale University Press.

May, E., & Hood, M. (1962). Javanese music for American children. *Music Educators Journal, 48*(5), 38-41.

Ornstein, R. (1971). The five-tone gamelan angklung of north Bali. *Ethnomusicology*, 15 (1), 71-80.

Pickvance, R. (2005). *A gamelan manual: A player's guide to the central Javanese gamelan*. London: James Mas Books.

Rainbow, B. (2001). Galin-Paris-Chevé Method. In S. Sadie & J. Tyrell (Ed.), *The New Grove Dictionary of Music and Musicians 2nd Ed., Vol. 9* (pp. 440 – 441).

Shamrock, M., & Wenten, I. N. (2000). The challenge of 'kotekan.' In A. de Quadros (Ed.), *Many seeds, different flowers: The music education legacy of Carl Orff* (pp. 186-195). Nedlands: CIRCME.

Sorrell, N. (1990). *A guide to the gamelan*. London: Faber and Faber. (another edition: Society for Asian Music, 2000) On Javanese gamelan; highly recommended for beginners.

Spiller, H. (2004). *Gamelan: The traditional sounds of Indonesia*. Santa Barbara, CA. ABC-CLIO, Inc. (World music series) Includes gamelan traditions of Central Java, Bali and especially on Sunda plus good information on early music history of Southeast Asia (with a CD).

Sumarsam. (1995). *Gamelan: Cultural interaction and musical development in central Java*. Chicago: University of Chicago Press.

Tenzer, M. (1991). *Balinese music*. Seattle: University of Washington Press.

Tenzer, M. (2000). *Gamelan gong kebyar: The art of twentieth-century Balinese music*. Chicago: University of Chicago Press.

Endnotes

1   For teaching modern bamboo *angklung* music, see the author's article:
Han, K. H. (2010). Bamboo is fun: Bamboo angklung for the classroom. In M. C. Moore (Ed.), *Kaleidoscope of cultures, a celebration of multicultural research and practice: Proceedings of the MENC/University of Tennessee National Symposium on Multicultural Music* (pp. 59-62; 122-1280. Lanham, ML: Rowman & Littlefield Education.

2   McPhee's lovely children's tale published in 1948 (*A Club of Small Men*) was based on his experience in forming a children's *gamelan angklung* club in Sayan Village. It is a good reading assignment for students. In the 2002 new edition, the illustrations (by Trina Boham Tyrie) are interesting, but the metallophones keys should be four instead of five and the kettle number should be four instead of three (cover, pp. 28-29, p. 47). See **References**. In the summer of 1985, the author studied *gamelan angklung* in Sayan Village, Bali by using the very set of instruments purchased by McPhee and donated to this children's club. The instructors were Pak Kantor and Pak Reca (an original member of McPhee's club).

3   Other versions with different pitch sequences exist. The version presented in this chapter is the most common one.

The author's complete Balinese gamelan angklung made by I Made Gableran of Blahbatuh, Bali. Photo by the author, 2005.

Gamelan angklung at a tooth-filling ceremony, Ubud, Bali. Photo by the author, Aug. 1985.

The University of Kentucky Gamelan Angklung directed by the author. Photo by Roger Chui, Oct. 22, 2006

Kentucky Orff-Schulwerk Association Workshop directed by the author - *Old Man Dance*. Photo by Maria Han, Oct. 23, 2004.

Chapter 18

Neuroscience, Technology, and Music Education

Robyn Staveley

The challenge for all educators is how to best use resources to enhance the learning opportunities for their students. Technology in education has provided a strong way for storing and creating knowledge, quick and accessible pathways to information, and more avenues for providing specific learning programs for our students. Music technology has allowed us to access notation and audio software, repertoire and sound sources, authentic examples of music from many cultures, the ability to improvise and compose with many layers created by one's self or others, and so much more. We can even become a choir or ensemble across the globe in synchrony—such exciting possibilities. The challenge in using technology is how embodied the experience is.

Musical experience is embodied. When we play an instrument, sing or move, the conceptual understanding that develops is grounded in our sensory and motor systems. Our experiences shape our minds (Lakoff & Johnson, 1999). The specific qualities of our experiences allow us to build rich networks of knowledge in multimodal, neuronal structures. These networks are also deeply linked to our emotions. The joy of making music with others elicits levels of ecstatic participation that words often cannot express. That embodiment is dependent upon sensory-rich, real, and personal experience with being musical.

It is interesting that in the discussions and research about how to make technology more suited to the way that humans learn and perform in the environment, a similar debate about "form and matter" (Keller, 2011) has taken place in cognitive neuroscience in the mind/body debate. Computational models of the mind represent learning as modular, with information being processed in specific and separate modules with rules and codes that are content specific and interact with each other only through specific representations (Brooks, 1991). Computer science is now acknowledging that intelligence is not built through separate units of mind and body (in humans), or form and matter (in computer science), but that intelligence is developed through an active process between the body, the mind, tools (affordances) (Bonderup, 2009; Menin & Schiavio, 2012), and others in the environment (Vala, Ribeiro, & Paiva, 2012; Garbarini & Adenzato, 2004). Robotic science has followed these principles by developing robots that integrate motor sensory input with the environment (Davis & Markman, 2012). Arts, law, humanities, advertising, and other creative areas are all "profitably evaluating" the implications of embodied cognition (Davis et al., 2012). Embodied cognition asserts that the neural structures that allow us to learn from others also allow us to put ourselves into the minds of others to understand intention, emotions, and empathy (Aziz-Zadeh & Ivry, 2009; Gazzola, Aziz-Zadeh, & Keysers, 2006; Hickok, Gallese, Rochat, & Berchio, 2012). In evolutionary terms, embodied cognition allows us to understand others and be more successful socially and therefore, survive.

Just as architecture is building spaces that serve the bodies that will use the space, technology is becoming more responsive to how humans interact with the environment. Although in the past, technology has been a type of "extended brain" (Clark, 2005), iPads and other devices are now affording humans the ability to intuitively and kinesthetically interact and feed backward and forward between self and device.

Much of how we learn is through being responsive to others through reading their emotions. The structures in the brain that respond to facial expressions are mirror neurons and are situated in the motor systems in the brain. When we perceive a facial expression of others, we understand it through our own past experiences of when we had that expression on our faces. Our motor neurons fire in response to these expressions, and the memory "map" attached to that expression gives us the understanding of what the other person is likely to be feeling and thinking (Aziz-Zadeh & Ivry, 2009; Cartmill, Beilock, & Goldin-Meadow, 2012; Gazzola, Aziz-Zadeh, & Keysers, 2006; Ocampo & Kritikos, 2011). Much of how we perform when being musical is reliant on these structures for understanding the intent, the feeling, and the synchrony with others that musical endeavors so often involve. Without a human body to interact with, to respond and understand these motives, something of the essence of being musical can be missed.

We already know that some disembodied experiences are not as strongly represented in the brain as real, embodied experiences. For example, mirror neurons for visual and auditory stimuli respond more to biological stimuli than synthetic (Leveque, Giovanni, & Schon, 2012); that is, humans respond more to a human voice than an artificial voice as the human voice engenders more neuronal action because of rich, multimodal memories and experiences. Mirror neurons for an action were found to fire both when an action was performed and when the sound related to the action was heard (Kohler et al., 2002). This circumstance is because, again, when we hear that sound the whole network of neurons associated with that sound fires. When reading music, the motor cortex fires as if the reader is performing the act or watching the act. The strength of the firing is reliant on past experience of reading and playing an instrument or singing (Behmer & Jantzen, 2011). If there had never been the experience of a real instrument, only a two-dimensional image on a screen, the motor processing and conceptual development would be much less rich.

Imagine how the neurons would fire when we hear a marimba for example. Some of the memories included in that neuronal map might be:

- the size of the instrument and our spatial relationship to it;
- the weight of the instruments and the mallets;
- what our bodies did to make a sound;
- how much energy was exerted;
- the variations in sound in relation to exertion of the body;
- which body parts were involved;
- what the instrument looked like;

- the relationship of the size of the instrument and components, and the pitch;
- the audible range of pitches;
- the feel of the vibrations from the sound;
- the feel of the material the instrument and mallets were made of;
- how the body learned to play the instrument;
- other people who were involved with the learning process;
- other people who played together with you;
- the space where the instrument was played;
- the repertoire that was played;
- relationships of pitch to size of instrument, succession of notes; and
- how our bodies explored the instrument and responded to these explorations.

And the list would go on and on. Many people report that they love the smell of their instrument, the texture of the wood, or the smell of the resin. All these aspects are looped into the map of this instrument in the brain. Such rich representations of our bodies being musical, or even being the music, are only possible when our bodies are involved in the learning. Then, at a later time, when thinking about the sound of a marimba, all these neurons would fire, and there would be a representation—an imagination—for thinking abstractly about playing the marimba.

If technology can provide us with embodied experiences as rich and multisensory and active as our bodies can provide to develop conceptual knowledge, then we have a good justification for using it as a tool for enhancing student learning. Current trends in touch and sensory development of technology are indicating that this is beginning to be the case. I hope we will be able to look back and note our efforts to use every available technology to enhance learning and contribute to the research in developing these tools.

References

Aziz-Zadeh, L., & Ivry, R. B. (2009). The human mirror neuron system and embodied representations. In D. Sternad (Ed.), *Progress in motor control* (pp. 355-376). US: Springer Science + Business Media.

Behmer, L. P., & Jantzen, K. J. (2011). Reading sheet music facilitates sensorimotor mu-desynchronization in musicians. *Clinical Neurophysiology, 122*(7), 1342-1347.

Bonderup, D. N. (2009). Affordances revisited: Articulating a Merleau-Pontian view. *International Journal of Computer-Supported Collaborative Learning, 4*(2), 151-170.

Brooks, R. A. (1991). Intelligence without representation. *Artificial Intelligence, 47*(1), 139-159.

Cartmill, E. A., Beilock, S., & Goldin-Meadow, S. (2012). A word in the hand: Action, gesture and mental representation in humans and non-human primates. *Philosophical Transactions of the Royal Society B: Biological Sciences, 367*(1585): 129-143.

Clark, A. (2005). Intrinsic content, active memory and the extended mind. *Analysis, 65*(285): 1-11.

Davis, J. I., Benforado, A., Esrock, E., Turner, A., Dalton, R. C., van Noorden, L., & Leman, M. (2012). Four applications of embodied cognition. *Topics in Cognitive Science, 4*(4), 786-793.

Davis, J., & Markman, A. (2012). Embodied cognition as a practical paradigm: Introduction to the topic, the future of embodied cognition. *Topics in Cognitive Science, 4*(4): 685-691.

Gallese, V., Rochat, M. J., & Berchio, C. (2012). The mirror mechanism and its potential role in autism spectrum disorder. *Developmental Medicine & Child Neurology, 55*(1), 15-22.

Garbarini, F., & Adenzato, M. (2004). At the root of embodied cognition: Cognitive science meets neurophysiology. *Brain and Cognition, 56*, 100-106.

Gazzola, V., Aziz-Zadeh, L., & Keysers, C. (2006). Empathy and the somatotopic auditory mirror system in humans. *Current Biology, 16* (18), 1824-1829.

Hickok, G. (2012). Do mirror neurons subserve action understanding? *Neuroscience Letters.* Retrieved from http://dx.doi.org/10.1016/j.neulet.2012.11.001.

Keller, E. F. (2011). Towards a science of informed matter. *Studies in History and Philosophy of Science Part C: Studies in History and Philosophy of Biological and Biomedical Sciences, 42*(2), 174.

Kohler, E., Keysers, C., Umiltà, M. A., Fogassi, L., Gallese, V., & Rizzolatti, G. (2002). Hearing sounds, understanding actions: Action representation in mirror neurons. *Science, 297*(5582), 846-848.

Lakoff, G., & Johnson, M. (1999). *Philosophy in the flesh: The embodied mind and its challenge to western thought.* US: Basic Books.

Leveque, Y., Giovanni, A., & Schon, D. (2012). Pitch-matching in poor singers: Human model advantage. *Journal of Voice, 26*(3), 293-298.

Menin, D., & Schiavio, A. (2012). Rethinking musical affordances. *Avant,* 2, 201-215.

Ocampo, B., & Kritikos, A. (2011). Interpreting actions: The goal behind mirror neuron function. *Brain Research Reviews, 67*(1), 260-267.

Vala, M., Ribeiro, T., & Paiva, A. (2012). A model for embodied cognition in autonomous agents. In Y. Nakano, M. Neff, A. Paiva, & M. Walker (Eds.), *Intelligent virtual agents*, Vol. 7502 (pp. 505-507). Berlin: Springer.

ORFF SCHULWERK
Lesson Plans for the
Twenty-First-Century Classroom

Selected Resources for Orff Schulwerk

Books

Carley, I. M. (Ed.) (1977). *Orff Re-Echoes*. Book I. American Orff-Schulwerk Association.

Carley, I. M. (Ed.) (1985). *Orff Re-Echoes*. Book II. American Orff-Schulwerk Association.

Frazee, J. (1998). *Discovering Keetman*. Schott.

Frazee, J. (2007). *Orff Schulwerk Today: Nurturing Musical Expression and Understanding*. Schott.

Frazee, J. (2008). *Playing Together: An Introduction to Teaching Orff Instruments*. Schott.

Frazee, J. (2012). *Artful-Playful-Mindful*. Schott.

Frazee, J., and Kreuter, K. (1987). *Discovering Orff*. Schott.

Keetman, G. (1974). *Elementaria*. Translated by Margaret Murray. Schott.

Orff, C. (1976). *The Schulwerk*. Schott.

Saliba, K. K. (1990). *Accent on Orff*. Pearson.

Steen, A. (1992). *Exploring Orff*. Schott.

Warner, B. (1991). *Orff Schulwerk: Applications in the Classroom*. Prentice Hall.

Orff Schulwerk Literature

Aaron, T. et. al. (1977-1993). *Music for Children, American Edition, Vols. I-III*. Schott.

Goodkin, D. (2002). *Play, Sing, and Dance*. Schott.

Keetman, G. (1965). *Rhythmische ubung*. Schott.

Keetman, G. (1966). *Spielbuch fur xylophon*. I-III. Schott.

Orff, C., and Keetman, G. (1950). *Music for Children, Vols. I-V*. English version edited by Margaret Murray. Schott.

Books of Folk Song Orchestrations

Boshkof, R. (1984*). All Around the Buttercup*. Schott.

Frazee, J. (1983). *Singing in the Season*. MMB Music.

Frazee, J., and Steen, A. (1985). *Baker's Dozen*. Alfred.

McRae, S. (1980). *Chatter with the Angels*. MMB Music.

McRae, S. (1982). *Glow Ree Bee*. Memphis Musicraft Publications.

McRae, S. (1985). *American Sampler*. Memphis Musicraft Publications.

Folk Song Resources

Choksy, L. (1987). *One Hundred Twenty Singing Games and Dances*. Pearson.

Erdei, P. and Komlos, K. (2004). *150 American Folk Songs*. Boosey & Hawkes.

Johnson, R. (1984). *Folk Songs North America Sings*. E. C. Kerby Ltd.

Kersey, R. E. (1985). *Just Five*. Alfred.

Locke. E. (2004). *Sail Away*. Boosey & Hawkes.

Lomax. A. (1960). *The Folk Songs of North America*. Doubleday & Company.

Seeger. R. (2002). *American Folk Songs for Children*. Music Sales America.

Poetry and Other Resources

Childcraft Encyclopedia, Vol. 1-15. (1995). World Book, Inc.

de Regniers, B. S. (Ed.). (1988). *Sing a Song of Popcorn: Every Child's Book of Poems*. Scholastic, Inc.

Fitzgerald, M., McCord, K., & Berg, S. (2003). *Chop-Monster, Jr*. Alfred Music.

Goodkin, D. (2004). *Now's the Time: Teaching Jazz to All Ages*. Pentatonic Press.

Goodkin, D. (2009). *Intery Mintery*. Pentatonic Press.

Larrick, N. (1999), Ed. *Piping Down the Valleys Wild*. Horn Book.

Lopez-Ibor, S. (2011). *Blue is the Sea*. Pentatonic Press.

Mother Goose (many illustrated versions)

Prelutsky, J. (Ed.). (1983). *The Random House Book of Poetry for Children*. Random House.

Web Sites

American Orff-Schulwerk Association. (http://www.aosa.org).

Alliance for Active Music Making. (http://www.allianceamm.org/).

Key for Lesson Plans

S	Student(s)
T	Teacher
SR	Soprano Recorder
AR	Alto Recorder
SG	Soprano Glockenspiel
AG	Alto Glockenspiel
SX	Soprano Xylophone
AX	Alto Xylophone
BX	Bass Xylophone
SM	Soprano Metallophone
AM	Alto Metallophone
BM	Bass Metallophone
NPP	Non-Pitched Percussion
BP	Body Percussion

MFC   *Music for Children*, Carl Orff, Gunild Keetman, and English version adapted by Margaret Murray

A Note About the Lessons that Follow

The diverse lessons included in this volume were submitted by a number of individuals. As a result, the language used in these documents differs across lesson plans. Although some efforts were made to incorporate a consistent lesson plan format, the lesson plans are presented here using their original language to maximize and highlight the variety of successful uses of the Orff-Schulwerk approach by individuals from different perspectives and experiences.

These lessons represent a variety of cultural resources, the use of technology, and materials from the Orff literature as well as those beyond. All lessons have been field-tested to work well and you will find individual styles in the lesson process and original arrangements. Teachers in the Orff-Schulwerk approach are creative thinkers who adapt resources to fit the abilities and ages of their students. We hope you enjoy using these lesson samples and are encouraged to create more for your students.

In some of these lesson plans, musical scores for Orff arrangements are provided. In these scores, parts for all instruments are written with middle C as the lowest pitch, which represents the longest bar of that instrument. Sounding pitches may differ from written pitches (e.g., bass xylophones sound one octave lower than written pitches). Using the specified instruments will result in the intended registers.

LESSON PLANS

Lesson Plan 1: Gumboot Dancing
Written by Janice Evans, presented by Nicola Mason

Lesson Plan 2: Hop, Old Squirrel
Lori F. Gooding

Lesson Plan 3: Taiko and Technology, Part 1
Cindy Hall

Lesson Plan 3: Taiko and Technology, Part 2
Cindy Hall

Lesson Plan 4: Gamelan Angklung Lessons
Han, Kuo-Huang

Lesson Plan 5: Hold On
Jo Ella Hug

Lesson Plan 6: Rum Tum Tugger
Jo Ella Hug

Lesson Plan 7: Band Composition
K. Michelle Lewis

Lesson Plan 8: My Favorite Music
Nicola F. Mason

Lesson Plan 9: G Blues Improvisation
Kimberly McCord

Lesson Plan 10: Cai Shen Dao (财神到)
Orff Arrangement: Margaret Thong

Lesson Plan 1: Gumboot Dancing[1]
Written by Janice Evans, presented by Nicola Mason

Aim

In this lesson, students perform simple body percussion rhythms using gumboots. Gumboot dancing is performed by miners in South Africa.

Musical Objectives

- Students will imitate and explore simple rhythms presented by the teacher.
- Students will perform rhythmic patterns using gumboots while moving.

Materials

- Gumboots. For school children, any gumboots will do—the participants *must* have boots. Feel free to start without boots, using an alternative noisemaker such as plastic bags wrapped around the ankles, but the participants only feel as though they are gumboot dancing when they have boots on! Wrap foam or bubble wrap around the legs inside the boot, sealing the top of the boot, to create a "sound box" inside, just above the ankle.

Process

1. The action:

   A. The boot is struck with an open hand, relaxed at the wrist, above the ankle.

   B. Bend at the knees, not the lower back, to reach the best hitting spot.

   C. Take small steps, which helps to get a flowing rhythm.

2. Start with a basic rhythm, and then put it on the boots.

3. Gradually increase in complexity.

4. Be creative with a range of jumps, stamps, and slaps—in front of the body, behind the body, on the inside of the boot, on the outside of the boot, clicking boots together, etc.

5. Think of the form, e.g., balance the phrases; a dramatic ending on the first beat of the measure is always effective.

6. When you are familiar with basic four-beat patterns, try creating some surprises by changing the meter (careful to keep the rhythm flowing).

7. A useful basic rhythm:

   A. Keep the left foot in place while moving the right foot forward and back:

      i. Step onto the right foot in front.

      ii. Step onto the left foot.

      iii. Step onto the right foot behind.

      iv. Step onto the left foot.

      v. N.B. Keep the steps small; the right foot always only slightly in front of—or behind—the left foot.

8. This action creates a very simple "four beats to the bar" basic, which can be easily altered.

9. I have devised a simple notation of a dance sequence; please remember that the "notation" is just there to give you a starting point from which to create your own rhythms and to enjoy your own ideas.

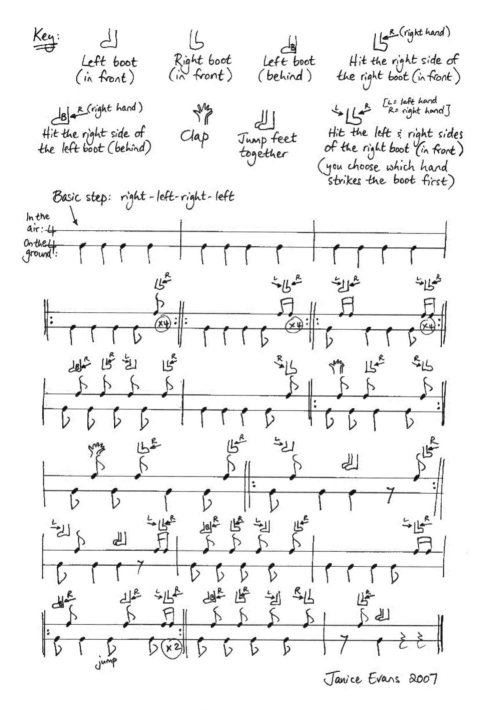

Endnotes

1   This lesson was presented at the *Global Connections in Orff Schulwerk: Reflections from Kentucky* by Nicola F. Mason with the approval of the author, Janice Evans. It was published in the *Orff Beat, 2010*, the yearly journal of the South African Orff-Schulwerk Association.

Lesson Plan 2: Hop, Old Squirrel
Lori F. Gooding

Target Audience Grades 2-3

Aim

In this lesson, students (including those with special needs) will sing a call-and- response song and then create their own call-and-response compositions.

Musical Objectives

- Students will sing *do, re, mi* patterns
- Students will recognize simple forms (call-and-response; AB)
- Students will practice ta and ti-ti rhythms
- Students will improvise a musical call-and-response composition

Non-Musical Objectives

- Students will develop basic conversational skills
- Students will develop impulse control
- Students will develop basic social skills

Materials

- Various NPP or xylophones, metallophones, etc.
- Adaptive mallet holders or hair scrunchies to hold mallets/instruments in place as needed.
- Adaptive instrument holders as needed.
- Visual song aid (song on board, SmartBoard, etc.)

Process

1. Pre-record song with two voices (one female, one male). Play recording.

2. State "This is a call-an-response song." Explain that it is similar to a conversation in which the girl asks a question and the boy responds.

3. Play recording again. Ask students to raise their hands on the question and lower them on the answer. Alternatively, students can "hop" on the question and stand still on the answer.

    A. *Be aware of students with gross motor deficits if hopping. Be prepared to adapt the movements, e.g., everyone does a "seated hop," etc.*

4. Place music on the board. Ask for a volunteer to find the "question"; circle it. Repeat for "answer" but underline it.

    A. *Encourage children with special needs to volunteer. Para-professionals can assist students as needed to facilitate participation.*

    B. *Keep in mind that you may need to musically guide the paraprofessional. They will assist the child, but often need your support and guidance to do so. Paraprofessionals are great resources!*

5. Divide the class into boys and girls; have them sing with the recording. (Girls with the female and boys with the male.) Point to the music on board as children sing.

    A. *Reinforcing educational concepts using multimodal presentations is extremely important for children with special needs. Pointing to the material as you sing encourages participation but also reinforces reading concepts, both musically and academically.*

    B. *If a child is struggling with the appropriate time to sing, visual aids such as stop/go signs or pictures of a boy and girl can be used as cues. Peer models can also be partnered with a child with special needs.*

6. Discuss ways in which the song is similar to a conversation. Use musical cues to prompt conversation points.

    A. *Example: Sing the call at a piano dynamic and the response at a forte dynamic. Ask "In conversation, what might be happening if one person is louder than the other? One person could be angry, yelling, etc.*

    B. *Other possible talking points: taking turns in conversation, listening, eye contact, making sure questions and answers are related, etc.*

7. Divide the class into a series of pairs. Give each child a NPP instrument. Make sure each child within a pair has a different instrument.

    A. *Alternative to hand percussion: Allow children to create conversations on various Orff instruments.*

    B. *For children with special needs, it may be necessary to remove all unwanted bars, i.e., only leave do, re, and mi on the instruments. This sets the child up for success.*

8. Ask them to create their own call-and-response song. The first child in the pair will have four beats to ask a question, and the second child will respond for four. Adding words will reinforce the conversational concept and may facilitate improvisation. If possible, have them write out the words.

    A. *Writing promotes academic skills as well as fine motor skills for children with cognitive and motor delays. Encourage children to make the questions and answers "fit" together, as they would in a conversation.*

    B. *This approach would be an excellent time to partner a child with a special need with a typically-developing child who can serve as a peer model. This would also work if using small groups instead of partners. In other words, a typically-developing child and a child with a special need can partner on the "call" while two other children partner on the "response." This may be especially useful if the child with special needs requires help to physically play an instrument.*

    C. *Encourage them to make eye contact, because it is necessary for both musical communication and verbal/nonverbal communication.*

9. Have each pair perform.

    A. Review the call-and-response form and discuss its similarities to conversation.

    B. It is important to help students transfer or generalize the musical concept (call-and-response) to the non-musical concept (conversational/social skills and impulse control) by talking about it.

Hop, Old Squirrel

Stanza 2: Jump, old squirrel, etc.
Stanza 3: Skip, old squirrel, etc.
Stanza 4: Run, old squirrel, etc.

Lesson Plan 3: Taiko and Technology, Part 1
Cindy Hall

Target Audience Grades 4-5

Aim
In this lesson, students explore Japanese taiko drumming with the use of YouTube video excerpts.

Musical Objectives
- Students will imitate and improvise in duple meter (quarter and eighth notes) within an aaba phrase form.
- Students will apply stylistic features of Japanese taiko drum playing, viewed on YouTube excerpts, to their rhythmic piece.

Materials
- *MFC*, Vol. 1, p. 67
- Large drums (taiko drums, tubano drums, and/or hand drums) with sticks/mallets
- YouTube sites:
  - YouTube #1: http://goo.gl/DWQae
  - YouTube #2: http://goo.gl/stH8f
  - YouTube #3: http://goo.gl/fSXdJ

Process

1. Students walk to steady beat as T plays hand drum.
2. Students clap, in place, when T taps rim of drum.
3. Students move/clap to pattern (clap on rests).

4. Students move/clap to new pattern:

5. Students listen to four phrases of rhythm and ID form aaba.

6. Students transfer rhythm to hand drums (notes = drum head, rests = taps on rim).
7. Students divide into two groups, one plays drum head part, one rim part; switch.
8. Students practice with a partner using both parts.
9. Watch YouTube Excerpt #1 (0:00 – 0:24 seconds, then 3:50 – 4:15) discuss observations about how drums are played (skin/rim), both hands together or alternating mallets.
10. Transfer piece to standing drums or hand drum held by partner.
11. Listen to change in pattern, spoken; identify which phrase does not change:

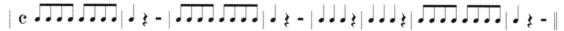

12. Experiment with way to play new rhythm on drum (alternating mallets?).
13. Watch YouTube Excerpt #2 (0:58 —1:28), observe mallets in air, jumping feet apart/together, yelling commands.
14. Work in small groups using combination of drum head and rim to play revised version of piece, share solutions, decide on one for the class, practice together.

15. Students imitate eight-beat phrases of new rhythm patterns (quarter, eighth, rest); Students become leaders to give eight-beat patterns.

16. Students, with partners or small groups, create new eight-beat pattern to share.

17. Listen to group patterns, choose two contrasting eight-beat phrases for new piece, decide how to arrange in aaba form.

18. Notate piece together.

19. Brainstorm how to play rhythm of piece using ideas from video.

20. Perform both pieces, ABA.

21. Back with hand drum, imitate down/up strokes, two patterns:

22. Listen to where patterns fit with known Part I, performed by T;

23. Imitate patterns, with Part I spoken.

24. Review Part I of piece.

25. Students play Part I, T plays Part 2 (switch).

26. Make change to Part I (see score in *Music for Children*, Vol. I, p. 67).

27. Make one change to Part 2 (see score, play on downbeat of fourth phrase).

28. In half groups, practice both parts.

29. Practice in small groups.

30. Transfer to taiko drum sticking, with student ideas.

31. Watch taiko drum Excerpt #3, (1:59 —2:35).

32. Discuss observations (karate-style sideways gestures, jumps).

33. Work as a class to create final choreography for piece.

34. Add "backbeat" rhythm (ti-tiri, ti-tiri).

35. Review B section piece, in small groups, use rhythm of B section but create original choreography.

36. Perform "rondo" style with small groups sharing their B section ideas.

Lesson Plan 3: Taiko and Technology, Part 2
Cindy Hall

Target Audience Grades 4-5

Aim

In this lesson extension, students explore Japanese melodic patterns and develop simple accompaniment and choreography.

Musical Objectives

- Students will extend the rhythmic piece to a melodic exploration of the Japanese scale found in the folk song *Sakura, Sakura*.
- Students will apply stylistic features of accompaniment to *Sakura, Sakura* using YouTube excerpts.
- Students will create a "fan" dance based upon stylistic features of YouTube excerpts.

Materials

- *MFC*, Vol. 1, p. 67
- Large drums (taiko drums, tubano drums, and/or hand drums) with sticks/mallets
- Orff instruments
- A variety of NPP instruments (wind chimes, woodblock, finger cymbals)
- Fans (can be made with paper plates)

- YouTube site:
  - YouTube #4: http://goo.gl/WC5KL

Process

1. Watch a selected YouTube clip of fan dancers.
2. Discuss movements fan dancers make.
3. Experiment with fans.
4. Listen to *Sakura, Sakura* melody (http://en.wikipedia.org/wiki/File:Sakura.song.png) on starting pitch A, played on alto recorder or other melodic instrument; identify repetition.
5. Together use pictures of four different types of fans to make a symbolic chart of melodic form: abcbcad.
6. Imitate phrases of song *Sakura, Sakura* (to simplify, sing on loo).
7. Sing while working on small group fan dances.
8. On barred instruments, figure out notes used for the first three phrases of melody (BC EF AB C).
9. Explore transferring rhythm of taiko drum piece (*MFC* Volume I, p. 67) to scale, beginning and ending on E, use student ideas to develop both parts:

10. For orchestration ideas for piece, listen to and discuss YouTube excerpt #4 (0:00-0:30).
11. For a final performance, divide into work groups: students use iPads or computers to further research and elaborate on their portion of the performance.
    A. Song (additional examples of song for pronunciation and style).
       i. http://goo.gl/Akm7Y
       ii. http://goo.gl/naMbc

B. Fan dance (a Chinese example of fan dancing with ideas for group choreography).

    i.   http://goo.gl/DtYiA

C. Taiko drumming (a longer video example by "Kodo" with many styles of drumming).

    i.   http://goo.gl/m4AYv

D. Additional work group if the project extends to language arts study:

    i.   http://goo.gl/44HrM

Lesson Plan 4: Gamelan Angklung Lessons
Han, Kuo-Huang

Target Audience Grades 4-6

Aim

In this lesson, students explore Indonesian culture by performing gamelan music on traditional classroom instruments.

Musical Objectives

- To introduce a new culture (in this case, Bali, Indonesia) as part of the multicultural education.
- To learn gamelan music through hands-on practice. Action (dance improvisation) in some pieces is possible to enhance interest.
- To use existing Orff and other classroom instruments as substitutes due to their similarities in structure.
- To cooperate with art (masks, costumes, props) and social studies (history, geography) classes.
- To understand music in relation to Balinese culture and compare that of Western culture.
- To showcase the results in a school assembly.

Materials

- SM, AM
- Gongs of various sizes with beaters

- Cymbals
- Recorder
- Two drums (on lap)
- Flowers
- Basket
- Young girl mask
- Old man mask
- Walking cane

General Teaching Procedures.

(All barred instruments should be set for diatonic pitches 1, 2, 3, and 5, or *do re mi sol*.)

1. Ask students to remove their shoes (leave them at the door, if possible) and never step over instruments. Respect Orff instruments the way they would have respected real gamelan instruments in the native environment. Sit on the floor behind or next (gongs) to instruments.

2. Inform them that the gong (especially the big gong) is always the spirit of the ensemble and the drum is always the leader, kind or king (queen), and prime minister (CEO) respectively.

3. In a public performance, offer flowers to the gong and distribute flowers to all members to be put in their hair or behind an ear.

4. Since the pieces are so short, dynamic alternation (*forte* once, *piano* once, or other ways) is recommended.

5. **Always teach by rote.** One group of students sings the melody and the other claps the punctuation (dividing into several smaller units for different instruments); then reverse the group assignment. These are short and easy pieces.

Process

For Lesson 1: *Tabuh Empat* (Appendix 1)

This is the last section of a multi-section traditional *lelambatan* (slow) ceremonial composition titled *Tabuh Emput*. The slow tempo makes it easier for beginners. *Tabuh* means "composition" (among others) and *empat* means "four." The best translation would be a *"Composition in Four (Phrases)."* The repeated first melodic line consists of phrases one and two. The notation is based upon the Javanese system with a little modification. This version is based upon the performance by Banjar (Ward) Belawan, Abiansemal Village.

1. The first line or half line is usually a solo introduction played by a leader (one medium metallophone).

2. Everyone (except medium gong and secondary time beater) comes in on the "gong beat," which is the last note of the introduction (enclosed with a big circle on the pitch). From there on, the piece is in ostinato. The gong beats at the end of the introduction and the end of the piece marked the cycle.

3. The lower line is for the bass instruments.

4. Leading drum comes in one and a half beats before the "gong beat." Two drums play alternatively after that point. Using only one drummer playing two drums is better. Drum part follows the melody most of the time. Limited improvisation is allowed.

5. A louder (loud enough to be heard by members only) drum beat on the third beat (medium gong stroke) of the fourth phrase indicates the piece is coming to an end, thus slowing down in tempo. If no louder stroke, keep going on in the cycle.

6. Recorder follows the melody with improvisation (using scale pitches 5 & 6 allowed). The cymbals follow the drums.

7. In gamelan theory, even beats are more important than odd beats (marked by "x" and performed by the primary time beater). The most important beat is the gong beat (marked by O and performed by the large gong and all melodic instruments).

8. A slash over a number indicates a muted (un-pitched) sound (striking the key with the mallet in one hand while dampening the very same key simultaneously with the other hand).

Process

For Lesson 2: *Waled* (Appendix II bottom)

This was a West Javanese (Sundanese) gamelan piece the author learned in 1974 and transcribed for *gamelan angklung*. Using some of the improvisation methods learned then, the author arranged it as an exercise in several parts for *gamelan angklung*. The tempo is *andante*.

1. The composition begins with a solo introduction (derived from the second half of the melody).

2. Everyone (except the medium gong and the secondary time beater) comes in at the gong beat at the end of the introduction. From there on, the piece is in ostinato.

3. The lower line is for the bass instruments.

4. The remaining three lines are some of the improvisations the author learned. Select one or two melody players for each line.

5. The bass and two melody players play the same thing continuously in ostinato to the end.

6. Select one or two melody players to play a simple doubling of the melody (first line). Come in after two cycles of (5) and continue in ostinato to the end.

7. Select one or two melody players also to play a simple doubling of the melody (second line) but ahead of the previous line (6). Come in after four cycles of (5) and continue in ostinato to the end.

8. Select one or two melody players to play the elaboration line (third line). Come in after six cycles of (5) and continue in ostinato to the end. This is a good melody for the recorder player with improvisation. Reminder: the dot indicates a half or an extension of the previous note.

9. Gongs, time beaters, cymbals, etc. come in at the beginning.

10. When everyone is tired, the drummer hits a louder stroke on beat 8 (medium gong beat). Slow down and end.

11. Teachers are encouraged to arrange other orders of entrances or exits for the different parts.

Process

For Lesson 3: *Flower Girl* (Appendix II top)

In March 1984, Professor John Emigh of Brown University came to give a lecture and performance of his work *The Little Red Riding Shawl* (a work combining Balinese *topeng* mask theater and Western elements) at Northern Illinois University. The author's student Balinese *gamelan angklung* group was invited to provide the musical accompaniment. One of the pieces he taught us was this one-phrase happy tune to accompany the flower girl character (Red Riding Shawl). Following Prof. Emigh, the author always uses a student wearing a girl mask and mimicking a girl giving flower petals to the audience.

1. The solo introduction is derived from the phrase itself. Everyone, except the medium gong, comes in at the gong beat. Note: Due to its fast speed (*allegretto*), the secondary time beater is omitted. But, it can be used by playing with the primary time beater simultaneously on beats 2 and 4 (pitches 5 and 2 respectively).

2. The piece is in ostinato until the dancer exits. At that moment the drummer strikes a louder stroke on beat 3 (pitch 3) to slow everyone down to the end.

3. A young girl's mask is recommended. A basket with flower petals or paper flowers is needed.

Process

For Lesson 4: *Topeng Tua* (*Old Man Dance*) (Appendix II middle)

Also taught by Prof. John Emigh, this is a simplified version of a longer composition accompanying a dance. This composition is another good example for action (dance improvisation). The general tempo is that of *largo*. But, unlike the *Flower Girl*, the tempo changes with the action of the dancer who mimics an old man's walking and action (including teasing the audience).

1. At the end of the solo introduction, everyone except the medium gong and secondary time beater comes in with the gong. From there on the piece is in ostinato.

2. The dancer can change movements in accordance with an old man's movement while the tempo of the music changes accordingly. The drummer watches the movement and directs the band.

3. As the dancer exits, the drummer strikes a louder stroke on beat 8 (medium gong; pitch 2) to slow everyone down to end.

4. An old man's mask and a walking cane are recommended. See Chapter 17 for a performance of *Topeng Tua* with Orff instruments.

Appendix I

Tabuh Empat   (Balinese Gamelan Angklung)

1 2 3 5 = G A B d

O = big gong
( ) = medium gong
x = primary time beater
° = secondary time beater
top line = small and medium metallophones
bottom line = large metallophones

1, 2, 3 etc. = ♩ ♩ ♩

33 32 = ♫ ♫

2 ·3 = ♪. ♩

♪ = un-pitched   K. H. Han <khan@niu.edu>

Appendix II

Simple Pieces for Balinese Gamelan Angklung

FLOWER GIRL

5 5 33 $\overline{2\,5\,3\,2}$ 1 ⟦ 1　55　33　$\overline{2\,5\,3\,2}$　1⟧
　　　　　①　　5　　3　　2　　　　①
　　　　　x　　x　　x　　x　　　　x

OLD MAN DANCE

$\overline{2\,3\,1\,2}$ 3 · 5 · 3 1 12 1
　　　　　　　　　　　　　　①
　　　　　　　　　　　　　　x

⟦ 2　12　13　35　35　35　32　23　23　23　23　35　35　35　31　12　1⟧
　　　　　　3　　　　　　(2)　　　　　　　3　　　　　　　①
　₀　X　₀　X　₀　X　₀　X　₀　X　₀　X　₀　X　₀　X

WALED

5　2　5　3　5　2　5　3
　　　　　　　　　③
　　　　　　　　　x

⟦ 3　1　3　2　|　3　1　3　2　|　5　2　5　3　|　5　2　5　3 ⟧
　1　　2　　　1　(2)　　2　　3　　　2　　③
　₀　X　₀　X　　₀　X　₀　X　　₀　X　₀　X　　₀　X　₀　X

3 3 1 1 3 3 2 2 3 3 1 1 3 3 2 2 5 5 2 2 5 5 3 3 5 5 2 2 5 5 3

3 3 1 1 3 3 2 2 3 3 1 1 3 3 2 2 5 5 2 2 5 5 3 3 5 5 2 2 5 5 3 3

3 5 1 2 3 5 2 ·|3 5 1 2 3 5 2 ·|5 3 2 3 5 2 3 ·|5 3 2 3 5 2 3 ·|

O = large gong　　　　　( ) = medium gong

x = primary time beater　　　₀ = secondary time beater

K.H. Han

LESSON PLAN 5: HOLD ON
Jo Ella Hug

Target Audience Grades 6-8

Aim
In this lesson, students will improvise on Orff instruments and vocally in la pentatonic.

Musical Objectives
- Students will learn a folk melody from Kentucky and perform in canon
- Students will identify change of metric grouping from 2 to 3
- Students will improvise using notes from the pentatonic scale (la tonal center)

Materials
- Chart of pentatonic scale in solfege syllables
- Sticky note
- Orff instruments (SX, AX, BX, contrabass bars C, D, E, F)

Process
1. Listen as teacher models song *Hold On*.
2. Using chart of pentatonic scale, listen again and analyze notes used in melody.

3. Song initially appears to be in F pentatonic with *la* as the tonal center: note D. Determine that it is not a pentatonic scale as it doesn't use syllable *sol*. Musicians describe this scale as a tetratonic scale – pentatonic minus one of the usual players on the team.

4. Use the sticky note to cover syllable *sol*. Teacher sings again and shows the melodic shape on the pentatonic scale chart.

5. Focus attention on last three measures of song. Add clap on strong beat (words *KEEP* and *ON*) and chest thump(s) on weak beat(s).

6. Discover the meter change and identify the octave leap that precedes the three beat measure.

7. Sing the repeating phrase (measure 5-7, 10-12) but leave space for teacher to sing the unknown material in measures 8 & 9.

8. Assimilate melody and perform in circle formation. Feet are stationary but weight shifts into the circle with the clap on strong beats and out with the chest thump(s) on weak beat(s).

9. Divide group into two circles and sing in two-part canon at the interval of 2 beats.

Improvisation

1. Return to chart of pentatonic scale in solfege syllables and determine that improvisation will use pentatonic scale even though *Hold On* was missing one of the notes in the pentatonic scale.

2. Have students identify notes that will be used for improvisation: D, F, G, A, C2, D2

3. Set up SX, AX, BX and identify note D as the tonal center in the F pentatonic scale.

4. Transfer 3 note pitch patterns sung by the teacher in solfege syllables to the barred instruments.

5. Imitate various logical (usually stepwise in the pentatonic scale) patterns to secure comfort.

6. Select 3 or 4 patterns that students like and write them in a visible place for easy reference.

7. During the improvisation, maintain meter in 2.

8. Direct students toward elemental patterns for improvisation to avoid random and chaotic choices: (a) choose a pattern, (a) repeat the same pattern, (b) choose a different pattern, and (a) return to the first pattern. Other easy patterns for students:

    a a b b   a b a b   a b a c   a a b c

9. Add a supportive ostinato on the contrabass bars.

10. Transfer experience of improvising on barred instruments to vocal improvisation.

11. Review chart of pentatonic scale and use for vocal echo preparation of potential patterns:

    LA
    SOL

    MI
    RE
    DO

    LA

12. Apply same rules about repetition as in step #8.

13. When improvisation is familiar, encourage the use of word phrases from the text to substitute for solfege syllables.

14. Create a plan for performance that includes the song *Hold On* as well as vocal and/or barred improvisation.

Hold On

Kentucky

One of these days a-bout four o' clock, This old world's goin' to reel and rock.

Keep your hand, keep your hand to the plow, hold on. Hold on, Hold on, Keep your hand, keep your hand to the plow, hold on.

My source for this song: *My Recorder Reader 2* , by Isabel McNeill Carley, Brasstown Press

LESSON PLAN 6: RUM TUM TUGGER
Jo Ella Hug

Target Audience Grades 4-6

Aim

In this lesson, students explore the concept of Same, Similar, and Different and improvise in speech, body percussion, and barred instruments.

Musical Objectives

- Students will understand how to construct an 8 beat phrase that has two similar parts
- Students will improvise using notes from the C pentatonic scale

Materials

- Visual representation:

#1	#2	#3	RUMTUM	#5	#6	#7	CAT

- Orff instruments (SG, AG, SX, AX, BX)

Process

1. Learn text of *Rum Tum Tugger* through participation:

> Rum Tum Tugger is a curious cat.
> C – U – R – I – O – U – S
> Rum Tum Tugger is a curious cat.
> C – U – R – I – O – U – S

> *(Adapted from the poem The Rum Tum Tugger by T. S. Elliot;*
> *contained in Old Possums's Book of Practical Cats)*

2. Use various body percussion beat patterns to reinforce underlying beat.

3. Transfer rhythm of words to body percussion:

> Rum Tum Tugger is a curious cat.
> *(Alternating pats on shoulders)*

> C – U – R – I – O – U – S
> *(Pat Clap Snap Clap **Pat Clap Snap**)*

> Rum Tum Tugger is a curious cat.
> *(Alternating pats on shoulders)*

> C – U – R – I – O – U – S
> *(Pat Clap Snap Clap **Pat   Pat   Pat**)*

4. Transfer rhythm established by word patterns and body percussion to barred instruments in C pentatonic (C, D, E, G, A). Notice the relationship between the body percussion and the note choices. Body percussion prepares the student for success:

Rum Tum Tugger is a curious cat.	*(note G)*
C – U – R – I – O – U – S	*(C D E D C D E --)*
Rum Tum Tugger is a curious cat.	*(note G)*
C – U – R – I – O – U – S	*(C D E D C C C --)*

5. Label this melody as the repeating section of a rondo to be constructed after the improvisation part of the lesson. Add simple bordun to assist in rhythmic accuracy.

Improvisation

6. When poem and melody are familiar, focus attention to word rhythms as raw material for improvisation. The goal is playing with the rhythmic sound of language, rather than reading rhythmic notation.

Cat = ♩   Rum Tum = ♪ ♩   Curious = ♪♪♩

7. Using the 3 possibilities above, fill in the empty squares:

#1	#2	#3	RUMTUM	#5	#6	#7	CAT

8. Create unity by using the same choices for boxes 5, 6, & 7 that were made for boxes 1, 2 & 3.

•Curious	Cat	Curious	<u>Rum Tum</u>	Curious	Cat	Curious	<u>Cat</u>
•Cat	Cat	Rum Tum	<u>Rum Tum</u>	Cat	Cat	Rum Tum	<u>Cat</u>
•Curious	Curious	Rum Tum	<u>Rum Tum</u>	Curious	Curious	Rum Tum	<u>Cat</u>

9. In elemental style, the two very similar, parts are called a and a'. Learning to recognize same, similar, and different "bits" leads to quicker understanding of the overall structure of melody.

10. Share your improvisation in a small group of 3 - 4. Perform your example with a repeat for a total of 16 beats.

11. Create a group example and transfer it to body percussion. Perform for the larger group.

12. Transfer rhythm established by word patterns / body percussion to barred instruments in C pentatonic (C, D, E, G, A). Save as the contrasting sections in a rondo.

13. Create a rondo that incorporates various components of the lesson into an extended musical experience:

    A = melody as learned in step #4.

    B = first improvisation section as created in step #12.

    A = melody as learned in step #4 in a canon 2 beats apart.

    C = second improvisation section as created in step #12.

    A = melody as learned in step #4 with ostinati.

    Etc.

14. The entire poem *The Rum Tum Tugger* is easily available on the web.

LESSON PLAN 7: BAND COMPOSITION

K. Michelle Lewis

Target Audience Grades 7-8

Aim

In this lesson, students learn how to compose their own band work and perform it in a concert.

Musical Objectives

- Students will compare and contrast music and stories.
- Students will have a deeper understanding of how melody, harmony, and rhythm work together.
- Students will create and perform an original band composition in front of an audience.
- Students will use prior knowledge of music to make connections to old and new works.
- Students will create a bridge in performing and composing music through literary devices.

Materials

- Band instruments

Process

1. Entering Activities (Imitation):
   A. Imitation of rhythm through body percussion.
   B. Imitation of three pitches (do, re, mi) in varying patterns of quarter notes/eighth notes on instruments.

2. Anticipatory Set (Exploration):
   A. Students will compare and contrast stories and music. For example, how are characters in a story introduced? Now, compare this to a new melody in music.

3. Interactive Instruction:
   A. Students will learn basic building blocks of music theory such as intervals, key signatures, chords, rhythm, and scales to use as a springboard to write their piece.

4. Guided Practice:
   A. Students have a choice of working in a small group or alone.
   B. Students spend warm-up time imitating body percussion patterns with the teacher.
   C. Students break into small groups and create a BP piece using four different parts. Exploration of BP in four parts is getting the students to perform rhythmic ostinati independently and will in turn make them a stronger musician when they add the melody and harmony to the part.
   D. Students apply BP to their instruments. They explore rhythmic and melodic ostinati until they get the sound they want.
   E. Students decide key signature, style, time signature, and rhythmic devices used. They will continue to explore a variety of timbres, ostinati, harmonies, etc.
   F. Students begin writing music on manuscript paper.

5. Closure:
   A. Students reflect on the process they took to develop their compositions. They are instructed to answer a reflection sheet honestly; this information will be used for setting goals for improvements for the next composition exercise.

6. Independent Practice:

    A. Students will independently practice their band parts for the composition in preparation for the public performance.

Nota Bene: *This unit is to be completed in several lessons over time. This is the process used in in the research study in Chapter 10 titled "Orff in Band: Research and Implementation" where the students produced and performed their composition "Aftershock".*

LESSON PLAN 8: MY FAVORITE MUSIC
Nicola F. Mason

Target Audience Grades 6-8

Aim
In this lesson, band students improvise and notate rhythmic patterns using rhythmic building blocks based on their favorite type of music.

Musical Objectives
- Students will explore quarter- and eighth-note rhythms through body percussion.
- Students will imitate body percussion rhythms and perform these rhythms on their band instruments.
- Students will improvise eight-beat rhythmic patterns using rhythmic building blocks.
- Students will notate their eight-beat rhythmic patterns.

Materials
- Band instruments
- Smartboard, dry erase board, or chalkboard

Process
1. Teacher presents topic of interest to students, viz. country music, rap music, etc.

2. Students provide related words that comply with rhythms after teacher engages in active listening questions: What word has only one sound? What word has two sounds? (one sound = ♩, 2 sounds = ♫)

3. Teacher demonstrates word selections with body percussion.

4. Students explore appropriate body percussion for various rhythms.

5. Students imitate body percussion and perform rhythm on instrument, concert B-flat.

6. In groups, students improvise their own eight-beat rhythmic building blocks and notate rhythms.

7. Students perform improvisation on instruments on concert B-flat.

8. Time permitting, allow students to perform each other's improvisations

Sample of rhythmic building blocks:

Tay - lor	Swift	Coun-try	Mu-sic

LESSON PLAN 9: G BLUES IMPROVISATION
Kimberly McCord

Kimberly McCord

Target Audience Grades 6-8

Aim
In this lesson, students will improvise on Orff instruments or recorders while playing G Blues arrangement on Orff instruments.

Musical Objectives
- Students will identify I, IV, and V7 chords
- Students will improvise using notes from the three blues scales

Materials
- B. B. King, "Blues in G" from *Blues on the Bayou* (recording available on iTunes)
- Orff instruments (SG, AG, SX, AX, BX, contrabass bars [G, C, and D])
- Ride cymbal or drum set (optional if you have a student who can play drum set)
- Recorders (optional for improvised solos)

Process
1. Listen to B.B. King's *Blues in G* (available on iTunes). Students *patschen* to shuffle feel.

2. Raise and lower hand quickly to show changing of chords. Ask students "who notices a pattern? What is it?" (G,G,G,G,C,C,G,G,D7,C,G,G)

3. "This is the twelve-bar blues." Explain each letter name is one measure and that jazz people call it a "bar" instead of a measure.

4. Teach the bass line first as quarter notes for each pitch. Use mallet visual to help with figuring out what the pattern is for the chord changes.

5. Have BX change to shuffle pattern for students who can play the pattern (listen to bass part on the recording and let students figure out the shuffle rhythm). If you have CBB keep CBB playing on the quarter notes.

6. Teach AX, having students notice notes change via the same chordal pattern.

7. Same step as #6 with SX.

8. Glocks fill in on count four after the SX/AX pattern.

9. Teach drum set shuffle pattern.

Improvised solos use notes from blues scales. Have students identify which notes are used in all three scales (G, C, F).

> G Blues Scale: G, B-flat, C, D-flat or C-sharp, D, and F.
> C Blues Scale: C, E-flat, F, G-flat or F-sharp, G and B-flat.
> D Blues Scale: D, F, G, A-flat or G-sharp, A and C.

Students who struggle with shuffle bass rhythm can play quarter notes on BX.

G Blues

arr. Kimberly McCord

G Blues Notes: G, A, B-flat, B natural, D, E, F natural, G

LESSON PLAN 10: CAI SHEN DAO (财神到)
Orff Arrangement: Margaret Thong

Target Audience Grades 6-8

Aim
Students will perform a traditional Chinese New Year melody arranged for mixed Chinese, Western, and Orff instruments. These assignments will require several lessons to prepare for performance in the Chinese New Year Celebration Concert.

Musical Objectives
Students will:
- identify the ostinato and melodies;
- identify the notes of the C-pentatonic scale;
- describe the stylistic features of the Chinese tune; and
- perform the ensemble and discuss the effect of the different combinations of Chinese, Orff, and other available instruments.

Materials
- Music score: *Cai Shen Dao* anon., arr. Margaret Thong.
  (Tune transcribed as heard on the radio.)
- Ostinato: BX, marimba.
- Rhythm :   Chinese drums, Chinese cymbals, drum set
- Melody 1: SM, pianicas, Chinese flutes
- Melody 2: B-flat clarinet

- Melody 3: Yang Qin
- Melody 4: A repeat of melody 3 played by pianicas, recorders, Chinese flutes, keyboard

Process

1. Cai Shen Dao is a traditional Chinese New Year song that uses the pentatonic scale. Discuss the meaning of this song title and the culture. Chinese New Year is a time when one wishes everyone else good fortune.

2. Teach the ostinato using the listen and echo technique on bass xylophone and marimba.

3. Students spell the C-pentatonic scale.

4. Teach the rhythm part using body percussion, handclaps for drums first. Add stomping for the cymbal part.

5. Transfer to instruments, clapping on the drums, stomping on the cymbals. For the drum set part, the hi-hat cymbal part is notated with Xs on the space above the staff. The snare drum part is notated on the third space of the staff, and the bass drum part is notated on the first space.

6. Provide scores for different instruments available, class performs Melody One on soprano metallophones, pianicas, and Chinese flutes. Students describe the timbral effect of different combinations.

7. Add clarinet and yanqin solo to the ensemble.

8. Students practice the piece in the final arrangement (see score attached).

9. Students perform the piece in the final arrangement in a concert.

10. Extension: Perform "Winter Jasmine" using same process as above

Cai Shen Dao

Anonymous, arr. Margaret Thong

2

Cai Shen Dao

Cai Shen Dao

4   Cai Shen Dao

Cai Shen Dao

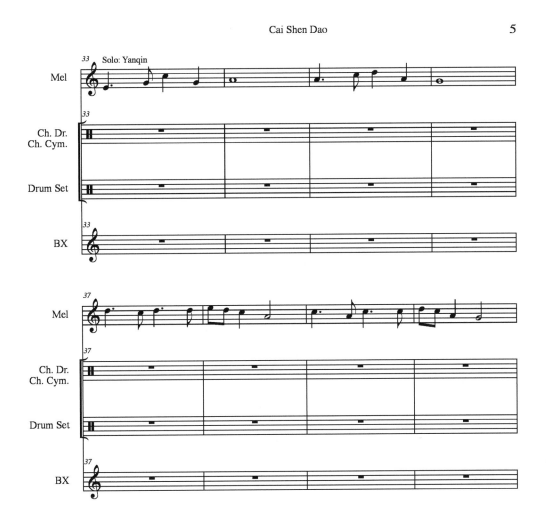

6   Cai Shen Dao

Cai Shen Dao

8   Cai Shen Dao

Winter Jasmine

Traditional, arr. Margaret Thong

2   Winter Jasmine

Winter Jasmine 3

4   Winter Jasmine

Winter Jasmine

5

6 Winter Jasmine

ORFF SCHULWERK
Biographies of Authors

Dr. Carlos R. Abril is associate professor and director of undergraduate music education at the University of Miami Frost School of Music. He was previously associate professor and coordinator of music education at Northwestern University. He has presented at numerous state, national, and international conferences, including AOSA, NAfME, and ISME. Abril has taught Orff Levels courses and presented for Orff chapters around the country. His work is published in books and journals including: *Music Educators Journal, Orff Echo, Journal of Research in Music Education, International Journal of Music Education,* and *General Music Today.* He has served on many editorial boards, including the *Orff Echo* and *Journal of Research in Music Education,* and co-edited the book, *Musical Experience in Our Lives.* His music arrangements and instructional materials are published by World Music Press and found in the Macmillan/McGraw-Hill textbook series, *Spotlight on Music.*

Dr. Judith W. Bond is professor of music and coordinator of music education at the University of Wisconsin Stevens Point, where she also directs the UWSP Women's Choir. She is a past-president of the American Orff-Schulwerk Association, and currently serves as co-chair of the Alliance for Active Music Making. As a church musician, she served on the board of the Presbyterian Association of Musicians. She has presented Orff sessions and courses at national and state conferences as well as internationally, and has taught Orff Levels 1, 2, and 3. Her international teaching includes courses taught for the

Chinese Orff Association. She is an author of *Share The Music* and *Spotlight On Music*, K – 8 music textbook series, published by Macmillan/McGraw-Hill.

Jay Broeker is an elementary music specialist, and college instructor with certification in both Orff and Kodály approaches. He has taught, conducted, and arranged music for children and adults in Indiana, Texas, Oklahoma, and Pennsylvania. He frequently presents workshops in Orff Schulwerk, recorder, and curriculum materials at national conferences and workshops in many states. He teaches at Blake Elementary School in Minneapolis. Jay is also a regular summer faculty at the University of St. Thomas and is one of the authors of *Share the Music*.

Jane Frazee is founder and former director of Graduate Music Education Programs at the University of St. Thomas in St. Paul MN. Her thirty years of Orff work in the classroom and with music educators has brought her local, state, national and international recognition. A former Fulbright teaching scholar at the Orff Institute in Austria, she has presented workshops and courses throughout the U.S., Canada, and Australia.

Frazee's six books for Orff teachers in print from Schott Music include her most recent contribution *Artful-Playful-Mindful* released in 2012. Her first book *Ten Folk Carols for Christmas*, published in 1977, was followed by several other best-selling titles, including *Discovering Orff, Discovering Keetman, Playing Together* and *Orff Schulwerk Today*.

Dr. Ana Lucía Frega is a lifelong Argentinean music educator, having taught at all levels of the general and artistic educational system in her own country, and served as Head of the School of Performing Arts at the Teatro Colón De Buenos Aires for ten years. She holds a PhD in music with a special focus in education. Currently she is Head of the Music Education Center at the Music Department of the National University of Arts in Buenos Aires and previously at the University CAECE, she created and ran the first Master's Program in Music Education, established in 2004. Dr. Frega has conducted in-service teacher training courses in all the Argentinean provinces and throughout Latin

America. She has taught and lectured many times in France, Spain, Portugal, Canada, Italy, UK, Greece, and the USA. She has written sixty books about music education, published in her own country and abroad, including *All for Music, Music for All*, published by the University of Pretoria, South Africa. Dr. Frega is an Honorary Life Member of the International Society for Music Education (ISME); she first joined ISME in1966, served ten years on the Board of the Research Commission, and two years as its chair. In 1990, she was appointed to the Board of Directors of ISME and later became President. In 2012 and with Wayne Bowman, she co-authored *The Oxford Handbook in Philosophy of Music Education*, at OUP, New York.

Dr. Lori Gooding, PhD, MT-BC is assistant professor and Director of Music Therapy at the University of Kentucky (UK). Dr. Gooding teaches music therapy and music education courses in the UK as well as provides music therapy services for children, adolescents, and adult patients in the UK Healthcare system. Additionally, she conducts music therapy assessments for students in several Kentucky counties. Gooding, who is Orff-Schulwerk Level II certified, implements many Orff-based techniques in her work with individuals with physical and mental health needs. She has published in several journals, including *General Music Today*, the Journal of *Music Therapy, Music Therapy Perspectives*, and the *Arts in Psychotherapy*. Dr. Gooding has presented nationally and internationally, and she currently serves at the regional and national levels in the American Music Therapy Association.

Dr. Han, Kuo-Huang (K. H. Han), PhD (Northwestern University), is a Distinguished Teaching Professor Emeritus, Northern Illinois University. He has been teaching world music, ethnomusicology, and Chinese and Southeast Asian musical instruments for thirty years, and has given workshops in many colleges and at scholarly conferences. After retirement, he taught at the University of Kentucky for a short period (2004-2008 and in 2010). As an author, he has contributed articles to *Ethnomusicology, Asian Music, New Grove Dictionary of Music and Musicians* (2nd edition), *Garland Encyclopedia of World Music, Encyclopedia Britannica, Encyclopedia of*

Contemporary China, Association for Chinese Music Research Reports, and book chapters in *Multicultural Perspectives in Music Education*, 3rd ed. (ed. by William Anderson and Patricia Campbell), *Musics in Many Cultures* (ed. by Elizabeth May), *Kaleidoscope of Cultures* (ed. by Marvelene Moore), etc. His research on contemporary Chinese music history is the subject of a master's thesis by Shishi Liu of Xian Conservatory of Music, China (2010) and his experience in establishing a world music program at Northern Illinois University is the subject of a research paper by Dr. Jui-Ching Wang (Northern Illinois University) to be published in the *Journal of Historical Research in Music Education*.

Cindy Hall teaches Orff certification courses at the University of St. Thomas and the University of Kentucky. She is an active conference and workshop clinician. She has taught music to children in public and private schools, directed an after school arts program, and conducted church children's choirs. She served as a contributing writer of recorder materials for the Macmillan/McGraw-Hill series, *Share the Music*. Cindy holds a B.A. in music from Duke University, M.A. in music education from the University of Oklahoma, and Orff Certification from Memphis State University and Hamline University. She currently teaches first through fifth grade music and chorus at Rowland Hall-St. Mark's school in Salt Lake City.

Jo Ella Hug, recently retired, is a teacher from Missoula, Montana. In thirty-eight years of public school teaching, she taught all ages of students from Kindergarten through adults, but her most recent and long-lasting specialty was teaching emerging adolescent learners in middle school. In the summer, she teaches Orff-Schulwerk Teacher Education at various universities including the University of St Thomas in St. Paul, MN. Jo Ella has been published numerous times with articles in the *Orff Echo* and *Reverberations* as well as the *Ostinato* (Carl Orff Canada) and *Orff-Schulwerk Informationen* (Orff-Schulwerk Forum Salzburg). Jo Ella has been included four times in the annual publication of *Who's Who Among America's Teachers*. She frequently presents workshops in the USA and Canada and for AOSA National Conference Sessions. Jo Ella has been a headliner at the National

Conference of Carl Orff Canada in 2000 and 2010; has presented for NAfME All-Northwest and the NAfME 2008 National Conference. She is a Past-President of AOSA.

Terri Brown Lenzo is currently a PhD candidate in music education at Kent State University. Her dissertation research is focused on the development and implementation of an online music education-training program for preschool classroom teachers. She has taught infants through adults as an early childhood music teacher, band director, and university instructor. Her areas of interest include early childhood music education, pre-service teacher education, shared delivery of the arts, and music education history.

K. Michelle Lewis is currently in her fourth year as the director of middle and high school bands and elementary music at the J. Graham Brown School in Louisville, Kentucky. Michelle received a BME from Morehead State University, MM in percussion performance from Rutgers University, a Graduate Orff Certificate from the University of Kentucky, and an Educational Administration Certificate from the University of Louisville). Michelle has also developed a jazz curriculum for the Jazz Band and Jazz Combo at Brown and created a steel drum ensemble that consists of third through fifth graders called "Brown Steel." She holds the following leadership positions: Kentucky Music Educators Association Elementary Music Chair, District 12 Elementary Music chair, and her school's SBDM committee. Michelle was awarded the Gheens Innovative Teaching Grant for two consecutive years, to advance her middle school and high school band students in the area of music composition. She is a lifetime advisory board member for the Composers and Schools in Concert organization in Sacramento, California. In addition to a full teaching schedule, Michelle enjoys performing as a percussionist with local musicians, the Jewish Community CenterStage, Pandora Productions, VOICES of Kentuckiana, Louisville Winds, and Sacred Winds.

Dr. Nicola F. Mason is an assistant professor of music education in the Department of Curriculum and Instruction at Eastern Kentucky University. She is Vice-President of the Kentucky Orff-Schulwerk Association and assists in the organization of the annual Orff- Schulwerk Teacher Training program at the University of Kentucky. As a high school band director in South Africa, Nicola performed regularly with the Cape Town Symphony Orchestra and performed solo with the KwaZulu Natal Philharmonic Orchestra. Nicola presents regularly at local and national, professional conferences.

Dr. Kimberly McCord is a professor of music education at Illinois State University. She teaches courses in General Music, Integrated Arts, and Music for the Exceptional Child. Previously, she taught music and special education in the Denver Public Schools for ten years. Her books include *Strategies for Teaching Technology, Chop Monster, Jr.* and chapters in *Music Experience in Our Lives,* and *The Jazz Educators Resource Guide and Handbook* and *Together We Can Improvise!* Her articles have been published in the *Bulletin for the Council for Research in Music Education, Australian Journal of Music Education,* International Society for Music Education (ISME) Commission on Music in Special Education, *Music Therapy and Music Medicine Journal, General Music Today, Update, Jazz Educators Journal, Orff Echo, Illinois Music Educators Journal,* Connecticut *Music Educators* Journal and *Journal of Technology in Music Learning.* She is the a board member for the International Society for Music Education (ISME) and the founder and chair of the Special Interest Group on Jazz for ISME. She has held leadership positions with the International Association for Jazz Education (IAJE), National Association for Music Education (MENC/NAfME), Illinois Music Educators Association (IMEA), and the Connecticut Music Educators Association. She has presented in China, Taiwan, Italy, Spain, Malaysia, Norway, Finland, Greece, Canada, and forty states. She has worked on jazz projects for the Smithsonian Institute, Jazz at Lincoln Center and the Kennedy Center in Washington D.C. She frequently presents workshops for teachers about teaching jazz , including six IAJE Teacher Training Institutes. She was a teaching artist-in-residence at the Henry Viscardi School in Long Island, New York. Her many honors include National Endowment grants, the IAJE Education Award and the ISU College of Fine Arts Senior Researcher Award. She coordinates the summer teacher-training program in Orff Schulwerk at ISU.

Dr. Mary Shamrock returned to her home state upon retirement in 2003 and now lives in Minneapolis, Minnesota. She holds a Ph.D. in Ethnomusicology and Music Education from UCLA; her academic service includes longtime professorships and administrative experience at West Virginia University and California State University, Northridge. The Orff-Schulwerk pedagogical approach has been a major area of interest; she has taught Schulwerk teacher training courses and served as workshop clinician at many institutions throughout the U.S. and abroad. Her dissertation focused on Schulwerk dispersal and adaptation in three Asian countries—Japan, Taiwan, and Thailand. She served the American Orff-Schulwerk Association as national board member, *Orff Echo* editor, national president, and chair of two national conferences; she received AOSA's Distinguished Service Award in 1999. Her record of publication combines the interest in Orff Schulwerk with that in World Music Education. Currently, she is executive director for Sumunar Indonesian Music and Dance in Minnesota that promotes Indonesian arts and culture through performance and education.

Dr. David Sogin is a professor of music education at the University of Kentucky. Before his UK appointment he taught at East Texas State University in Commerce, Texas, and served as a visiting professor of music education at Florida State University in Tallahassee, Florida. Dr. Sogin's work has been published in the *Journal for Research in Music Education, Psychology of Music, Contributions to Music Education* and the *Bulletin of the Council of Research in Music Education*. He is also the co-editor of the American String Teachers Association's *String Research Journal* and has been awarded the ASTA *String Researcher Award* in 2012. Dr. Sogin has presented papers both nationally and internationally on many facets of the Orff Schulwerk in Asia, Europe, North America, and Australia.

Dr. D. Gregory Springer is Director of Music Education and an assistant professor of music at the Boise State University Department of Music. He completed teacher training in Orff Schulwerk (Levels I-III) at the University of Kentucky while also pursuing a PhD in music education from the same institution. Prior to his doctoral study, he taught middle school and high school band in Mississippi. He has presented research and research-to-practice papers at regional, national, and international conferences on topics related to creative thinking in music, musical practice behaviors, assessment, and popular/vernacular music learning.

Robyn Staveley is Senior Lecturer in Music, Movement, and Dance Education at the University of Technology Sydney, Kuring-gai Campus. She is one of two representatives to the Australian National Orff Association from New South Wales. Robyn is well versed in the Orff training programs and organizational structures in her country. Robyn has written many resources and materials and presented many workshops and courses throughout Australia and internationally. In 2003 Robyn was recipient of the ASME (Australian Society for Music Education) Excellence in Teaching award. Her research interests are in educational psychology, neuroscience and music education and how a multi-modal approach to music education produces strong learning. Her workshops take you on a journey that is provocative, reflective, invigorating and best of all an enjoyable musical experience.

Arvida Steen was the first director of the Orff Teacher Certification Course at the University of Kentucky, beginning with Level 1 in 1987. She continued as director and instructor in each level for ten years. She later taught Orff Curriculum and Master Classes at UK. She began her Orff Teacher Training career at the University of Minnesota in 1974 and continued with that program until 2007 at the University of St. Thomas. There she developed the course in Curriculum Development and guided teaching practice using videotaping of classroom work. Arvida taught at the Blake Schools, using a K-5 Orff Schulwerk curriculum as the complimentary part of her career, 1972 – 2000. She holds AOSA's Distinguished Service Award, and is a member of the Minnesota Music Educators' Hall of Fame. *Exploring Orff: A Teacher's Guide*, published by Schott, 1992 reflected her combined interests in children, teaching Orff Schulwerk, pedagogy and curriculum.

Margaret Thong is an elementary school music teacher in the Concordia International School in Shanghai, where she has taught for almost 12 years.

Trained in the Institute of Education in Singapore, Margaret majored in trumpet and developed a strong interest in band and dance. She has taught marching bands, award-winning recorder groups, and choirs in Malaysia, where she also hails from. In her years of teaching, Margaret has started and directed jazz band, concert band, and rock band for middle and high school students. Certified in the Orff approach from the University of Kentucky, she is currently the creator and director of the elementary school Rockin' Rhythm Revelers Orff band at Concordia International School. She teaches, conducts and arranges the music played by the Orff band. Margaret enjoys transcribing music and her hobby when she is not teaching is to arrange music to suit her students in her band. Margaret's other hobbies include choreographing dances for school concerts, learning new instruments, and participating in her local zumba class.

Dr. Cecilia Wang is the director of the Orff-Schulwerk Program and professor of Music Education at the University of Kentucky. She teaches courses in general music education, research, arts in education, psychology of music, tests and measurements and directs theses and dissertations in these areas. She presents research papers and publishes regularly and internationally. Her research interests include music perception, music learning and development, creative thinking in music, and teacher effectiveness. She has served on the editorial board of the *Journal of Research in Music Education*, and several other research journals. She was one-time chair of the Research Interest Group of AOSA and MENC, and the AOSA Research Advisory Panel for several years. She served as leader in creating the Webliography for *Research Studies in Orff Schulwerk*, now posted on the AOSA website.

ORFF SCHULWERK

Index